C-107 CAREER EXAMINATION SERIES

This is your
PASSBOOK for...

Blacksmith

Test Preparation Study Guide
Questions & Answers

NATIONAL LEARNING CORPORATION®

COPYRIGHT NOTICE

This book is SOLELY intended for, is sold ONLY to, and its use is RESTRICTED to individual, bona fide applicants or candidates who qualify by virtue of having seriously filed applications for appropriate license, certificate, professional and/or promotional advancement, higher school matriculation, scholarship, or other legitimate requirements of education and/or governmental authorities.

This book is NOT intended for use, class instruction, tutoring, training, duplication, copying, reprinting, excerption, or adaptation, etc., by:

1) Other publishers
2) Proprietors and/or Instructors of "Coaching" and/or Preparatory Courses
3) Personnel and/or Training Divisions of commercial, industrial, and governmental organizations
4) Schools, colleges, or universities and/or their departments and staffs, including teachers and other personnel
5) Testing Agencies or Bureaus
6) Study groups which seek by the purchase of a single volume to copy and/or duplicate and/or adapt this material for use by the group as a whole without having purchased individual volumes for each of the members of the group
7) Et al.

Such persons would be in violation of appropriate Federal and State statutes.

PROVISION OF LICENSING AGREEMENTS – Recognized educational, commercial, industrial, and governmental institutions and organizations, and others legitimately engaged in educational pursuits, including training, testing, and measurement activities, may address request for a licensing agreement to the copyright owners, who will determine whether, and under what conditions, including fees and charges, the materials in this book may be used them. In other words, a licensing facility exists for the legitimate use of the material in this book on other than an individual basis. However, it is asseverated and affirmed here that the material in this book CANNOT be used without the receipt of the express permission of such a licensing agreement from the Publishers. Inquiries re licensing should be addressed to the company, attention rights and permissions department.

All rights reserved, including the right of reproduction in whole or in part, in any form or by any means, electronic or mechanical, including photocopying, recording, or by any information storage and retrieval system, without permission in writing from the Publisher.

Copyright © 2025 by
National Learning Corporation

212 Michael Drive, Syosset, NY 11791
(516) 921-8888 • www.passbooks.com
E-mail: info@passbooks.com

PASSBOOK® SERIES

THE *PASSBOOK® SERIES* has been created to prepare applicants and candidates for the ultimate academic battlefield – the examination room.

At some time in our lives, each and every one of us may be required to take an examination – for validation, matriculation, admission, qualification, registration, certification, or licensure.

Based on the assumption that every applicant or candidate has met the basic formal educational standards, has taken the required number of courses, and read the necessary texts, the *PASSBOOK® SERIES* furnishes the one special preparation which may assure passing with confidence, instead of failing with insecurity. Examination questions – together with answers – are furnished as the basic vehicle for study so that the mysteries of the examination and its compounding difficulties may be eliminated or diminished by a sure method.

This book is meant to help you pass your examination provided that you qualify and are serious in your objective.

The entire field is reviewed through the huge store of content information which is succinctly presented through a provocative and challenging approach – the question-and-answer method.

A climate of success is established by furnishing the correct answers at the end of each test.

You soon learn to recognize types of questions, forms of questions, and patterns of questioning. You may even begin to anticipate expected outcomes.

You perceive that many questions are repeated or adapted so that you can gain acute insights, which may enable you to score many sure points.

You learn how to confront new questions, or types of questions, and to attack them confidently and work out the correct answers.

You note objectives and emphases, and recognize pitfalls and dangers, so that you may make positive educational adjustments.

Moreover, you are kept fully informed in relation to new concepts, methods, practices, and directions in the field.

You discover that you are actually taking the examination all the time: you are preparing for the examination by "taking" an examination, not by reading extraneous and/or supererogatory textbooks.

In short, this PASSBOOK®, used directedly, should be an important factor in helping you to pass your test.

BLACKSMITH

DUTIES AND RESPONSIBILITIES
Under direction, does general blacksmith work in forging and shaping metal in building, maintenance and repair of equipment and appurtenances; performs related work.

EXAMPLES OF TYPICAL TASKS
Forges and shapes, manually or by power hammer, angle iron, bridle irons, tools, automobile parts and other similar pieces of equipment. Forge welds iron components, repairs metal parts of trucks, automobiles, carts, enclosures, sweepers and other equipment. Is responsible for, and directs the work of Blacksmith's Helpers. Keeps records and makes reports.

TESTS
The test may include demonstration of knowledge of working heats in the fabrication of tools and parts; shaping of metal, using hand forge, gas furnace, steam hammer, and related machines and hand tools, forge welding, and tool hardening and tempering; properties of various metals (primarily hot-rolled structural steel) in fabrication and application; basic arithmetic and measurement; sketch reading; safety; identification of tools and equipment; and other related areas.

HOW TO TAKE A TEST

I. YOU MUST PASS AN EXAMINATION

A. *WHAT EVERY CANDIDATE SHOULD KNOW*

Examination applicants often ask us for help in preparing for the written test. What can I study in advance? What kinds of questions will be asked? How will the test be given? How will the papers be graded?

As an applicant for a civil service examination, you may be wondering about some of these things. Our purpose here is to suggest effective methods of advance study and to describe civil service examinations.

Your chances for success on this examination can be increased if you know how to prepare. Those "pre-examination jitters" can be reduced if you know what to expect. You can even experience an adventure in good citizenship if you know why civil service exams are given.

B. *WHY ARE CIVIL SERVICE EXAMINATIONS GIVEN?*

Civil service examinations are important to you in two ways. As a citizen, you want public jobs filled by employees who know how to do their work. As a job seeker, you want a fair chance to compete for that job on an equal footing with other candidates. The best-known means of accomplishing this two-fold goal is the competitive examination.

Exams are widely publicized throughout the nation. They may be administered for jobs in federal, state, city, municipal, town or village governments or agencies.

Any citizen may apply, with some limitations, such as the age or residence of applicants. Your experience and education may be reviewed to see whether you meet the requirements for the particular examination. When these requirements exist, they are reasonable and applied consistently to all applicants. Thus, a competitive examination may cause you some uneasiness now, but it is your privilege and safeguard.

C. *HOW ARE CIVIL SERVICE EXAMS DEVELOPED?*

Examinations are carefully written by trained technicians who are specialists in the field known as "psychological measurement," in consultation with recognized authorities in the field of work that the test will cover. These experts recommend the subject matter areas or skills to be tested; only those knowledges or skills important to your success on the job are included. The most reliable books and source materials available are used as references. Together, the experts and technicians judge the difficulty level of the questions.

Test technicians know how to phrase questions so that the problem is clearly stated. Their ethics do not permit "trick" or "catch" questions. Questions may have been tried out on sample groups, or subjected to statistical analysis, to determine their usefulness.

Written tests are often used in combination with performance tests, ratings of training and experience, and oral interviews. All of these measures combine to form the best-known means of finding the right person for the right job.

II. HOW TO PASS THE WRITTEN TEST

A. NATURE OF THE EXAMINATION

To prepare intelligently for civil service examinations, you should know how they differ from school examinations you have taken. In school you were assigned certain definite pages to read or subjects to cover. The examination questions were quite detailed and usually emphasized memory. Civil service exams, on the other hand, try to discover your present ability to perform the duties of a position, plus your potentiality to learn these duties. In other words, a civil service exam attempts to predict how successful you will be. Questions cover such a broad area that they cannot be as minute and detailed as school exam questions.

In the public service similar kinds of work, or positions, are grouped together in one "class." This process is known as *position-classification*. All the positions in a class are paid according to the salary range for that class. One class title covers all of these positions, and they are all tested by the same examination.

B. FOUR BASIC STEPS

1) Study the announcement

How, then, can you know what subjects to study? Our best answer is: "Learn as much as possible about the class of positions for which you've applied." The exam will test the knowledge, skills and abilities needed to do the work.

Your most valuable source of information about the position you want is the official exam announcement. This announcement lists the training and experience qualifications. Check these standards and apply only if you come reasonably close to meeting them.

The brief description of the position in the examination announcement offers some clues to the subjects which will be tested. Think about the job itself. Review the duties in your mind. Can you perform them, or are there some in which you are rusty? Fill in the blank spots in your preparation.

Many jurisdictions preview the written test in the exam announcement by including a section called "Knowledge and Abilities Required," "Scope of the Examination," or some similar heading. Here you will find out specifically what fields will be tested.

2) Review your own background

Once you learn in general what the position is all about, and what you need to know to do the work, ask yourself which subjects you already know fairly well and which need improvement. You may wonder whether to concentrate on improving your strong areas or on building some background in your fields of weakness. When the announcement has specified "some knowledge" or "considerable knowledge," or has used adjectives like "beginning principles of..." or "advanced ... methods," you can get a clue as to the number and difficulty of questions to be asked in any given field. More questions, and hence broader coverage, would be included for those subjects which are more important in the work. Now weigh your strengths and weaknesses against the job requirements and prepare accordingly.

3) Determine the level of the position

Another way to tell how intensively you should prepare is to understand the level of the job for which you are applying. Is it the entering level? In other words, is this the position in which beginners in a field of work are hired? Or is it an intermediate or advanced level? Sometimes this is indicated by such words as "Junior" or "Senior" in the class title. Other jurisdictions use Roman numerals to designate the level – Clerk I, Clerk II, for example. The word "Supervisor" sometimes appears in the title. If the level is not indicated by the title, check the description of duties. Will you be working under very close supervision, or will you have responsibility for independent decisions in this work?

4) Choose appropriate study materials

Now that you know the subjects to be examined and the relative amount of each subject to be covered, you can choose suitable study materials. For beginning level jobs, or even advanced ones, if you have a pronounced weakness in some aspect of your training, read a modern, standard textbook in that field. Be sure it is up to date and has general coverage. Such books are normally available at your library, and the librarian will be glad to help you locate one. For entry-level positions, questions of appropriate difficulty are chosen – neither highly advanced questions, nor those too simple. Such questions require careful thought but not advanced training.

If the position for which you are applying is technical or advanced, you will read more advanced, specialized material. If you are already familiar with the basic principles of your field, elementary textbooks would waste your time. Concentrate on advanced textbooks and technical periodicals. Think through the concepts and review difficult problems in your field.

These are all general sources. You can get more ideas on your own initiative, following these leads. For example, training manuals and publications of the government agency which employs workers in your field can be useful, particularly for technical and professional positions. A letter or visit to the government department involved may result in more specific study suggestions, and certainly will provide you with a more definite idea of the exact nature of the position you are seeking.

III. KINDS OF TESTS

Tests are used for purposes other than measuring knowledge and ability to perform specified duties. For some positions, it is equally important to test ability to make adjustments to new situations or to profit from training. In others, basic mental abilities not dependent on information are essential. Questions which test these things may not appear as pertinent to the duties of the position as those which test for knowledge and information. Yet they are often highly important parts of a fair examination. For very general questions, it is almost impossible to help you direct your study efforts. What we can do is to point out some of the more common of these general abilities needed in public service positions and describe some typical questions.

1) General information

Broad, general information has been found useful for predicting job success in some kinds of work. This is tested in a variety of ways, from vocabulary lists to questions about current events. Basic background in some field of work, such as sociology or economics, may be sampled in a group of questions. Often these are principles which have become familiar to most persons through exposure rather than through formal training. It is difficult to advise you how to study for these questions; being alert to the world around you is our best suggestion.

2) Verbal ability

An example of an ability needed in many positions is verbal or language ability. Verbal ability is, in brief, the ability to use and understand words. Vocabulary and grammar tests are typical measures of this ability. Reading comprehension or paragraph interpretation questions are common in many kinds of civil service tests. You are given a paragraph of written material and asked to find its central meaning.

3) Numerical ability

Number skills can be tested by the familiar arithmetic problem, by checking paired lists of numbers to see which are alike and which are different, or by interpreting charts and graphs. In the latter test, a graph may be printed in the test booklet which you are asked to use as the basis for answering questions.

4) Observation

A popular test for law-enforcement positions is the observation test. A picture is shown to you for several minutes, then taken away. Questions about the picture test your ability to observe both details and larger elements.

5) Following directions

In many positions in the public service, the employee must be able to carry out written instructions dependably and accurately. You may be given a chart with several columns, each column listing a variety of information. The questions require you to carry out directions involving the information given in the chart.

6) Skills and aptitudes

Performance tests effectively measure some manual skills and aptitudes. When the skill is one in which you are trained, such as typing or shorthand, you can practice. These tests are often very much like those given in business school or high school courses. For many of the other skills and aptitudes, however, no short-time preparation can be made. Skills and abilities natural to you or that you have developed throughout your lifetime are being tested.

Many of the general questions just described provide all the data needed to answer the questions and ask you to use your reasoning ability to find the answers. Your best preparation for these tests, as well as for tests of facts and ideas, is to be at your physical and mental best. You, no doubt, have your own methods of getting into an exam-taking mood and keeping "in shape." The next section lists some ideas on this subject.

IV. KINDS OF QUESTIONS

Only rarely is the "essay" question, which you answer in narrative form, used in civil service tests. Civil service tests are usually of the short-answer type. Full instructions for answering these questions will be given to you at the examination. But in case this is your first experience with short-answer questions and separate answer sheets, here is what you need to know:

1) Multiple-choice Questions

Most popular of the short-answer questions is the "multiple choice" or "best answer" question. It can be used, for example, to test for factual knowledge, ability to solve problems or judgment in meeting situations found at work.

A multiple-choice question is normally one of three types—
- It can begin with an incomplete statement followed by several possible endings. You are to find the one ending which *best* completes the statement, although some of the others may not be entirely wrong.
- It can also be a complete statement in the form of a question which is answered by choosing one of the statements listed.

- It can be in the form of a problem – again you select the best answer.

Here is an example of a multiple-choice question with a discussion which should give you some clues as to the method for choosing the right answer:

When an employee has a complaint about his assignment, the action which will *best* help him overcome his difficulty is to
- A. discuss his difficulty with his coworkers
- B. take the problem to the head of the organization
- C. take the problem to the person who gave him the assignment
- D. say nothing to anyone about his complaint

In answering this question, you should study each of the choices to find which is best. Consider choice "A" – Certainly an employee may discuss his complaint with fellow employees, but no change or improvement can result, and the complaint remains unresolved. Choice "B" is a poor choice since the head of the organization probably does not know what assignment you have been given, and taking your problem to him is known as "going over the head" of the supervisor. The supervisor, or person who made the assignment, is the person who can clarify it or correct any injustice. Choice "C" is, therefore, correct. To say nothing, as in choice "D," is unwise. Supervisors have and interest in knowing the problems employees are facing, and the employee is seeking a solution to his problem.

2) True/False Questions

The "true/false" or "right/wrong" form of question is sometimes used. Here a complete statement is given. Your job is to decide whether the statement is right or wrong.

SAMPLE: A roaming cell-phone call to a nearby city costs less than a non-roaming call to a distant city.

This statement is wrong, or false, since roaming calls are more expensive.

This is not a complete list of all possible question forms, although most of the others are variations of these common types. You will always get complete directions for answering questions. Be sure you understand *how* to mark your answers – ask questions until you do.

V. RECORDING YOUR ANSWERS

Computer terminals are used more and more today for many different kinds of exams.

For an examination with very few applicants, you may be told to record your answers in the test booklet itself. Separate answer sheets are much more common. If this separate answer sheet is to be scored by machine – and this is often the case – it is highly important that you mark your answers correctly in order to get credit.

An electronic scoring machine is often used in civil service offices because of the speed with which papers can be scored. Machine-scored answer sheets must be marked with a pencil, which will be given to you. This pencil has a high graphite content which responds to the electronic scoring machine. As a matter of fact, stray dots may register as answers, so do not let your pencil rest on the answer sheet while you are pondering the correct answer. Also, if your pencil lead breaks or is otherwise defective, ask for another.

Since the answer sheet will be dropped in a slot in the scoring machine, be careful not to bend the corners or get the paper crumpled.

The answer sheet normally has five vertical columns of numbers, with 30 numbers to a column. These numbers correspond to the question numbers in your test booklet. After each number, going across the page are four or five pairs of dotted lines. These short dotted lines have small letters or numbers above them. The first two pairs may also have a "T" or "F" above the letters. This indicates that the first two pairs only are to be used if the questions are of the true-false type. If the questions are multiple choice, disregard the "T" and "F" and pay attention only to the small letters or numbers.

Answer your questions in the manner of the sample that follows:

32. The largest city in the United States is
    A. Washington, D.C.
    B. New York City
    C. Chicago
    D. Detroit
    E. San Francisco

1) Choose the answer you think is best. (New York City is the largest, so "B" is correct.)
2) Find the row of dotted lines numbered the same as the question you are answering. (Find row number 32)
3) Find the pair of dotted lines corresponding to the answer. (Find the pair of lines under the mark "B.")
4) Make a solid black mark between the dotted lines.

VI. BEFORE THE TEST

Common sense will help you find procedures to follow to get ready for an examination. Too many of us, however, overlook these sensible measures. Indeed, nervousness and fatigue have been found to be the most serious reasons why applicants fail to do their best on civil service tests. Here is a list of reminders:

- Begin your preparation early – Don't wait until the last minute to go scurrying around for books and materials or to find out what the position is all about.
- Prepare continuously – An hour a night for a week is better than an all-night cram session. This has been definitely established. What is more, a night a week for a month will return better dividends than crowding your study into a shorter period of time.
- Locate the place of the exam – You have been sent a notice telling you when and where to report for the examination. If the location is in a different town or otherwise unfamiliar to you, it would be well to inquire the best route and learn something about the building.
- Relax the night before the test – Allow your mind to rest. Do not study at all that night. Plan some mild recreation or diversion; then go to bed early and get a good night's sleep.
- Get up early enough to make a leisurely trip to the place for the test – This way unforeseen events, traffic snarls, unfamiliar buildings, etc. will not upset you.
- Dress comfortably – A written test is not a fashion show. You will be known by number and not by name, so wear something comfortable.

- Leave excess paraphernalia at home – Shopping bags and odd bundles will get in your way. You need bring only the items mentioned in the official notice you received; usually everything you need is provided. Do not bring reference books to the exam. They will only confuse those last minutes and be taken away from you when in the test room.
- Arrive somewhat ahead of time – If because of transportation schedules you must get there very early, bring a newspaper or magazine to take your mind off yourself while waiting.
- Locate the examination room – When you have found the proper room, you will be directed to the seat or part of the room where you will sit. Sometimes you are given a sheet of instructions to read while you are waiting. Do not fill out any forms until you are told to do so; just read them and be prepared.
- Relax and prepare to listen to the instructions
- If you have any physical problem that may keep you from doing your best, be sure to tell the test administrator. If you are sick or in poor health, you really cannot do your best on the exam. You can come back and take the test some other time.

VII. AT THE TEST

The day of the test is here and you have the test booklet in your hand. The temptation to get going is very strong. Caution! There is more to success than knowing the right answers. You must know how to identify your papers and understand variations in the type of short-answer question used in this particular examination. Follow these suggestions for maximum results from your efforts:

1) Cooperate with the monitor

The test administrator has a duty to create a situation in which you can be as much at ease as possible. He will give instructions, tell you when to begin, check to see that you are marking your answer sheet correctly, and so on. He is not there to guard you, although he will see that your competitors do not take unfair advantage. He wants to help you do your best.

2) Listen to all instructions

Don't jump the gun! Wait until you understand all directions. In most civil service tests you get more time than you need to answer the questions. So don't be in a hurry. Read each word of instructions until you clearly understand the meaning. Study the examples, listen to all announcements and follow directions. Ask questions if you do not understand what to do.

3) Identify your papers

Civil service exams are usually identified by number only. You will be assigned a number; you must not put your name on your test papers. Be sure to copy your number correctly. Since more than one exam may be given, copy your exact examination title.

4) Plan your time

Unless you are told that a test is a "speed" or "rate of work" test, speed itself is usually not important. Time enough to answer all the questions will be provided, but this does not mean that you have all day. An overall time limit has been set. Divide the total time (in minutes) by the number of questions to determine the approximate time you have for each question.

5) Do not linger over difficult questions

If you come across a difficult question, mark it with a paper clip (useful to have along) and come back to it when you have been through the booklet. One caution if you do this – be sure to skip a number on your answer sheet as well. Check often to be sure that you have not lost your place and that you are marking in the row numbered the same as the question you are answering.

6) Read the questions

Be sure you know what the question asks! Many capable people are unsuccessful because they failed to *read* the questions correctly.

7) Answer all questions

Unless you have been instructed that a penalty will be deducted for incorrect answers, it is better to guess than to omit a question.

8) Speed tests

It is often better NOT to guess on speed tests. It has been found that on timed tests people are tempted to spend the last few seconds before time is called in marking answers at random – without even reading them – in the hope of picking up a few extra points. To discourage this practice, the instructions may warn you that your score will be "corrected" for guessing. That is, a penalty will be applied. The incorrect answers will be deducted from the correct ones, or some other penalty formula will be used.

9) Review your answers

If you finish before time is called, go back to the questions you guessed or omitted to give them further thought. Review other answers if you have time.

10) Return your test materials

If you are ready to leave before others have finished or time is called, take ALL your materials to the monitor and leave quietly. Never take any test material with you. The monitor can discover whose papers are not complete, and taking a test booklet may be grounds for disqualification.

VIII. EXAMINATION TECHNIQUES

1) Read the general instructions carefully. These are usually printed on the first page of the exam booklet. As a rule, these instructions refer to the timing of the examination; the fact that you should not start work until the signal and must stop work at a signal, etc. If there are any *special* instructions, such as a choice of questions to be answered, make sure that you note this instruction carefully.

2) When you are ready to start work on the examination, that is as soon as the signal has been given, read the instructions to each question booklet, underline any key words or phrases, such as *least, best, outline, describe* and the like. In this way you will tend to answer as requested rather than discover on reviewing your paper that you *listed without describing*, that you selected the *worst* choice rather than the *best* choice, etc.

3) If the examination is of the objective or multiple-choice type – that is, each question will also give a series of possible answers: A, B, C or D, and you are called upon to select the best answer and write the letter next to that answer on your answer paper – it is advisable to start answering each question in turn. There may be anywhere from 50 to 100 such questions in the three or four hours allotted and you can see how much time would be taken if you read through all the questions before beginning to answer any. Furthermore, if you come across a question or group of questions which you know would be difficult to answer, it would undoubtedly affect your handling of all the other questions.

4) If the examination is of the essay type and contains but a few questions, it is a moot point as to whether you should read all the questions before starting to answer any one. Of course, if you are given a choice – say five out of seven and the like – then it is essential to read all the questions so you can eliminate the two that are most difficult. If, however, you are asked to answer all the questions, there may be danger in trying to answer the easiest one first because you may find that you will spend too much time on it. The best technique is to answer the first question, then proceed to the second, etc.

5) Time your answers. Before the exam begins, write down the time it started, then add the time allowed for the examination and write down the time it must be completed, then divide the time available somewhat as follows:
   - If 3-1/2 hours are allowed, that would be 210 minutes. If you have 80 objective-type questions, that would be an average of 2-1/2 minutes per question. Allow yourself no more than 2 minutes per question, or a total of 160 minutes, which will permit about 50 minutes to review.
   - If for the time allotment of 210 minutes there are 7 essay questions to answer, that would average about 30 minutes a question. Give yourself only 25 minutes per question so that you have about 35 minutes to review.

6) The most important instruction is to *read each question* and make sure you know what is wanted. The second most important instruction is to *time yourself properly* so that you answer every question. The third most important instruction is to *answer every question*. Guess if you have to but include something for each question. Remember that you will receive no credit for a blank and will probably receive some credit if you write something in answer to an essay question. If you guess a letter – say "B" for a multiple-choice question – you may have guessed right. If you leave a blank as an answer to a multiple-choice question, the examiners may respect your feelings but it will not add a point to your score. Some exams may penalize you for wrong answers, so in such cases *only*, you may not want to guess unless you have some basis for your answer.

7) Suggestions
   a. Objective-type questions
      1. Examine the question booklet for proper sequence of pages and questions
      2. Read all instructions carefully
      3. Skip any question which seems too difficult; return to it after all other questions have been answered
      4. Apportion your time properly; do not spend too much time on any single question or group of questions

5. Note and underline key words – *all, most, fewest, least, best, worst, same, opposite,* etc.
6. Pay particular attention to negatives
7. Note unusual option, e.g., unduly long, short, complex, different or similar in content to the body of the question
8. Observe the use of "hedging" words – *probably, may, most likely,* etc.
9. Make sure that your answer is put next to the same number as the question
10. Do not second-guess unless you have good reason to believe the second answer is definitely more correct
11. Cross out original answer if you decide another answer is more accurate; do not erase until you are ready to hand your paper in
12. Answer all questions; guess unless instructed otherwise
13. Leave time for review

b. Essay questions
   1. Read each question carefully
   2. Determine exactly what is wanted. Underline key words or phrases.
   3. Decide on outline or paragraph answer
   4. Include many different points and elements unless asked to develop any one or two points or elements
   5. Show impartiality by giving pros and cons unless directed to select one side only
   6. Make and write down any assumptions you find necessary to answer the questions
   7. Watch your English, grammar, punctuation and choice of words
   8. Time your answers; don't crowd material

8) Answering the essay question

Most essay questions can be answered by framing the specific response around several key words or ideas. Here are a few such key words or ideas:

M's: manpower, materials, methods, money, management
P's: purpose, program, policy, plan, procedure, practice, problems, pitfalls, personnel, public relations

   a. Six basic steps in handling problems:
      1. Preliminary plan and background development
      2. Collect information, data and facts
      3. Analyze and interpret information, data and facts
      4. Analyze and develop solutions as well as make recommendations
      5. Prepare report and sell recommendations
      6. Install recommendations and follow up effectiveness

   b. Pitfalls to avoid
      1. *Taking things for granted* – A statement of the situation does not necessarily imply that each of the elements is necessarily true; for example, a complaint may be invalid and biased so that all that can be taken for granted is that a complaint has been registered

2. *Considering only one side of a situation* – Wherever possible, indicate several alternatives and then point out the reasons you selected the best one
3. *Failing to indicate follow up* – Whenever your answer indicates action on your part, make certain that you will take proper follow-up action to see how successful your recommendations, procedures or actions turn out to be
4. *Taking too long in answering any single question* – Remember to time your answers properly

IX. AFTER THE TEST

Scoring procedures differ in detail among civil service jurisdictions although the general principles are the same. Whether the papers are hand-scored or graded by machine we have described, they are nearly always graded by number. That is, the person who marks the paper knows only the number – never the name – of the applicant. Not until all the papers have been graded will they be matched with names. If other tests, such as training and experience or oral interview ratings have been given, scores will be combined. Different parts of the examination usually have different weights. For example, the written test might count 60 percent of the final grade, and a rating of training and experience 40 percent. In many jurisdictions, veterans will have a certain number of points added to their grades.

After the final grade has been determined, the names are placed in grade order and an eligible list is established. There are various methods for resolving ties between those who get the same final grade – probably the most common is to place first the name of the person whose application was received first. Job offers are made from the eligible list in the order the names appear on it. You will be notified of your grade and your rank as soon as all these computations have been made. This will be done as rapidly as possible.

People who are found to meet the requirements in the announcement are called "eligibles." Their names are put on a list of eligible candidates. An eligible's chances of getting a job depend on how high he stands on this list and how fast agencies are filling jobs from the list.

When a job is to be filled from a list of eligibles, the agency asks for the names of people on the list of eligibles for that job. When the civil service commission receives this request, it sends to the agency the names of the three people highest on this list. Or, if the job to be filled has specialized requirements, the office sends the agency the names of the top three persons who meet these requirements from the general list.

The appointing officer makes a choice from among the three people whose names were sent to him. If the selected person accepts the appointment, the names of the others are put back on the list to be considered for future openings.

That is the rule in hiring from all kinds of eligible lists, whether they are for typist, carpenter, chemist, or something else. For every vacancy, the appointing officer has his choice of any one of the top three eligibles on the list. This explains why the person whose name is on top of the list sometimes does not get an appointment when some of the persons lower on the list do. If the appointing officer chooses the second or third eligible, the No. 1 eligible does not get a job at once, but stays on the list until he is appointed or the list is terminated.

X. HOW TO PASS THE INTERVIEW TEST

The examination for which you applied requires an oral interview test. You have already taken the written test and you are now being called for the interview test – the final part of the formal examination.

You may think that it is not possible to prepare for an interview test and that there are no procedures to follow during an interview. Our purpose is to point out some things you can do in advance that will help you and some good rules to follow and pitfalls to avoid while you are being interviewed.

What is an interview supposed to test?

The written examination is designed to test the technical knowledge and competence of the candidate; the oral is designed to evaluate intangible qualities, not readily measured otherwise, and to establish a list showing the relative fitness of each candidate – as measured against his competitors – for the position sought. Scoring is not on the basis of "right" and "wrong," but on a sliding scale of values ranging from "not passable" to "outstanding." As a matter of fact, it is possible to achieve a relatively low score without a single "incorrect" answer because of evident weakness in the qualities being measured.

Occasionally, an examination may consist entirely of an oral test – either an individual or a group oral. In such cases, information is sought concerning the technical knowledges and abilities of the candidate, since there has been no written examination for this purpose. More commonly, however, an oral test is used to supplement a written examination.

Who conducts interviews?

The composition of oral boards varies among different jurisdictions. In nearly all, a representative of the personnel department serves as chairman. One of the members of the board may be a representative of the department in which the candidate would work. In some cases, "outside experts" are used, and, frequently, a businessman or some other representative of the general public is asked to serve. Labor and management or other special groups may be represented. The aim is to secure the services of experts in the appropriate field.

However the board is composed, it is a good idea (and not at all improper or unethical) to ascertain in advance of the interview who the members are and what groups they represent. When you are introduced to them, you will have some idea of their backgrounds and interests, and at least you will not stutter and stammer over their names.

What should be done before the interview?

While knowledge about the board members is useful and takes some of the surprise element out of the interview, there is other preparation which is more substantive. It *is* possible to prepare for an oral interview – in several ways:

1) Keep a copy of your application and review it carefully before the interview

This may be the only document before the oral board, and the starting point of the interview. Know what education and experience you have listed there, and the sequence and dates of all of it. Sometimes the board will ask you to review the highlights of your experience for them; you should not have to hem and haw doing it.

2) Study the class specification and the examination announcement

Usually, the oral board has one or both of these to guide them. The qualities, characteristics or knowledges required by the position sought are stated in these documents. They offer valuable clues as to the nature of the oral interview. For example, if the job involves supervisory responsibilities, the announcement will usually indicate that knowledge of modern supervisory methods and the qualifications of the candidate as a supervisor will be tested. If so, you can expect such questions, frequently in the form of a hypothetical situation which you are expected to solve. NEVER go into an oral without knowledge of the duties and responsibilities of the job you seek.

3) Think through each qualification required

Try to visualize the kind of questions you would ask if you were a board member. How well could you answer them? Try especially to appraise your own knowledge and background in each area, *measured against the job sought*, and identify any areas in which you are weak. Be critical and realistic – do not flatter yourself.

4) Do some general reading in areas in which you feel you may be weak

For example, if the job involves supervision and your past experience has NOT, some general reading in supervisory methods and practices, particularly in the field of human relations, might be useful. Do NOT study agency procedures or detailed manuals. The oral board will be testing your understanding and capacity, not your memory.

5) Get a good night's sleep and watch your general health and mental attitude

You will want a clear head at the interview. Take care of a cold or any other minor ailment, and of course, no hangovers.

What should be done on the day of the interview?

Now comes the day of the interview itself. Give yourself plenty of time to get there. Plan to arrive somewhat ahead of the scheduled time, particularly if your appointment is in the fore part of the day. If a previous candidate fails to appear, the board might be ready for you a bit early. By early afternoon an oral board is almost invariably behind schedule if there are many candidates, and you may have to wait. Take along a book or magazine to read, or your application to review, but leave any extraneous material in the waiting room when you go in for your interview. In any event, relax and compose yourself.

The matter of dress is important. The board is forming impressions about you – from your experience, your manners, your attitude, and your appearance. Give your personal appearance careful attention. Dress your best, but not your flashiest. Choose conservative, appropriate clothing, and be sure it is immaculate. This is a business interview, and your appearance should indicate that you regard it as such. Besides, being well groomed and properly dressed will help boost your confidence.

Sooner or later, someone will call your name and escort you into the interview room. *This is it.* From here on you are on your own. It is too late for any more preparation. But remember, you asked for this opportunity to prove your fitness, and you are here because your request was granted.

What happens when you go in?

The usual sequence of events will be as follows: The clerk (who is often the board stenographer) will introduce you to the chairman of the oral board, who will introduce you to the other members of the board. Acknowledge the introductions before you sit down. Do not be surprised if you find a microphone facing you or a stenotypist sitting by. Oral interviews are usually recorded in the event of an appeal or other review.

Usually the chairman of the board will open the interview by reviewing the highlights of your education and work experience from your application – primarily for the benefit of the other members of the board, as well as to get the material into the record. Do not interrupt or comment unless there is an error or significant misinterpretation; if that is the case, do not hesitate. But do not quibble about insignificant matters. Also, he will usually ask you some question about your education, experience or your present job – partly to get you to start talking and to establish the interviewing "rapport." He may start the actual questioning, or turn it over to one of the other members. Frequently, each member undertakes the questioning on a particular area, one in which he is perhaps most competent, so you can expect each member to participate in the examination. Because time is limited, you may also expect some rather abrupt switches in the direction the questioning takes, so do not be upset by it. Normally, a board member will not pursue a single line of questioning unless he discovers a particular strength or weakness.

After each member has participated, the chairman will usually ask whether any member has any further questions, then will ask you if you have anything you wish to add. Unless you are expecting this question, it may floor you. Worse, it may start you off on an extended, extemporaneous speech. The board is not usually seeking more information. The question is principally to offer you a last opportunity to present further qualifications or to indicate that you have nothing to add. So, if you feel that a significant qualification or characteristic has been overlooked, it is proper to point it out in a sentence or so. Do not compliment the board on the thoroughness of their examination – they have been sketchy, and you know it. If you wish, merely say, "No thank you, I have nothing further to add." This is a point where you can "talk yourself out" of a good impression or fail to present an important bit of information. Remember, *you close the interview yourself*.

The chairman will then say, "That is all, Mr. _____, thank you." Do not be startled; the interview is over, and quicker than you think. Thank him, gather your belongings and take your leave. Save your sigh of relief for the other side of the door.

How to put your best foot forward

Throughout this entire process, you may feel that the board individually and collectively is trying to pierce your defenses, seek out your hidden weaknesses and embarrass and confuse you. Actually, this is not true. They are obliged to make an appraisal of your qualifications for the job you are seeking, and they want to see you in your best light. Remember, they must interview all candidates and a non-cooperative candidate may become a failure in spite of their best efforts to bring out his qualifications. Here are 15 suggestions that will help you:

1) Be natural – Keep your attitude confident, not cocky

If you are not confident that you can do the job, do not expect the board to be. Do not apologize for your weaknesses, try to bring out your strong points. The board is interested in a positive, not negative, presentation. Cockiness will antagonize any board member and make him wonder if you are covering up a weakness by a false show of strength.

2) Get comfortable, but don't lounge or sprawl

Sit erectly but not stiffly. A careless posture may lead the board to conclude that you are careless in other things, or at least that you are not impressed by the importance of the occasion. Either conclusion is natural, even if incorrect. Do not fuss with your clothing, a pencil or an ashtray. Your hands may occasionally be useful to emphasize a point; do not let them become a point of distraction.

3) Do not wisecrack or make small talk

This is a serious situation, and your attitude should show that you consider it as such. Further, the time of the board is limited – they do not want to waste it, and neither should you.

4) Do not exaggerate your experience or abilities

In the first place, from information in the application or other interviews and sources, the board may know more about you than you think. Secondly, you probably will not get away with it. An experienced board is rather adept at spotting such a situation, so do not take the chance.

5) If you know a board member, do not make a point of it, yet do not hide it

Certainly you are not fooling him, and probably not the other members of the board. Do not try to take advantage of your acquaintanceship – it will probably do you little good.

6) Do not dominate the interview

Let the board do that. They will give you the clues – do not assume that you have to do all the talking. Realize that the board has a number of questions to ask you, and do not try to take up all the interview time by showing off your extensive knowledge of the answer to the first one.

7) Be attentive

You only have 20 minutes or so, and you should keep your attention at its sharpest throughout. When a member is addressing a problem or question to you, give him your undivided attention. Address your reply principally to him, but do not exclude the other board members.

8) Do not interrupt

A board member may be stating a problem for you to analyze. He will ask you a question when the time comes. Let him state the problem, and wait for the question.

9) Make sure you understand the question

Do not try to answer until you are sure what the question is. If it is not clear, restate it in your own words or ask the board member to clarify it for you. However, do not haggle about minor elements.

10) Reply promptly but not hastily

A common entry on oral board rating sheets is "candidate responded readily," or "candidate hesitated in replies." Respond as promptly and quickly as you can, but do not jump to a hasty, ill-considered answer.

11) Do not be peremptory in your answers

A brief answer is proper – but do not fire your answer back. That is a losing game from your point of view. The board member can probably ask questions much faster than you can answer them.

12) Do not try to create the answer you think the board member wants

He is interested in what kind of mind you have and how it works – not in playing games. Furthermore, he can usually spot this practice and will actually grade you down on it.

13) Do not switch sides in your reply merely to agree with a board member

Frequently, a member will take a contrary position merely to draw you out and to see if you are willing and able to defend your point of view. Do not start a debate, yet do not surrender a good position. If a position is worth taking, it is worth defending.

14) Do not be afraid to admit an error in judgment if you are shown to be wrong

The board knows that you are forced to reply without any opportunity for careful consideration. Your answer may be demonstrably wrong. If so, admit it and get on with the interview.

15) Do not dwell at length on your present job

The opening question may relate to your present assignment. Answer the question but do not go into an extended discussion. You are being examined for a *new* job, not your present one. As a matter of fact, try to phrase ALL your answers in terms of the job for which you are being examined.

Basis of Rating

Probably you will forget most of these "do's" and "don'ts" when you walk into the oral interview room. Even remembering them all will not ensure you a passing grade. Perhaps you did not have the qualifications in the first place. But remembering them will help you to put your best foot forward, without treading on the toes of the board members.

Rumor and popular opinion to the contrary notwithstanding, an oral board wants you to make the best appearance possible. They know you are under pressure – but they also want to see how you respond to it as a guide to what your reaction would be under the pressures of the job you seek. They will be influenced by the degree of poise you display, the personal traits you show and the manner in which you respond.

ABOUT THIS BOOK

This book contains tests divided into Examination Sections. Go through each test, answering every question in the margin. We have also attached a sample answer sheet at the back of the book that can be removed and used. At the end of each test look at the answer key and check your answers. On the ones you got wrong, look at the right answer choice and learn. Do not fill in the answers first. Do not memorize the questions and answers, but understand the answer and principles involved. On your test, the questions will likely be different from the samples. Questions are changed and new ones added. If you understand these past questions you should have success with any changes that arise. Tests may consist of several types of questions. We have additional books on each subject should more study be advisable or necessary for you. Finally, the more you study, the better prepared you will be. This book is intended to be the last thing you study before you walk into the examination room. Prior study of relevant texts is also recommended. NLC publishes some of these in our Fundamental Series. Knowledge and good sense are important factors in passing your exam. Good luck also helps. So now study this Passbook, absorb the material contained within and take that knowledge into the examination. Then do your best to pass that exam.

EXAMINATION SECTION

EXAMINATION SECTION
TEST 1

DIRECTIONS: Answer the following questions directly, briefly, and succinctly.

1. What is used in a slack tub besides water to temper ordinary steel for hard rock drilling?
2. What tool is used to smooth and straighten up the work?
3. In making a sharp bend in piping, what is used to keep it from buckling?
4. What quenching usually makes steel MOST brittle?
5. What is used to keep a tool from sticking when punching a soft piece of steel?
6. What is the name of the tool used for reducing a piece of stock to three-quarters diameter?
7. What is used for tempering steel springs?
8. Name two common fluxes for welding, besides compounds.
9. What would happen to the weld if anything like lead, tin foil, or sulphur got into the fire?
10. What is the pointed end of an anvil called?

KEY (CORRECT ANSWERS)

1. Salt (brine)

2. Flatter

3. Sand

4. Water (ice water)(cold water)

5. Coal (slag)(coal dust)
   Soap
   Sawdust
   Ashes
   Grease

6. Swedge

7. Oil

8. Borax
   Sand
   Glass
   Iron filings
   Soap

9. Would not weld (weld would not stick)

10. Horn

TEST 2

DIRECTIONS: Answer the following questions directly, briefly, and succinctly.

1. What is used for casehardening steel?
2. What tool is used for spreading or grooving iron?
3. What is a good color of heat for forging iron?
4. What tool is used to put in the heel of the anvil for cutting?
5. Name two different kinds of welds.
6. By what name does one refer to the action of a trotting horse who strikes his front foot with his hind foot?
7. How does a deep-seated corn usually shown on a sole?
8. What is the ring called that appears around the top of the horse's hoof?
9. What disease necessitates that a horse be shod with lowered toes and raised heels?
10. What is the lower part of a horse's leg between the hoof and fetlock called?

KEY (CORRECT ANSWERS)

1. Potassium cyanide
   Raw ground bone
   Potash

2. Fuller tool

3. White
   Lemon (high yellow)

4. Hardie

5. Scarf (lap)
   Butt (jump)
   Cleft (vee)(split)
   Male
   Female
   Fargot (roller)

6. Forging (overreaching)(overstriding)

7. Red spots (red)(purple)(bloody)

8. Coronet band (coronet)(coronary band)

9. Navicular
   Tendons
   Founder

10. Pastern
    Coffin joint (coffin)

EXAMINATION SECTION
TEST 1

DIRECTIONS: Answer the following questions directly, briefly, and succinctly.

1. In molding a half core, where is the LONGEST reinforcing rods usually put?
2. What is meant by *2-off* marked on a core box?
3. What is used to secure cores to keep them from floating during pouring?
4. What is a core called which has not been naked in an oven?
5. What is the process of painting called that paints the core with graphite and charcoal mixed in molasses water?
6. What tool is used to make the top of the sand level with the top edges of the core box?
7. What liquid is used on metal core boxes to keep the cores from sticking?
8. What are the end parts of a core called which are used only to locate the core in the mold?
9. What is the taper called that is given to a core box to make it easy to withdraw?
10. Name two materials used as binders in core sand.
11. Name two materials used to vent cores.
12. What tool has a flat end at right angles to the stem, and is used to remove loose sand from deep pockets of a mold?
13. Name two tools used to smooth and touch up green cores.
14. What is used to lighten large cores?
15. What are the rounded edges of a core called?

KEY (CORRECT ANSWERS)

1. Center Weak point
2. Make two cores
   Number of cores to be made
3. Chaplets (anchors) (studs)
4. Green sand core (green core)
5. Blacking (coating) (facing) (swabbing) (core wash)
6. Strike-off
   Trowel
7. Kerosene (coal oil)
8. Prints (core prints)
9. Draft
10. Glutrin   Core Compound   Linseed oil
    Lincoal   Tux   Flour
    Resin   Dextrine   Pitch
11. Wires   Rods   Coke
    Cinders   Wax (tapers)   Hay
12. Lifter
13. Spoon slick   Heart tool   Trowel
    Double-ender Lifter   Yankee tool
14. Coke   Cinders   Ashes
15. Fillets

TEST 2

DIRECTIONS: Answer the following questions directly, briefly, and succinctly.

1. What are the shapes of the two ends of a double-ender slick?
2. What is put on the cope to properly guide it on the drag?
3. What are the two ends of a rammer called?
4. In what part of the casting are shrink holes MOST often found?
5. What is used to support the core besides core prints and to make sure it will stay in place when the metal is poured?
6. By what means can one tell a pattern print from a core print?
7. What is the taper called that is given to a core box to make it easy to withdraw?
8. What is a flask called which is fastened at one corner with a snap?
9. What is used to keep the cope and drag from sticking together?
10. What tool is used to cut gates in the drag?
11. What is used as a binder for cores?
12. What part of the rammer is USUALLY used first?
13. What tool is used to clean out a flange?
14. What is the surface between the cope and drag of a mold called?
15. What is the middle part of a three-part flask called?

KEY (CORRECT ANSWERS)

1. Heart (flat)
   Spoon (spade)
2. Pins and eyes (pins) (guides)
3. Peen
   Butt
4. Heaviest (thickest) part
   Cope (top)
5. Chaplets (anchors) (studs)
6. Painted different colors
7. Draft
8. Snap flask
9. Parting sand (parting dust) (parteen) (partimold)
10. Gate stick (sprue cutter)
11. Molasses   Oil   Resin
    Core compound Flour   Glutrin
    Dextrine
12. Peen (point)
13. Lifter
    Flange tool
14. Joint (face) (parting)
15. Cheek

TEST 3

DIRECTIONS: Answer the following questions directly, briefly, and succinctly.

1. What is put in the cope to reinforce and help hold the sand together?
2. What is used on the face of a mold to give a smooth surface to the casting?
3. Why are patterns made oversize?
4. What is used to support cores when they cannot be held in place otherwise?
5. What is the slope or taper called that is given to a pattern to allow for the clean removal of the pattern from the mold?
6. What is used to keep the cope and drag from sticking together?
7. What tool is used to slick a deep part of the mold?
8. What is done to prevent the molten metal from running out at the parting line?
9. Into what are gaggers dipped to help the sane stick to them?
10. What is used to reinforce the corners and edges of the sand in a mold?
11. What is ramming sand around the edges of the flask called?
12. What are iron bars or rods called that are put in a mold when certain parts are to cool before others?
13. Where are the cheek flasks located?
14. What is a mold called that does not have to be dried before pouring?
15. What part of the lifter is used to slick a very deep part of the mold?

KEY (CORRECT ANSWERS)

1. Gaggers
2. Graphite (blacking) (plumbago) (silver lead) (sea coal)
   Facing sand
   Parting dust
3. Allow for shrinkage (contraction)
4. Chaplets (anchors) (studs)
5. Draft
6. Parting sand (parting dust) (parteen) (partimold)
7. Lifter
8. Clamp
   Weight
   Paste (daub) (clay)
9. Clay wash (paste)
10. Nails
    Rods (bars)
11. Peening (peen ramming) (tucking)
12. Chills
13. Between cope and drag (in center) (in middle)
14. Green sand mold (green mold)
15. Heel (foot) (hub) (butt)

EXAMINATION SECTION
TEST 1

DIRECTIONS: Answer the following questions directly, briefly, and succinctly.

1. What is used to oxidize and darken red brass and copper?
2. What metal plate is formed by the combination of two or more metals?
3. What is done to the circuit to remove old plating?
4. Why are objects dipped in a weak acid between the cleaning and plating process?
5. What chemical is added to a brass solution in order to keep the copper and zinc mixed thoroughly?
6. What commonly used plating metal is the hardest?
7. What is the negative rod in the plating tank called?
8. What is added to a nickel solution to raise the pH?
9. What type of electroplating is often called rust-proofing?
10. What acid is used to remove sand from castings?

KEY (CORRECT ANSWERS)

1. Sulphur compound (liver of sulphur)(sulphate)(sulphide)(polysulphide)(liquid of sulphur)(sulphurette)

2. Brass
   Bronze
   Alloy
   Green gold

3. Reverse

4. Remove oxide (remove rust)(remove tarnish)(remove stains)(remove film)(remove scales)
   Neutralize (kill)(cut) the alkali cleaner
   Clean it

5. Cyanide (sodium cyanide)
   Ammonia; salammoniac

6. Chromium (chrome)

7. Cathode
   Work rod

8. Ammonia (ammonium hydroxide)(ammonia water)
   Nickel carbonate
   Alkali
   Soda
   Ammonium carbonate

9. Cadmium
   Zinc
   Tin

10. Muriatic (hydrochloric)
    Hydrofluoric
    Sulphuric

TEST 2

DIRECTIONS: Answer the following questions directly, briefly, and succinctly.

1. What is the machine called which keeps the bath stirred up?
2. What acid is used to prepare an acid copper-plating solution?
3. What two chemicals are added to water to prepare a cadmium solution?
4. What is the term to describe a rough surface caused by pickling?
5. What two kinds of nickel salts are used in nickel plating?
6. What two chemicals are added to water to prepare a chrome solution?

KEY (CORRECT ANSWERS)

1. Agitator

2. Sulphuric

3. Cyanide (sodium cyanide)(potassium cyanide)(cyanide salt)
   Cadmium (cadmium oxide)(cadmium chloride)(cadmium sulphate)(cadmium cyanide)(salts of cadmium)

4. Etched
   Pitted

5. Single (S) (nickel chloride)(nickel sulphate)
   Double (d) (nickel ammonium sulphate)(ammonium sulphate)

6. Chromic acid and sulphuric acid
   Chrome salt and sulphuric acid

EXAMINATION SECTION
TEST 1

DIRECTIONS: Each question or incomplete statement is followed by several suggested answers or completions. Select the one that BEST answers the question or completes the statement. *PRINT THE LETTER OF THE CORRECT ANSWER IN THE SPACE AT THE RIGHT.*

1. Before splicing together the ends of two steel columns, the ends are *usually*

   A. coped   B. milled   C. broached   D. blocked

   1.____

2. Of the following heat treatment processes, the one that brings steel to the LOWEST hardness is

   A. tempering   B. normalizing
   C. annealing   D. nitriding

   2.____

3. A riveted girder consists of flange angles, flange plates, web, and stiffeners. Of the structural members listed above, the one that would MOST likely be crimped is the

   A. flange angles   B. flange plates
   C. web   D. stiffeners

   3.____

4. In the installation of steel studs on the flange of a beam with an automatic-end welder, the ceramic part that is removed from the stud after the completion of the welding process is known as a

   A. yoke   B. batten   C. collar   D. ferrule

   4.____

5. Of the following, the machine that should be used to make an angle from a flat plate is the

   A. shaper   B. turret lathe
   C. brake   D. mandrel press

   5.____

6. According to the AISC Code, the MINIMUM edge distance permitted for drilled holes in structural steel plate when the edges of the plate are sheared and when 5/8" diameter bolts are to be used is

   A. 7/8"   B. 1 1/8"   C. 1 1/2"   D. 1 3/4"

   6.____

7. Of the following welding processes, the one that is presently MOST widely used in the fabrication of structural steel is _____ welding.

   A. friction   B. braze   C. arc   D. forge

   7.____

8. The COMMON fabrication practice for structural steel is to make rivet holes _____ the size of the rivet.

   A. 1/32" smaller than   B. equal to
   C. 1/32" larger than   D. 1/16" larger than

   8.____

9. The tool that should be used to taper the top of a hole in a steel plate is a

   A. boring bar   B. reamer
   C. spot facer   D. countersink

   9.____

10. The type of rivet head MOST often used for structural steel is the _____ head.

    A. truss
    B. flat
    C. button
    D. wagon box

11.

    The sketch shown above is a profile of a type of defective weld. This type of defect is known as

    A. insufficient throat
    B. overlap
    C. excessive convexity
    D. excessive concavity

12. Of the following profiles of welds shown in cross-section, the one that shows an undercut is

    A.   B.   C.   D.

13. Of the following measuring devices, the one that gives the MOST precise measurement of thickness is the

    A. micrometer caliper
    B. machinists steel scale
    C. combination square
    D. protractor

14. Of the following methods, the BEST one to use in order to check the curvature of a curved steel beam is the

    A. chord-offset
    B. radius-offset
    C. tangent-offset
    D. deflection angle-chord

15. A testing machine that measures hardness is the

    A. Riehle
    B. Tinius Olsen
    C. Scott
    D. Brinnel

16. Brittleness of steel is measured by the _____ Test.

    A. Rockwell
    B. Charpy
    C. Proctor
    D. Spark

17. The micrometer reading shown at the right is
    A. .318"
    B. .346"
    C. .377"
    D. .392"

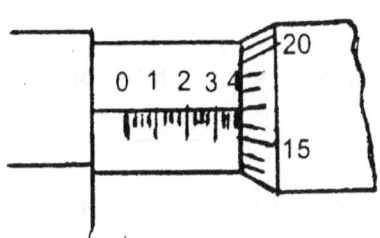

18.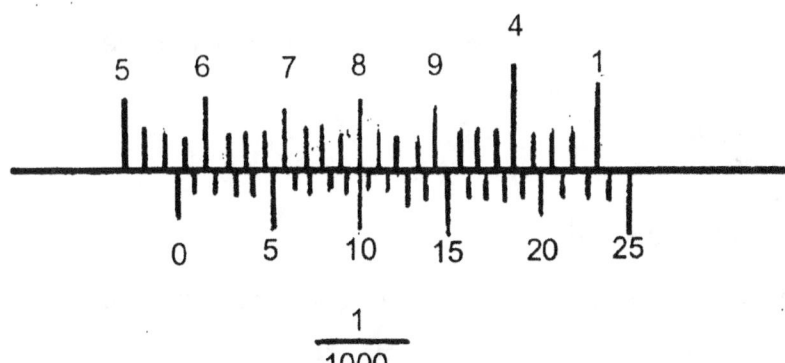

    The reading on the height gauge, with vernier shown above, is MOST NEARLY

    A. A.3.274   B. 3.560   C. 4.615   D. 4.916

19.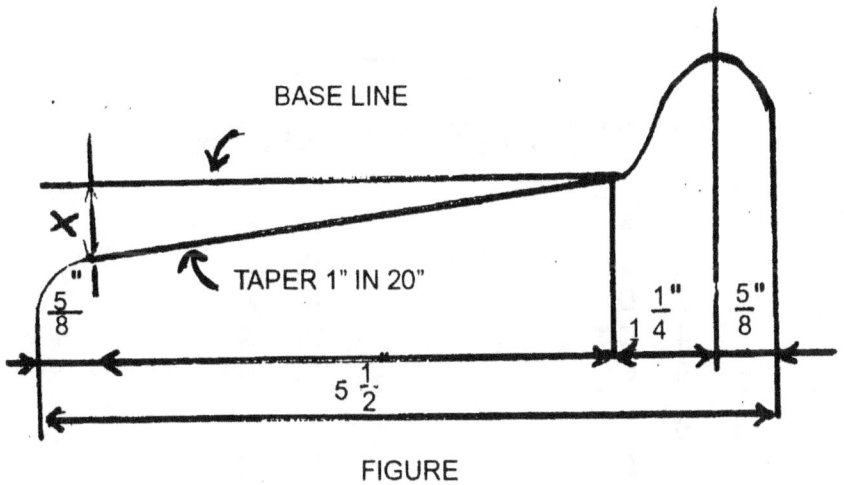

    FIGURE

    The distance X in the figure shown above is MOST NEARLY

    A. 3/32"   B. 1/8"   C. 5/32"   D. 3/16"

20. Of the following atmospheric conditions, the one under which it is MOST harmful to store welding electrodes is

    A. dampness   B. dryness   C. heat   D. cold

21. Of the following, the BEST tool to use to check the length of the circumference of the tread of a new railroad car wheel is a

    A. trammel   B. tape
    C. back-to-back gage   D. protractor

22. Specifications state that the tolerance for camber of a steel beam is equal to

    $1/8" \times \dfrac{\text{total length}}{5}$

    The tolerance for camber for a beam 30 feet long is

    A. 1/2"   B. 5/8"   C. 3/4"   D. 7/8"

23. The MAIN reason for making a ladle analysis of steel is to determine the _____ of the steel.

    A. chemical composition
    B. corrosion rate
    C. fatigue limit
    D. expansion and contraction

24. The machine that is NOT used in the physical testing of steel products is the

    A. Tinnius Olsen   B. Riehle
    C. Brinnel   D. Scott

25. An electrode has a designation of E7018. The digit that designates the position or positions it is suitable for is the

    A. 7   B. 0   C. 1   D. 8

KEY (CORRECT ANSWERS)

1. B		11. C	
2. C		12. B	
3. D		13. A	
4. D		14. A	
5. C		15. D	
6. B		16. B	
7. C		17. D	
8. D		18. B	
9. D		19. C	
10. C		20. A	

21. B
22. C
23. A
24. D
25. C

TEST 2

DIRECTIONS: Each question or incomplete statement is followed by several suggested answers or completions. Select the one that BEST answers the question or completes the statement. *PRINT THE LETTER OF THE CORRECT ANSWER IN THE SPACE AT THE RIGHT.*

1. A test that is NON-DESTRUCTIVE is the _____ test. 1._____

   A. ultrasonic B. tensile
   C. charpy D. strip

2. The symbol shown below that represents the cross-section of steel is 2._____

   A. [cross-hatched] B. [diagonal lines] C. [horizontal lines] D. [vertical lines]

3. The turn-of-nut method is to be used to tighten A325 bolts. The outer faces of the bolted parts are parallel to each other and perpendicular to the bolt axis (bevel washers not used). The additional required nut rotation from the *snug tight* condition is a _____ turn. 3._____

   A. 1/4 B. 1/2 C. 3/4 D. full

4. In the tensile testing of bolts, which of the following strength measurements are recorded? 4._____

   A. Yield point and ultimate strength
   B. Elastic limit and ultimate strength
   C. Yield point and fracture strength
   D. Elastic limit and fracture strength

5. In a guided bend test for weld ductility, the weld specimen is bent through an angle of 5._____

   A. 45° B. 90° C. 135° D. 180°

6. 6._____

   The type of butt weld shown above is a double
   A. bevel B. J C. U D. V

7. The conventional sign that represents a countersunk and chipped shop rivet is 7._____

   A. ⌀ B. ⊘ C. [symbol] D. [symbol]

8. The structural shape represented by the designation C15 x 40 is 8._____

   A. □ B. ⊥ C. I D. ⌐

9. Galvanizing of steel, when specified for grating, means coating the steel with

   A. lead B. titanium C. zinc D. tin

10. The shop coat of paint MOST often specified for structural steel is

    A. vermiculite B. red lead
    C. vinyl resin D. latex

11. A contract states that the material in steel piles and splices shall conform to structural steel specification ASTM A36. The 36 in the specification refers to the _____ steel.

    A. thickness of the
    B. minimum length of rolled section of
    C. weight per foot of the
    D. yield point of the

12. A rectangular bar, 1 3/4" thick, must have a minimum area of .36 square inches. Of the following, the MINIMUM acceptable width of the bar is

    A. 3/32" B. 5/32" C. 7/32" D. 9/32"

13. The rounded interior corners of structural steel shapes are called

    A. fillets B. kerfs C. dogs D. chamfers

14. A structural steel member having a designation of 18H5 is a

    A. girt B. purlin C. joist D. lintel

15. A hexagonal steel gusset plate is shown on a shop drawing with six equally spaced holes on the circumference of a 9-inch diameter circle. The distance between the centers of the adjacent holes is

    A. 4" B. 4 1/4" C. 4 1/2" D. 4 3/4"

16. Shown at the right is a sketch of the top of a bolt.
    The marking A490 on the head of the bolt is the _____ number of the bolt.

    A. heat
    B. shipment
    C. hardness
    D. specification

Questions 17-19.

DIRECTIONS: The drawing shown below refers to Questions 17 through 19. These questions should be answered in accordance with this drawing.

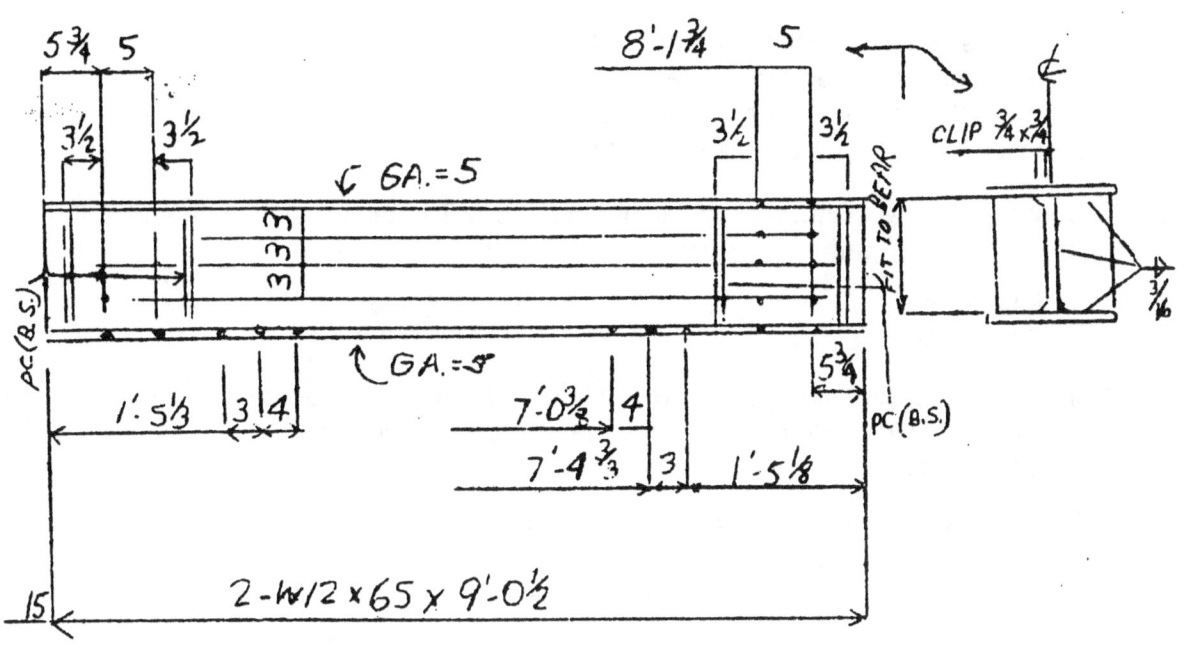

17. The welding symbol shown on the above diagram designates a _____ weld.

    A. spot   B. plug   C. butt   D. fillet

18. The abbreviation GA. appearing on the drawing means

    A. gage   B. galvanize   C. gap   D. gam

19. In the designation pc(B.S.) appearing on the shop drawing, the B.S. means

    A. billet steel   B. bearing steel
    C. both sides   D. beam stiffener

20. A specification states that in the shop assembly of structural steel, the parts of riveted structural members shall be well pinned and firmly drawn together with bolts before riveting is commenced. The pins used for aligning and holding the fabricated steel in place before bolting are known as _____ pins.

    A. linch   B. drift   C. clevis   D. finnegan

21. Of the following items relating to a written weekly report on the status of a fabrication contract, the MOST important item is that the report should be

    A. brief   B. accurate
    C. subjective   D. creative

22. Of the following, in preparing a monthly report of the work inspected in a steel fabrication shop, the BEST source of data is

    A. the contract CPM diagram   B. the fabricator's log book
    C. the shop drawings   D. his diary

23. Of the following items, the one that is LEAST important in qualifying a steel fabricator is the number of

    A. strikes suffered by the company in the last five years
    B. paid holidays given employees
    C. years the firm has been in existence
    D. miles the plant is from the nearest railroad

24. In writing a shop accident report, it is generally BEST to make each sentence in the report _____ and with _____ idea(s).

    A. long; one
    B. long; many
    C. short; one
    D. short; many

25. A specification states that gratings which show black or uncoated spots, *dross,* improper or insufficient galvanizing or any other defects shall be rejected.
    In the above specification, *dross* means

    A. dirt
    B. gloss
    C. flat
    D. clear

KEY (CORRECT ANSWERS)

1. A
2. B
3. C
4. A
5. D
6. B
7. D
8. D
9. C
10. B

11. D
12. C
13. A
14. C
15. C
16. D
17. D
18. A
19. C
20. B

21. B
22. D
23. B
24. C
25. A

EXAMINATION SECTION
TEST 1

DIRECTIONS: Each question or incomplete statement is followed by several suggested answers or completions. Select the one that BEST answers the question or completes the statement. *PRINT THE LETTER OF THE CORRECT ANSWER IN TE SPACE AT THE RIGHT.*

1. The hole size for a 1/2"-13" NC tapped hole maintaining a 65% thread height is 1.____

    A. 25/64"   B. 7/16"   C. 31/64"   D. 33/64"

2. A good flux for black iron is 2.____

    A. zinc chloride   B. rosin
    C. resin   D. sal ammoniac

3. The unified thread system which provides for an interchange of parts manufactured in the United States, Great Britain, and Canada is a combination of the _____ thread and the _____ thread. 3.____

    A. American national form; whitworth
    B. sharp V; acme
    C. American national form; acme
    D. American national form; sellers

4. The pan head of self-tapping screw, with a gimlet point, used for fastening light sheet metal, is referred to as type 4.____

    A. A   B. B   C. C   D. D

5. Terne plate is black iron coated with a mixture of 5.____

    A. lead and tin   B. lead and zinc
    C. lead and nickel D. tin and zinc

6. The worm gear of a thread chasing dial is designed to mesh with the 6.____

    A. feed screw   B. split nut
    C. lead screw   D. gear rack

7. The taper per foot for an American standard taper pin is 7.____

    A. 1/16"   B. 1/8"   C. 3/32"   D. 1/4"

8. To give a cutting speed of 35 f.p.m., a 3/4" drill should be run at about _____ r.p.m. 8.____

    A. 70   B. 176   C. 280   D. 350

9. The kaws on a pair of combination snips are 9.____

    A. curved   B. serrated   C. notched   D. straight

10. The taper that MOST closely resembles the Morse taper is known as the 10.____

    A. Pratt and Whitney   B. Sellers
    C. Jarno   D. Brown and Sharpe

11. The gage used to set the threading tool in the lathe is called a(n) _____ gage.   11._____
    A. center B. thread C. pitch D. angle

12. Ten-point steel has a carbon content of   12._____
    A. .010% B. .10% C. 1% D. 10%

13. The conductor stake used in sheet metal work has   13._____
    A. a round, slender horn and a rectangular horn
    B. two tapered horns of different diameters
    C. one slender horn and two shanks
    D. two cylindrical horns of different diameters

14. When draw filing a piece of cold rolled steel 1/2" x 1/2" x 6", the BEST file to use is the   14._____
    A. vixon B. XF
    C. mill   D. double cut smooth

15. Babbitt is an alloy of copper, tin, and   15._____
    A. antimony B. zinc C. aluminum D. nickel

16. The hand reamer that lends itself BEST to reaming a pulley hole with a keyway is the _____ reamer.   16._____
    A. adjustable hand B. straight tooth
    C. spiral tooth   D. increment cut

17. An acme thread has an included angle of   17._____
    A. 29° B. 55° C. 59 1/2° D. 60°

18. The straight single depth of a 1/2"-13 American national form thread is   18._____
    A. .0375 B. .0423 C. .0499 D. .0562

19. A four inch cylinder made of 1 X tin, joined with a #4 grooved seam, should have a stock allowance for the seam equal to   19._____
    A. 2 1/2 times the width of the seam plus 4 times the thickness of the metal
    B. 3 times the width of the seam
    C. 3 1/2 times the width of the seam plus twice the thickness of the metal
    D. 3 times the width of the seam plus three times the thickness of the metal

20. The process of heating cold rolled steel, impregnating with a carbonaceous material, and quenching is known as   20._____
    A. normalizing   B. nitriding
    C. case-hardening D. spherodizing

21. A solder made of 60% tin and 40% lead melts at _____ °F.   21._____
    A. 370 B. 415 C. 430 D. 461

22. A steel or wrought-iron block, other than the anvil, that is used for forge work is the _____ block.

   A. forming   B. vee   C. shaping   D. swage

23. A gate for a mold should always be shaped so that it

   A. is parallel to the drag surface
   B. slopes toward the mold
   C. slopes away from the mold
   D. connects with the heavy section of the pattern

24. Graphite is sometimes used in foundry practice as a

   A. binder for the sand
   B. binder for small cores
   C. mold facing
   D. material for making gaggers and chaplets

25. A newly developed structural steel that puts weather to work to protect itself and requires no painting is known as

   A. Stan-Steel   B. Ketos
   C. Cor-Ten   D. Armco

26. The process of heating and quenching tool steel from a temperature either within or above the critical temperature range is known as

   A. annealing   B. tempering
   C. hardening   D. normalizing

27. Of the following, the information that is NOT part of the manufacturer's grinding wheel marking symbols is

   A. grain size   B. grade
   C. wheel shape   D. structure

28. The rapid dulling of a twist drill, especially at the outer end of the lips (corners), is evidence that the

   A. drill has excessive lip clearance
   B. drill is revolving too rapidly
   C. point has been ground to an angle of less than 118°
   D. drill is riding on its *heel*

29. The size of a lathe mandrel or arbor is designated

   A. on the small end
   B. in accordance with standards set by individual manufacturers
   C. on the large end
   D. on both ends

30. The numbered lines on the barrel of a micrometer are in increments of 30._____
    A. .001"   B. .005"   C. .025"   D. .100"

KEY (CORRECT ANSWERS)

1. B
2. A
3. A
4. A
5. A

6. C
7. D
8. B
9. D
10. C

11. A
12. B
13. D
14. C
15. A

16. C
17. A
18. C
19. B
20. C

21. A
22. D
23. C
24. C
25. C

26. C
27. C
28. B
29. C
30. D

TEST 2

DIRECTIONS: Each question or incomplete statement is followed by several suggested answers or completions. Select the one that BEST answers the question or completes the statement. *PRINT THE LETTER OF THE CORRECT ANSWER IN THE SPACE AT THE RIGHT.*

1. To tap a hole for 1/8" standard pipe, one should use a tap designated 1/8 -   1.____

    A. 13 NSP   B. 20 NPT   C. 23 NTP   D. 27 NPT

2. A promising development in steel technology to produce BETTER steel more efficiently is   2.____

    A. modern blooming   B. continuous casting
    C. wet rolling   D. rapid ingot teaming

3. The spindle bore of an engine lathe is USUALLY equipped with a _____ taper.   3.____

    A. Morse   B. Brown and Sharpe
    C. Pratt and Whitney   D. Sellers

4. The space from the edge of the metal to the center of the rivet line should be AT LEAST _____ times the diameter of the rivet.   4.____

    A. 1 1/2   B. 2   C. 3   D. 4

5. A good forging heat for steel is   5.____

    A. cherry red (1375° F)   B. blood red (1075° F)
    C. light yellow (1975° F)   D. white (2200° F)

6. The tools BEST suited to forge a shoulder are the _____ and sledge.   6.____

    A. top fuller   B. bottom fuller
    C. set hammer   D. hardie

7. A base box is the unit of measure for tin plate and contains _____ sheets _____.   7.____

    A. 56; 18" x 20"   B. 100; 20" x 28"
    C. 112; 14" x 20"   D. 128; 18" x 20"

8. Of the following, the stake BEST suited for forming a common funnel is the   8.____

    A. creasing   B. blow horn
    C. beakhorn   D. candlemold

9. The body of sand used to form a recess or opening in a casting is called a   9.____

    A. core   B. core print
    C. fillet   D. cored hole

10. Tin plate with a light coating of tin is called _____ plate.   10.____

    A. coke tin   B. charcoal tin
    C. dairy   D. terne

11. The gage used to measure the thickness of iron and steel sheet metal is

    A. American
    B. United States standard
    C. Brown and Sharpe
    D. stubs

12. If a cross-feed screw on a lathe has eight threads per inch, and the micrometer dial is graduated so that a single division indicates a movement of one one-thousandth of an inch, the micrometer dial will have _____ equal divisions.

    A. 90   B. 100   C. 125   D. 250

13. Screws for use in metal, whose size is designated by a gage number indicating the diameter of the body of the screw, are called

    A. set screws
    B. machine bolts
    C. cap screws
    D. machine screws

14. An accurate method of checking the size of a twist drill would be to use a micrometer to measure the

    A. body of the drill
    B. point of the drill across the land
    C. point of the drill across the margin
    D. flute of the drill

15. If the cutting speed of steel is 75 feet per minute when using a high speed steel cutter to turn a 1 1/2" diameter piece of steel, the spindle speed of the lathe should be _____ RPM.

    A. 75   B. 186   C. 200   D. 340

16. In foundry, the process of making a mold in sand from a pattern with an irregular parting line USUALLY involves

    A. coping down
    B. a lost wax process
    C. a split pattern
    D. a sweep mold

17. The cutting action of a twist drill is aided by a *rake* action which is provided for on the drill by the

    A. web   B. flute   C. land   D. margin

18. The included angle on the head of a standard flat-head machine screw is

    A. 60°   B. 90°   C. 82°   D. 59°

19. The main alloying elements in monel metal are

    A. nickel, zinc, copper
    B. chrome, nickel, copper
    C. copper, zinc, tin
    D. nickel, copper

20. When turning a slender rod in a lathe, springing is minimized by using a

    A. compound rest
    B. follower rest
    C. cross rest
    D. draw-in bar

21. In foundry practice, a strike bar is used for

    A. loosening the pattern
    B. striking off flashing
    C. separating cope and drag
    D. making sand even with top of flask

21._____

22. The forge operation of enlarging the cross-sectional area of a bar is called

    A. upsetting   B. drawing out
    C. fullering   D. spreading

22._____

23. A screw thread that is NOT used much today is the

    A. acme   B. square
    C. American standard D. S.A.E.

23._____

24. One of the first men to produce carbide tools was

    A. Johannson   B. Metcalf   C. Jarno   D. Moissan

24._____

25. The twist drill that is exactly the same diameter as the letter *E* drill is

    A. 1/4"   B. #40   C. #1   D. 5/16"

25._____

26. The cross-sectional shape of a warding file is

    A. square
    B. tapered wedge
    C. rectangular (wide and thin)
    D. rectangular (wide and thick)

26._____

27. The steel that would lend itself BEST for making a center punch is

    A. high speed   B. 1020 machinery
    C. cold rolled   D. drill rod

27._____

28. One thousand 10 oz. rivets weigh about

    A. 1000 x 10 oz.   B. 10 oz.
    C. 1 lb.   D. 10 lbs.

28._____

29. A good flux for tin plate is

    A. zinc chloride   B. muriatic acid
    C. rosin   D. cut acid

29._____

30. The material that gives high-speed steel its hardness and ability to keep an edge is

    A. tungsten   B. vanadium   C. chromium   D. platinum

30._____

KEY (CORRECT ANSWERS)

1.	D	16.	A
2.	B	17.	B
3.	A	18.	C
4.	B	19.	D
5.	C	20.	B
6.	C	21.	D
7.	C	22.	A
8.	B	23.	B
9.	A	24.	D
10.	A	25.	A
11.	B	26.	C
12.	C	27.	D
13.	D	28.	B
14.	C	29.	C
15.	C	30.	B

TEST 3

DIRECTIONS: Each question or incomplete statement is followed by several suggested answers or completions. Select the one that BEST answers the question or completes the statement. *PRINT THE LETTER OF THE CORRECT ANSWER IN THE SPACE AT THE RIGHT.*

1. A metal that has a coating of zinc is known as a(n) _____ metal.
   A. nitrided B. anodized
   C. galvanized D. normalized

2. A set of hand taps includes _____ taps.
   A. machine, plug, and bottom
   B. taper, plug, and machine
   C. taper, machine, and bottom
   D. taper, plug, and bottom

3. The pitch of the threads in a micrometer sleeve is _____ threads per inch.
   A. 25   B. 40   C. 100   D. 1,000

4. The motion of the shaper ram is.
   A. circular B. rotary
   C. reciprocating D. semi-circular

5. A split die
   A. is damaged beyond repair
   B. can be adjusted
   C. requires two wrenches to operate
   D. contains two separate cutters

6. The diameter of a twist drill is measured across the
   A. margin   B. web   C. flutes   D. shank

7. A template is a
   A. type of hand shears B. metal cutting saw
   C. pattern D. type of pin punch

8. The tool post is mounted in the clapper box in a
   A. lathe B. drill press
   C. milling machine D. shaper

9. To remove a taper shank drill from a drill press, use a
   A. drift punch B. pin punch
   C. pipe wrench D. chuck key

10. One complete turn of the handle on the index head of a milling machine will turn the work
    A. 180°   B. 9°   C. 40°   D. 90°

11. Offsetting the tailstock on the lathe will   11._____

    A. facilitate boring
    B. enable threads to be cut accurately
    C. center-drill without oil
    D. produce a taper

12. A rack and pinion on a lathe give movement to the   12._____

    A. carriage   B. tailstock
    C. headstock   D. compound rest

13. A knurling tool is used in a   13._____

    A. milling machine   B. shaper
    C. lathe   D. drill press

14. The dead center in a lathe is found in the   14._____

    A. headstock   B. compound rest
    C. cross slide   D. tailstock

15. Lathe tool bits are made of _____ steel.   15._____

    A. low carbon   B. high speed
    C. machine   D. case hardened

16. The products of the blast furnace are   16._____

    A. waste gases, steel, and slag
    B. coke, slag, and pig iron
    C. waste gases, pig iron, and slag
    D. waste gases, coke, and slag

17. Solder is composed of _____ and lead.   17._____

    A. zinc   B. tin   C. copper   D. spelter

18. On a double thread, the lead is equal to   18._____

    A. the pitch   B. one-half the pitch
    C. twice the pitch   D. diameter

19. A vernier scale can be found on a   19._____

    A. height gage   B. surface plate
    C. dial indicator   D. telescope gage

20. The lines on the sleeve of a micrometer are _____ of an inch apart.   20._____

    A. .075   B. .025   C. .100   D. .001

21. An Allen head screw is tightened with a   21._____

    A. regular screwdriver
    B. spanner wrench
    C. cross-shaped screwdriver
    D. hexagon-shaped wrench

22. The handle of a file fits on the   22.____
    A. tang   B. heel   C. tail   D. sole

23. Countersinks for flat head screws have an included angle of   23.____
    A. 60°   B. 75°   C. 82°   D. 90°

24. A hand groover is used to   24.____
    A. remove chips from a groove or keyway
    B. lock a seam
    C. fold over a wired edge
    D. shape soft metal on a lathe

25. An example of a ferrous metal is   25.____
    A. brass   B. aluminum   C. iron   D. copper

26. The cold chisel commonly used to shape a keyway is a   26.____
    A. cape chisel   B. flat chisel
    C. round chisel   D. diamond point

27. A foundry flask is used to   27.____
    A. analyze the sand   B. clean the pattern
    C. support the sand   D. clean the casting

28. A sprue pin is used to   28.____
    A. ram a pattern
    B. provide a hole through which the metal is poured
    C. locate the two halves of a split pattern
    D. clean the slag off molten metal

29. The sand used to separate the cope from the drag is _____ sand. 29.____
    A. parting   B. green   C. core   D. tempered

30. Fillets are used to   30.____
    A. simplify construction of the mold
    B. strengthen the casting
    C. strengthen the pattern
    D. support sand cores

KEY (CORRECT ANSWERS)

1.	C	16.	C
2.	D	17.	B
3.	B	18.	C
4.	C	19.	A
5.	B	20.	B
6.	A	21.	D
7.	C	22.	A
8.	D	23.	C
9.	A	24.	B
10.	B	25.	C
11.	D	26.	A
12.	A	27.	C
13.	C	28.	B
14.	D	29.	A
15.	B	30.	B

TEST 4

DIRECTIONS: Each question or incomplete statement is followed by several suggested answers or completions. Select the one that BEST answers the question or completes the statement. *PRINT THE LETTER OF THE CORRECT ANSWER IN THE SPACE AT THE RIGHT.*

1. The suggested cutting speed for high-speed drills when drilling steel is APPROXIMATELY _____ surface feet per minute.   1._____

    A. 200-250 B. 150-200 C. 100-150 D. 50-100

2. When a strong joint is needed to connect the bottom of a sheet-metal container to the body, the BEST joint to use is a   2._____

    A. burr or flange B. single seam
    C. double seam D. dovetail seam

3. The candle-mould stake   3._____

    A. is used for shaping sheet-metal candlestick holders
    B. has a slender horn for tube forming
    C. is used mainly for corner seam closing
    D. is used for wiring and beading

4. Left-hand aviation snips are designed to   4._____

    A. cut a curve to the left
    B. be used by left-handed people
    C. cut a curve to the right
    D. cut aluminum airplane parts

5. Ammonium chloride is also known as   5._____

    A. sal ammoniac
    B. bauxite
    C. amino acid
    D. a good electro-plating electrolyte

6. As the percentage of lead in soft solder increases, the   6._____

    A. melting point becomes higher
    B. melting point becomes lower
    C. strength of the joint decreases
    D. percentage of zinc decreases

7. To improve the machinability and resistance to corrosion of aluminum, the alloying metal is   7._____

    A. silicon B. copper C. manganese D. magnesium

8. Borax can be used   8._____

    A. as a flux in brazing
    B. for pickling silver

C. as an adhesive in copper enameling
D. as a cutting compound

9. A 42-tooth driving gear rotating at 400 RPM in a clockwise direction is connected to a 14-tooth gear by means of an idler gear.
   The speed and direction of rotation of the (14-tooth) driven gear is

   A. 1200 RPM and rotating clockwise
   B. 1200 RPM and rotating counter-clockwise
   C. 133 1/3 RPM and rotating counter-clockwise
   D. 133 1/3 RPM and rotating clockwise

9.____

10. Rouge used in metal polishing is made of

    A. decomposed shale   B. iron oxide
    C. powdered lava   D. silicon carbide

10.____

11. The BEST thickness of copper for doing repousse projects is _____ gauge.

    A. 14   B. 18   C. 24   D. 36

11.____

12. Copper is often pickled with

    A. a solution of sulphuric acid and water
    B. a solution of ammonium sulphide
    C. powdered tragacenth and alcohol
    D. kasenit

12.____

13. Liver of sulphur is also known as

    A. ferric sulphide   B. hyposulphite of soda
    C. potassium sulphide   D. sulphur dioxide

13.____

14. *German Silver* is USUALLY made of about

    A. 92% tin, 6% antimony, and 2% copper
    B. 64% copper, 18% nickel, and 18% zinc
    C. 925 parts of silver and 75 parts of copper
    D. 85% copper and 15% zinc

14.____

15. Blowholes in castings can be avoided by the use of

    A. a gate   B. vents
    C. a sprue pin   D. a core print

15.____

16. Chaplets are used

    A. with match-plate patterns
    B. to support cores
    C. in investment casting
    D. in shell mold casting

16.____

17. Muriatic acid is the same as

    A. hydrochloric acid   B. nitric acid
    C. sulphuric acid   D. aqua regia

17.____

18. Most of the steel made today is made in a(n).

    A. open-hearth furnace   B. Bessemer converter
    C. electric furnace   D. blast furnace

19. Nitriding is a process used for hardening

    A. special steel alloys by using ammonia gas
    B. low carbon steels
    C. steel parts requiring shallow surface hardness
    D. steel by exposing it while heated to a carbonaceous material

20. An aluminum oxide abrasive wheel is intended especially for grinding

    A. brass   B. iron   C. aluminum   D. steel

21. A scleroscope is used to

    A. examine crystalline structure
    B. determine hardness
    C. measure with extreme accuracy
    D. identify metal

22. The United States Standard (USS) gauge is used for measuring

    A. drills from #1 to #80
    B. steel wire, sheets, and plates
    C. copper, brass, and aluminum
    D. machine screw sizes #0 to #12

23. Back gears are USUALLY used on a lathe when

    A. knurling
    B. boring a hole
    C. reversing the feed
    D. high spindle speed is needed

24. The axes of spur gears are aligned so that they GENERALLY

    A. intersect at right angles
    B. intersect at acute angles
    C. intersect at obtuse angles
    D. are parallel to each other

25. The BEST file for filing steel on the lathe is a _____ file.

    A. vixen
    B. double-cut warding
    C. second-cut pillar
    D. long angle single-cut mill

26. In lathe work, the formula to use to determine the correct spindle speed when V = cutting speed in feet per minute, and D = diameter of workpiece in inches, is:

    A. $RPM = \dfrac{12\pi}{VD}$ B. $RPM = \dfrac{12V}{\pi D}$ C. $RPM = \dfrac{\pi D}{12V}$ D. $RPM = \dfrac{\pi V}{12D}$

27. The CORRECT sequence of drill sizes from smallest to largest is:

    A. #60, #30, 7/32", M
    B. #7, #50, 1/4", F
    C. #14, #2, Q, 1/8"
    D. B, R, 3/8", #12

28. The taper per foot on a part 2 5/16" in length and with a 15/16" diameter at one end and 11/16" at the other end, is

    A. .578"   B. .770"   C. .925"   D. 1.297"

29. The MAJOR diameter of a 5-40 NC machine screw is

    A. .125"   B. .140"   C. .155"   D. .170"

30. The usual amount left for removal with a reamer is

    A. 1/8" to 1/16"
    B. 1/16" to 1/32"
    C. 1/32" to 1/64"
    D. 1/64" to .005"

KEY (CORRECT ANSWERS)

1.	D	16.	B
2.	C	17.	A
3.	B	18.	A
4.	C	19.	A
5.	A	20.	D
6.	A	21.	B
7.	D	22.	B
8.	A	23.	A
9.	A	24.	A
10.	B	25.	D
11.	D	26.	B
12.	A	27.	A
13.	C	28.	D
14.	B	29.	A
15.	B	30.	D

EXAMINATION SECTION
TEST 1

DIRECTIONS: Each question or incomplete statement is followed by several suggested answers or completions. Select the one that BEST answers the question or completes the statement. *PRINT THE LETTER OF THE CORRECT ANSWER IN THE SPACE AT THE RIGHT.*

1. A nonferrous metal is

    A. cast iron B. pig iron C. steel alloys
    D. gold E. wrought iron

2. The industry employing MORE workers than any other is

    A. automotive B. plastic C. woodworking
    D. metal E. drug

3. That part of the base determined by the rate is

    A. percentage B. rate C. base
    D. top E. foundation

4. The number of parts into which a unit is divided is

    A. denominator of the fraction
    B. numerator of the fraction
    C. proper fraction
    D. improper fraction
    E. mixed number

5. The height of all printing characters from the feet to the top of the printing face is 11/12 inches and is known as

    A. body type B. display type C. condensed type
    D. extended type E. type high

6. Of the following, the oldest and still MOST widely used process of printing is

    A. offset B. gravure C. itaglio
    D. letter press E. mimeograph

7. The power plant of an automobile is assembled

    A. onto the frame
    B. in the body
    C. onto the front axle
    D. onto the front suspension
    E. in the car's center of gravity

8. The two MAJOR parts of a passenger car are _____ and _____.

    A. body; engine B. body; brakes
    C. engine; transmission D. body; chassis
    E. chassis; frame

9. The pictorial shop drawing with a single drawing representing the object with three visible surfaces is

   A. isometric B. oblique C. pictorial
   D. orthographic E. plan

10. The FIRST thing that a student in woodwork should do is

    A. lay out the pieces
    B. make out bill of materials
    C. read the drawing
    D. select a drawing
    E. select a project

11. Drawing pencils are *uniformly* graded by

    A. softness and hardness of lead
    B. thickness of the pencil
    C. length of the pencil
    D. size of the lead
    E. color

12. The type of brake MOST commonly used on a passenger car is

    A. air B. vacuum C. hydraulic
    D. electric E. mechanical

13. The purpose of a ballast in a fluorescent lamp circuit is to

    A. protect the lamp from high voltages
    B. protect the lamp from high current
    C. increase the resistance in the circuit
    D. provide a sudden high voltage to start the lamp
    E. provide a sudden high current to start the lamp

14. The OLDEST known wax is

    A. brown wax B. carnauba C. spermaceti
    D. white wax E. beeswax

15. In faceplate turning, the stock is ALWAYS screwed or fastened to

    A. faceplate B. back plate C. tailstock
    D. workbench E. dead center

16. The number that describes a hexagon BEST is

    A. 7 B. 6 C. 5 D. 8 E. 4

17. Masking tape

    A. holds sandpaper B. removes dust
    C. holds materials D. covers edges
    E. shields certain portions

3 (#1)

18. Large commercial generators are rotated by   18.____

    A. wind power   B. electric motors
    C. gasoline engines   D. water power
    E. diesel engines

19. The system in the human body MOST similar to the electrical system in a car is the   19.____
    _____ system.

    A. skeletal   B. digestive   C. muscular
    D. nervous   E. water

20. The drawing of a single piece that gives all the information necessary for making it is   20.____
    called _____ drawing.

    A. working   B. perspective   C. detail
    D. revolution   E. oblique

21. The QUICKEST way of drying lumber is   21.____

    A. kiln dried   B. air dried   C. gas dried
    D. all the same   E. none of the above

22. Before using multicolor paint, it should be mixed   22.____

    A. by hand
    B. with a vibrator
    C. by mixing colors
    D. by adding tung oil
    E. by pouring from can to can

23. The BEST description of dry cells which are connected in series is the   23.____

    A. amperage is increased   B. voltage is decreased
    C. amperage is decreased   D. voltage is increased
    E. none of the above

24. Lubricants are used to   24.____

    A. decrease friction in the steering mechanism
    B. preserve radiator hoses
    C. lengthen the life of various parts
    D. decrease engine compression
    E. increase the efficiency of shock absorbers

25. The BEST time to equalize the air pressure in your tires is   25.____

    A. before you start on a trip
    B. every time the pressure goes up or down
    C. after you have been driving for a few hours
    D. as soon as you stop after a trip
    E. anytime

26. The iron core of a transformer is made of laminated strips in order to   26.____

    A. reduce the cost of the transformer
    B. make the assembly of the transformer easier

C. reduce the weight of the transformer
D. cool the transformer
E. improve the operation of the transformer

27. The natural color of shellac is

    A. white   B. orange   C. brown   D. green   E. red

28. The tool that is used in holding a bit perpendicular to an edge while drilling dowel holes is known as a

    A. bit jig   B. dowel jig   C. hole jig
    D. twist drill   E. joint jig

29. The distance that the spray gun should be held from the surface which is being sprayed is _____ inches.

    A. 15   B. 4-6   C. 6-8   D. 12   E. 18

30. Pressure-sensitive tape should be stored

    A. in original carton   B. in cool place
    C. in dry place   D. on edge
    E. flat

31. The BASIC law of magnetism is that

    A. north magnetic poles attract each other
    B. south magnetic poles attract each other
    C. unlike poles attract each other
    D. unlike poles repel each other
    E. all magnets are artificial

32. The gauge on the instrument panel that indicates the speed of a moving car is the

    A. odometer   B. ammeter   C. generator
    D. speedometer   E. barometer

33. The part of the automobile that permits the engine to run while the car wheels stand still is the

    A. universal   B. clutch   C. timing gears
    D. differential   E. accelerator

34. The orthographic drawing is BEST described as

    A. two or more views at right angles to each other
    B. one view on a 30° angle
    C. one view on two 30° angles
    D. one-view drawing facing the front of the object
    E. three-view drawing

35. The wire edge of a plane iron is removed by

    A. grinding
    B. honing
    C. using a scrap of walnut

D. dragging the sharp edge across metal
E. none of the above

36. Lithopone is used in

    A. exterior paint
    B. interior paint
    C. white lead
    D. coloring of paint
    E. brookite

37. The product of the voltage and the current flowing in a circuit is

    A. resistance
    B. amperage
    C. wattage
    D. watt hours
    E. ohms

38. The carburetor

    A. distributes gas equally to all cylinders
    B. mixes the air and gasoline
    C. supplies the amount of gas needed by each cylinder
    D. cleans the gasoline
    E. separates any water from the gas

39. A production drawing is composed of

    A. simple sketches
    B. many sketches
    C. elaborate shaded drawings
    D. many drawings of different sizes
    E. all of the above

40. The dovetail joint is used almost ALWAYS for

    A. chairs
    B. drawers
    C. tables
    D. beds
    E. cabinets

KEY (CORRECT ANSWERS)

1. D	11. A	21. A	31. C
2. D	12. C	22. B	32. D
3. A	13. D	23. D	33. B
4. A	14. E	24. C	34. A
5. E	15. A	25. A	35. B
6. D	16. B	26. E	36. B
7. A	17. E	27. C	37. C
8. D	18. D	28. A	38. B
9. C	19. D	29. C	39. E
10. E	20. C	30. A	40. B

TEST 2

DIRECTIONS: Each question or incomplete statement is followed by several suggested answers or completions. Select the one that BEST answers the question or completes the statement. *PRINT THE LETTER OF THE CORRECT ANSWER IN THE SPACE AT THE RIGHT.*

1. The purpose of the compass is to draw

   A. circles
   B. oblong curves
   C. horizontal lines
   D. vertical lines
   E. a square corner

   1.____

2. The tool used for testing surface for trueness is

   A. try square
   B. marking gauge
   C. carpenter's square
   D. sliding rule
   E. T-bevel

   2.____

3. The HARDEST natural resin is _____ copals.

   A. kauri
   B. congo
   C. boea
   D. pontianak
   E. manilas

   3.____

4. The resistance of a conductor is NOT determined by _____ of the conductor.

   A. diameter
   B. length
   C. material
   D. temperature
   E. weight

   4.____

5. The development that contributed MOST to uniform braking is

   A. hydraulic control
   B. improved roads
   C. smaller braking
   D. lower center of gravity
   E. better tires

   5.____

6. The purpose of a perpendicular line is to

   A. cross another line
   B. angle across another line
   C. cross another line at a 90° angle
   D. run along side of another line
   E. run along the same angle as another line

   6.____

7. The number of board feet of lumber in a board 1" thick, 12" wide, and 36" long is

   A. 1   B. 2   C. 3   D. 4   E. 5

   7.____

8. One CHIEF component of aluminum paint is

   A. color-in oil
   B. linseed oil
   C. a vehicle
   D. metallic pigment
   E. alyda resin

   8.____

9. The MOST important use of electricity in the home is

   A. heating
   B. lighting
   C. motors
   D. refrigerators
   E. cooking

   9.____

10. The compression ratio of a diesel engine is *approximately* 10.____

    A. 10 to 1 through 14 to 1
    B. 7.5 to 1 through 9 to 1
    C. 15 to 1 through 20 to 1
    D. 21 to 1 through 30 to 1
    E. 4 to 1

11. The purpose of a sectional view is to 11.____

    A. expose the exterior
    B. expose the interior
    C. cut the object in half
    D. show a section of the drawing
    E. draw sections of an object

12. Perhaps the MOST complicated hand woodworking tool is the 12.____

    A. chisel   B. saw   C. hammer
    D. plane   E. rule

13. Shellac should be thinned with 13.____

    A. water   B. paint thinner
    C. lacquer thinner   D. gas
    E. soda solution

14. The kind of wire used in heating elements is 14.____

    A. copper   B. iron   C. steel
    D. tungsten   E. nichrome

15. The directional stability is established on MOST vehicles by 15.____

    A. camber   B. kingpin inclination
    C. caster   D. toe-in
    E. toe-out

16. Furniture and cabinet drawings are *usually* dimensioned in 16.____

    A. feet   B. inches   C. yards
    D. square feet   E. square yards

17. An open-wood requiring paste filler is 17.____

    A. maple   B. walnut   C. red gum
    D. cedar   E. cherry

18. Knots and pitchy spots should be treated with 18.____

    A. aluminum paint   B. multicolor paint
    C. lacquer   D. varnish
    E. prime coat

19. MOST electrical failures in portable heater appliances are located in the 19.____

    A. element   B. rheostat   C. thermostat
    D. frame   E. cord

3 (#2)

20. If the two gears in a gear set differ greatly in size, the SMALLER one is called   20.____
    A. pinion   B. ring gear   C. sun
    D. spur   E. annular

21. When making drawings of wood construction, the type of drawing sometimes used is   21.____
    A. oblique   B. isometric   C. cabinet
    D. detail   E. production

22. The number of 5 inch pieces (allowing for saw key) that can be cut from a board four feet   22.____
    long is
    A. 3   B. 4   C. 5   D. 8   E. 9

23. One type of natural finish is   23.____
    A. penetrating   B. intra-surface   C. surface
    D. colored   E. neutral

24. The hydrometer reading of a fully charged wet cell is   24.____
    A. 1.00   B. 1.15   C. 1.30   D. 1.50   E. 2.00

25. The control arms are held to the frame by   25.____
    A. shackle   B. pivot pins   C. lock pin
    D. kingpin   E. pivot shaft

26. The angl.es in a 30 x 60 triangle are _____ angle, _____ angle, _____ angle.   26.____
    A. 30; 60; 90   B. 30; 45; 45   C. 60; 75; 45
    D. 45; 45; 45   E. 60; 90; 90

27. The size of the circular saw is determined by its   27.____
    A. table
    B. diameter of saw blade
    C. RPM of the motor
    D. the depth the blade will cut
    E. number of blades that can be put on the motor shaft

28. Polystyrene is a _____ resin.   28.____
    A. thermoplastic B. thermosetting   C. alkyd
    D. natural   E. modified

29. The total voltage of two No. 6 dry cells and two flashlight cells connected in series is   29.____
    _____ volts.
    A. 3   B. 4   C. 6   D. 8   E. 12

30. The torque converter is a fluid coupling plus the   30.____
    A. impeller   B. roter   C. stator
    D. pump   E. follower

31. The gap between the FIRST dimension line and the object line should not be less than   31.____
    A. 1/4   B. 5/16   C. 3/8   D. 7/16   E. 1/2

32. The part of the circular saw tilted to cut a miter is 32.____

    A. fence   B. base   C. guard
    D. table   E. saw blade

33. The MAIN type of backing used for abrasives is 33.____

    A. cloth   B. paper
    C. wood   D. fiber
    E. combination of these

34. The metal with the LOWEST resistance is 34.____

    A. aluminum   B. carbon   C. copper
    D. gold   E. silver

35. The MAXIMUM voltage and current output of a two-brush generator is controlled by 35.____

    A. generator regulator   B. battery voltage
    C. cutout   D. third brush
    E. resistance unit

36. When sharpening the nibs of a ruling pen, one should use 36.____

    A. emery wheel   B. oil stone
    C. pocket knife   D. rough leather strap
    E. sand paper

37. The vertical members of the door frame are called 37.____

    A. stiles   B. sides   C. edges   D. rails   E. panels

38. The basic ingredient of nonflammable paint removers is 38.____

    A. naphtha   B. benzol
    C. acetone   D. nethylene chloride
    E. grain alcohol

39. A galvanometer measures 39.____

    A. voltage
    B. amperage
    C. quantity of electricity
    D. quantity of magnetism
    E. quantity of electron flow

40. The part of the carburetor that contains the venturi and throttle valve is the 40.____

    A. accelerating pump system
    B. metering jet
    C. main fuel supply system
    D. carburetor base
    E. mixing chamber

KEY (CORRECT ANSWERS)

1.	A	11.	B	21.	C	31.	C
2.	C	12.	D	22.	E	32.	E
3.	B	13.	E	23.	A	33.	B
4.	E	14.	E	24.	C	34.	C
5.	A	15.	C	25.	E	35.	A
6.	C	16.	B	26.	B	36.	B
7.	C	17.	B	27.	B	37.	A
8.	D	18.	A	28.	A	38.	D
9.	B	19.	E	29.	C	39.	E
10.	C	20.	A	30.	C	40.	E

EXAMINATION SECTION
TEST 1

DIRECTIONS: Each question or incomplete statement is followed by several suggested answers or completions. Select the one that BEST answers the question or completes the statement. *PRINT THE LETTER OF THE CORRECT ANSWER IN THE SPACE AT THE RIGHT.*

1. The one of the following which is a reason for using flux in soldering is to

    A. reduce the amount of heat required
    B. permit the use of a smaller soldering iron
    C. make the solder flow more smoothly
    D. clean the metal around the joint

2. A rivet set is a tool used to

    A. shape the head of a rivet
    B. mark off the spacing of rivets
    C. remove a loose rivet
    D. check the shank length of a rivet

3.

    The hammer shown in the above sketch is a _____ hammer.

    A. raising	B. ball peen	C. setting	D. cross-over

4. Of the following, the BEST tool to use to scribe a line parallel to the straight edge of a piece of sheet metal is a(n)

    A. outside caliper	B. pair of dividers
    C. template	D. scratch gage

5. Hardware for sheet metal shelving requires 1/4-20-1/2 bolts. The *1/2* stands for the

    A. diameter of the bolt	B. length of the bolt
    C. diameter of the head	D. pitch of the threads

6. The QUICKEST way to draw a 25° angle is to use a

    A. pair of dividers	B. combination square
    C. protractor	D. circumference rule

7. When laying out the centers of 6 equally-spaced holes on the circumference of a 7" diameter circle, the dividers should be set to

    A. 3 1/2"	B. 3 3/4"	C. 4"	D. 4 1/4"

8. If sheets of #16 and #22 USSG sheet steel are compared for thickness, it will be found that the #22 gage sheet is MOST NEARLY _____ as thick as the #16 gage sheet.

   A. 3 times   B. twice as   C. 1/4   D. 1/2

9. Connections between steel sheet metal work and copper should be made with insulating gaskets made of

   A. rubber   B. steel   C. lead   D. copper

10. A MAJOR advantage of pop rivets is that these rivets

    A. can be set with a light hammer
    B. require no pre-drilling of rivet holes
    C. are cheaper than ordinary tinners' rivets
    D. may be installed and set from one side of the work

11. An object having a hexagonal shape is to be laid out in sheet metal. When completed, the figure will have _____ sides.

    A. 4   B. 5   C. 6   D. 7

12. Following are steps that must be taken in order to draw the pattern for an ellipse:
    I. Draw a circle whose diameter is equal to the large diameter of the ellipse
    II. Using the same center, draw a circle whose diameter is equal to the small diameter of the ellipse
    III. Divide the small circle into a number of small equal parts
    The correct NEXT step is to draw _____ lines.

    A. radial   B. tangent   C. horizontal   D. vertical

13. It is required to draw a line through point A which will be perpendicular to line BC in the sketch shown above. The FIRST step is to

    A. draw two random lines through point A intersecting line BC
    B. draw another line through point A, parallel to line BC
    C. use point A as a center to draw an arc which intersects line BC at two points
    D. use any point on line BC as a center and draw an arc intersecting point A

14. The pattern for the transition piece shown above should be made by

    A. parallel line development   B. triangulation
    C. radial line development   D. auxiliary view development

15. Neglecting edging seam allowance, the stretchout length for a 12 1/2" inside diameter, 0.06" thick sheet metal pipe is MOST NEARLY

    A. 39 1/8"   B. 39 7/16"   C. 39 11/16"   D. 40 1/4"

16. The two patterns required for a T-joint should be made by

    A. radial line development
    B. parallel line development
    C. triangulation
    D. resection

17. Where there are no clearance problems, the layout of a 5-piece 90° elbow GENERALLY requires _____ patterns.

    A. two   B. three   C. four   D. five

18. The pattern required for a regular cone should be made by

    A. auxiliary view development
    B. parallel line development
    C. radial line development
    D. resection

19. When making a pattern for a rectangular duct, allowance should be made for joining the parts of the ductwork using which of the following?

    A. Crimped edges   B. Drive clips
    C. Dovetail seams   D. Spot welds

20. The sketch shown at the right shows the front view of a line $A_V B_V$ and the top view of the same line $A_V B_V$ in the drawing for making a pattern. The TRUE length of line AB is equal to the length of line

    A. $A_h C_h$
    B. $A_v C_v$
    C. $B_v C_v$
    D. $C_h C_v$

KEY (CORRECT ANSWERS)

1.	D	11.	C
2.	A	12.	A
3.	C	13.	C
4.	D	14.	B
5.	B	15.	B
6.	C	16.	B
7.	A	17.	A
8.	D	18.	C
9.	A	19.	B
10.	D	20.	B

TEST 2

DIRECTIONS: Each question or incomplete statement is followed by several suggested answers or completions. Select the one that BEST answers the question or completes the statement. *PRINT THE LETTER OF THE CORRECT ANSWER IN THE SPACE AT THE RIGHT.*

1. The instructions for the drawing of a pattern for a T-joint state the following: *Step off, locate, and number the element lines on the stretchout.*
   The *stepping off* is USUALLY done with

   A. a protractor
   B. a square
   C. dividers
   D. a circumference ruler

2. Of the following, the FIRST step to take in preparing to lay out a pattern directly on a piece of sheet metal is to make sure that the

   A. top and bottom edges of the sheet are parallel
   B. sides of the sheet are perpendicular to each other
   C. left and right sides of the sheet are parallel
   D. sheet lays flat on the work bench

3. A sheet metal worker is given a job to make a transition piece from an 8 1/2" diameter duct to an 11 1/4" diameter duct. If the length of the transition piece is 5 1/2" for each inch change in diameter, then the length of the transition piece is

   A. 14 7/8"   B. 15"   C. 15 1/8"   D. 15 1/4"

4. A duct layout is drawn to a scale of 3/8" to a foot.
   If the length of a run shown on the drawing scales 7 1/2", then the ACTUAL length of the run is

   A. 19'6"   B. 19'9"   C. 20'0"   D. 20'3"

5. An 18" x 24" duct is to be connected to a 24" x 24" duct by means of an eccentric transition piece (3 sides flush). If the taper is to be 1" in 4", then the length of the transition piece is

   A. 6"   B. 12"   C. 18"   D. 24"

6. Twenty-seven pairs of 3/8" diameter rods each 3'3 1/2" long are needed to support a duct.
   If the available rods are ten feet long, then the MINIMUM number of rods that will be needed to make the twenty-seven sets is

   A. 9   B. 12   C. 15   D. 18

7. A rectangular sheet metal air duct with open ends is 12 feet long and 15" x 20" in cross section. If one square foot of the sheet metal weighs 1/2 pound, then the TOTAL weight of the duct is _____ lbs.

   A. 10   B. 17 1/2   C. 35   D. 150

53

8.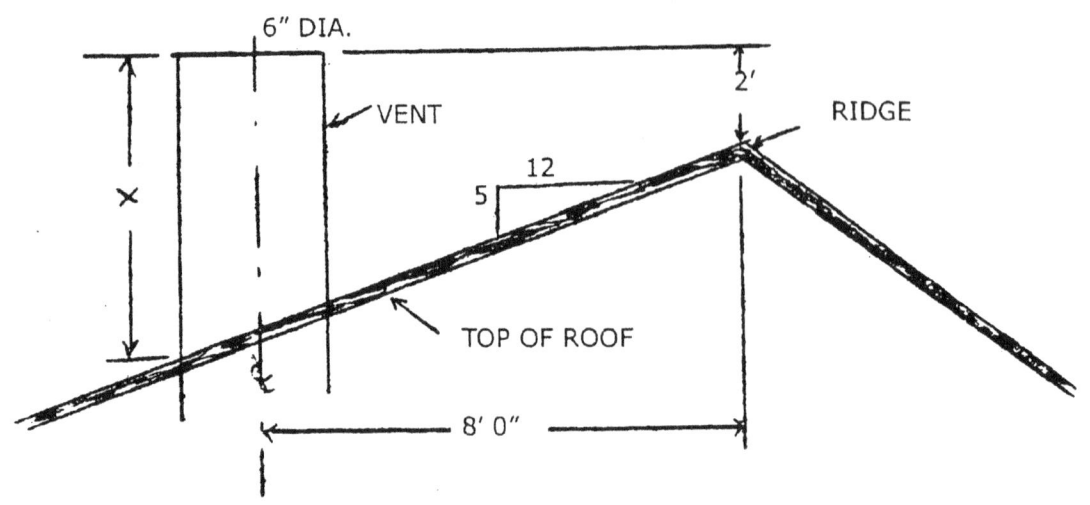

The above sketch represents a sheet metal vent going through a roof. The length X is

A. 5'2 3/4"   B. 5'4"   C. 5'5 1/4"   D. 5'6 1/2"

9.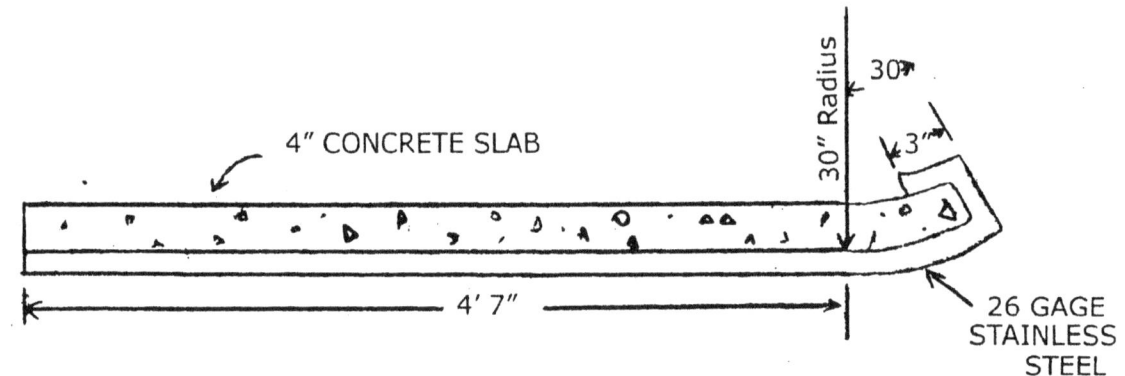

Shown above is a sketch of a concrete canopy which is to be covered with stainless steel as shown. The total length of slab to be covered is MOST NEARLY

A. 6'5 3/4"   B. 6'11 5/8"   C. 6'8 1/8"   D. 7'2"

10. The total number of 8-oz. solid flathead tin-plated tinners rivets which will weigh 3 ounces is MOST NEARLY

A. 250   B. 375   C. 450   D. 625

11. The sketch shown at the right shows the elevation of a part of a cone.
The length of the line XY is

A. 9"
B. 9 1/2"
C. 10"
D. 10 1/4"

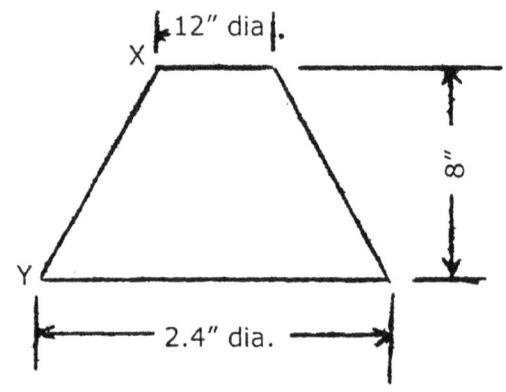

12. Two and two-thirds tees can be made from one sheet of steel. If 24 tees must be made, then the number of sheets required is MOST NEARLY

    A. 6 B. 7 C. 8 D. 9

13. Of the following materials, the BEST one to use as a tourniquet to stop bleeding from a severed artery is a(n)

    A. venetian blind cord
    B. electric extension cord
    C. leather belt
    D. shoelace

14. Of the following types of portable fire extinguishers, the one that should NOT be used to extinguish a fire around a blower motor is the _____ extinguisher.

    A. dry chemical
    B. carbon dioxide
    C. liquefied gas
    D. water solution

15. In setting a 16-foot extension ladder against a vertical wall, the SAFEST horizontal distance to set the foot of the ladder from the base of the wall is _____ ft.

    A. 2 B. 4 C. 6 D. 8

16. The sketch shown at the right represents a type of knot used in rigging. The knot is a

    A. clove hitch
    B. sheet bend
    C. square knot
    D. bowline

17. You are showing a new helper how to construct a complicated system of air ducts. Of the following, the helper is MOST likely to remember what you show him if you

    A. show him the entire job before permitting him to ask questions
    B. show him the hardest parts first, then go on to the easiest
    C. let him practice doing the things you show him
    D. show him both the right and the wrong ways to do it

18. Which of the following is the BEST way for you to make sure that your helper has understood a complicated instruction which you have given him?

    A. Ask the helper if he is sure that he has understood the instruction
    B. Ask the helper to repeat the instruction to you in his own words
    C. Watch the way the helper begins to follow the instruction
    D. Spot check the helper's progress in completing the instruction

Questions 19-20.

DIRECTIONS: Questions 19 and 20 are to be answered in accordance with the paragraph below.

The cabinet shall be *fabricated* entirely of 22-gage stainless steel with #4 satin finish on all exposed surfaces. The face trim shall be one piece construction with no mitres or welding, 1" wide and 1/4" to the wall. All doors shall be mounted on heavy duty stainless steel piano hinges and have a concealed lock.

19. As used in the above paragraph, the word *fabricated* means MOST NEARLY   19.____

    A. made   B. designed   C. cut   D. plated

20. According to the above paragraph, a satin finish is to be used on surfaces   20.____

    A. to be welded
    B. that are visible
    C. on which the hinges are mounted
    D. that are to be covered

KEY (CORRECT ANSWERS)

1.	C	11.	C
2.	D	12.	D
3.	C	13.	C
4.	C	14.	D
5.	D	15.	B
6.	D	16.	D
7.	C	17.	C
8.	C	18.	B
9.	A	19.	A
10.	B	20.	B

EXAMINATION SECTION
TEST 1

DIRECTIONS: Each question or incomplete statement is followed by several suggested answers or completions. Select the one that BEST answers the question or completes the statement. *PRINT THE LETTEE OF THE CORRECT ANSWER IN THE SPACE AT THE RIGHT.*

1. Of the following, the type of welding in which a filler rod is COMMONLY used is   1.____

   A. resistance   B. carbon arc   C. spot   D. pressure

2. A small short bead used as a temporary fastener is known as a(n) _____ weld.   2.____

   A. spot   B. edge   C. plug   D. tack

3. The one of the following which is the MOST important reason for using the step-back method of welding is to   3.____

   A. increase the strength of the weld
   B. speed the process of welding
   C. reduce the amount of warping
   D. decrease formation of slag

4. In butt welds, the purpose of open roots is to   4.____

   A. reduce the amount of electrode required
   B. secure more overlap
   C. aid slag formation
   D. obtain better penetration

5. Stresses in a welded piece may be relieved by   5.____

   A. annealing   B. case hardening
   C. cold drawing   D. quenching

6. Brazing is MOST commonly done at tempera.tures ranging from *approximately*   6.____

   A. 300° to 900° F   B. 1100° to 2000° F
   C. 2300° to 3000° F   D. 3300° to 3800° F

7. Bronze welding is MOST commonly used for welding   7.____

   A. wrought iron   B. aluminum
   C. white metal   D. chrome steel

Questions 8-11.

DIRECTIONS: In Questions 8 to 11, inclusive, there are shown in Column I various welding symbols. Column II gives types of welds. For each symbol listed in Column I, enter in the appropriate space on the right the capital letter in front *of* the type of weld listed in Column II which the symbol illustrates.

COLUMN I   COLUMN II

8. ⌒   A. flush
                                   B. plug
                                   C. weld all around
9. | D. square
                                   E. bevel
                                   F. fillet
                                   G. bead

10. ◺

11. ◯

12. The one of the following which indicates an intermittent weld is

    A. [symbol]   B. [symbol]
    C. [symbol]   D. [symbol]

13. The throat of a 1/2 inch fillet weld is MOST NEARLY _____ inches.

    A. .25   B. .35   C. .45   D. .55

14. Spelter is MOST commonly used in

    A. electric arc welding   B. oxy-acetylene fusion welding
    C. brazing   D. quenching

15. If one dozen 1/8" welding rods cost 48 cents, 37 rods would cost

    A. $1.44   B. $1.48   C. $1.52   D. $1.56

16. The sum of the following numbers, 6 5/8, 3 3/4, 4 1/2, 5 1/8, is

    A. 19 3/4   B. 19 7/8   C. 20   D. 20 1/8

17. Of the following, the one that is a method used to test completed welds is

    A. soaking bath   B. electrolytic resistance
    C. photo-elastic strain   D. acid-etch

18. Of the following, the term that defines a defect in a weld is

    A. scarf   B. tuyere   C. cold shut D. cohesion

19. When clean steel is heated to a faint straw color, the temperature of the steel, based upon this color, is APPROXIMATELY

    A. 400° F   B. 600° F   C. 800° F   D. 1000° F

20. Of the following metals, the one that has a fibrous structure is   20.____

    A. gray cast iron   B. manganese steel
    C. low carbon steel   D. wrought iron

21. Of the following alloying elements, the one that is MOST commonly used in tool steel is   21.____

    A. manganese   B. zirconium   C. titanium   D. tungsten

22. Of the following automotive parts, the one for which welding of any type would be LEAST desirable is   22.____

    A. crankcase   B. crankshaft
    C. cylinder block   D. body

23. Of the following metals, the one that is MOST commonly *hard-faced* is   23.____

    A. aluminum   B. bronze
    C. monel   D. high speed steel

24. Studs are frequently used to strengthen the welds in   24.____

    A. iron castings   B. structural steel
    C. bronze bushings   D. tool steel

25. Incomplete penetration in a weld is MOST likely to be caused by too   25.____

    A. rigid a joint   B. large a welding rod
    C. large a welding tip   D. slow a welding speed

26. Of the following, the metal with the LOWEST melting point is   26.____

    A. aluminum   B. bronze   C. monel   D. cast iron

27. Quenching to harden steel is MOST commonly done in a bath of   27.____

    A. lye   B. soda-ash   C. brine   D. muriatic acid

28. Shrinkage due to welding in non-preheated pieces can be reduced by   28.____

    A. open roots   B. peening
    C. large welds   D. increased number of welds

29. Brazing is MOST commonly used on   29.____

    A. lead   B. bronze   C. babbit   D. aluminum

30. Impact resisting pads on all types of machinery are MOST frequently made of   30.____

    A. monel   B. aluminum   C. bronze   D. inconel

31. Drag is usually determined in relation to the consumption of   31.____

    A. oxygen   B. acetylene   C. rod   D. power

Questions 32-35.

DIRECTIONS: Questions 32 to 35, inclusive, refer to the paragraph below. These questions are to be answered in strict accordance with the material in this paragraph.

Welds in sheet metal up to 1/16 inch in thickness can be made satisfactorily by flanging the edges of the joint. The edges are prepared by turning up a very thin lip or flange along the line of the joint. The height of this flange should be equal to the thickness of the sheet being welded. The edges should be alined so that the flanges stand up, and the joint should be tack-welded every 5 or 6 inches. Heavy angles or bars should be clamped on each side of the joint to prevent distortion or buckling. No filler metal is required for making this joint. The raised edges are quickly melted by the heat of the welding flame so as to produce an even weld bead which is nearly flush with the original sheet metal surface. By controlling the speed of welding and the motion of the flame, good fusion to the underside of the sheets can be obtained without burning through.

32. According to the above paragraph, satisfactory welds may be made in sheet metal by flanging the edges.
    The MAXIMUM thickness of metal recommended is

    A. 20 gauge   B. 18 gauge   C. 1/16"   D. 5/64"

33. According to the above paragraph, good fusion may be obtained without burning through of the metal by controlling the motion of the flame and the

    A. size of tip   B. speed of welding
    C. oxygen flow   D. acetylene flow

34. According to the above paragraph, if the thickness of the metal is 1/32", then the flange height should be

    A. 1/64"   B. 1/32"   C. 1/16"   D. 1/8"

35. According to the above paragraph, distortion in the welding of sheet metal may be prevented by

    A. controlling the speed of welding
    B. use of a flange of correct height
    C. use of proper filler metal
    D. clamping angles on each side of the joint

KEY (CORRECT ANSWERS)

1. B
2. D
3. C
4. D
5. A

6. B
7. A
8. G
9. D
10. F

11. C
12. D
13. B
14. C
15. B

16. C
17. D
18. C
19. A
20. D

21. D
22. B
23. C
24. A
25. B

26. A
27. C
28. B
29. B
30. C

31. A
32. C
33. B
34. B
35. D

TEST 2

DIRECTIONS: Each question or incomplete statement is followed by several suggested answers or completions. Select the one that BEST answers the question or completes the statement. *PRINT THE LETTER OF THE CORRECT ANSWER IN THE SPACE AT THE RIGHT.*

Questions 1-4.

DIRECTIONS: Questions 1 through 4, inclusive, refer to the jig for testing welded specimens shown below. The jig is to be built up from plate by welding.

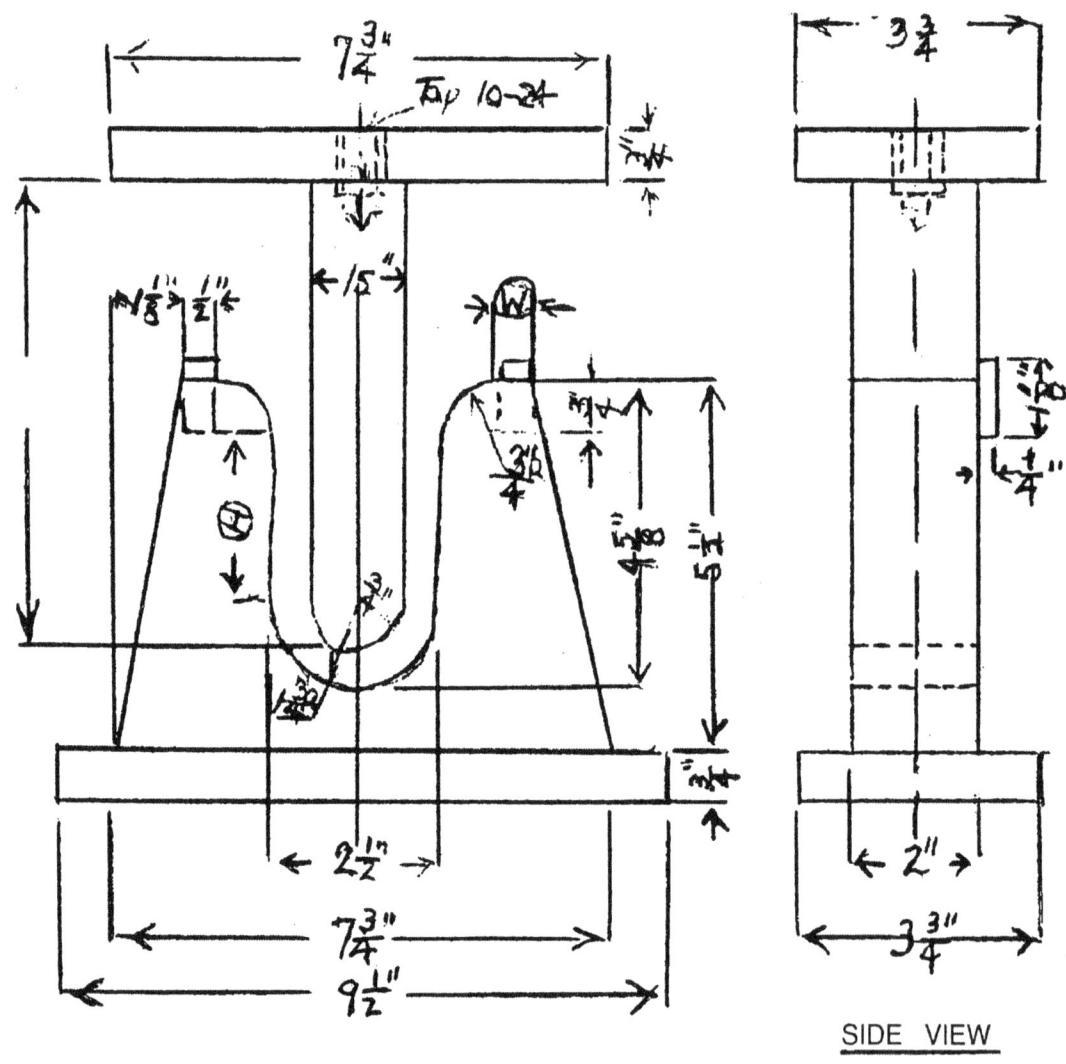

FRONT VIEW

SIDE VIEW

1. The type of weld that would MOST probably be used to weld the plates together is 1.___
   A. V bevel   B. U groove   C. plug   D. fillet

2. The symbol *Tap 10-24* at the top of the jig means that the hole is 2.___
   A. reamed   B. broached   C. threaded   D. punched

62

3. The length of the straight portion of the jig indicated by the letter *H* is

   A. 2 3/8"   B. 2 1/2"   C. 2 5/8"   D. 2 3/4"

4. The length of the straight portion of the jig indicated by the letter *W* is

   A. 3/4"   B. 7/8"   C. 1"   D. 1 1/8"

Questions 5-21.

DIRECTIONS: Questions 5 through 21, inclusive, are to be answered on the basis of welding with an electric arc welder.

5. Of the following, the MINIMUM voltage necessary to strike an arc with an alternating current machine is, in volts,

   A. 20   B. 40   C. 100   D. 140

6. According to the rules of the Department of Water Supply, Gas and Electricity, the MAXIMUM length of flexible cord or cable permitted for supplying current to a portable welder is _____ feet.

   A. 10   B. 20   C. 30   D. 40

7. The MINIMUM voltage required to strike an arc with a direct current welder is

   A. less than that required for an alternating current welder
   B. more than that required for an alternating current welder
   C. the same as that required for an alternating current welder
   D. more or less than that required for an alternating current welder depending on the type of electrode

8. Of the following, the one that would be MOST likely to appear on the name plate of an arc welder would be

   A. temperature of arc   B. number of feeders
   C. voltage   D. frequency

9. Splattering of the weld is caused by

   A. excessive current   B. too little current
   C. improper flux   D. lack of preheat

10. For a given voltage and current setting on an electric arc welder, decreasing the length of the arc

    A. increases the penetration
    B. decreases the penetration
    C. has no effect on the penetration
    D. may increase or decrease the penetration, depending on the voltage-current setting

11. For a given voltage and current setting on an electric arc welder, when the arc length is shortened, the arc voltage

    A. increases
    B. decreases
    C. stays constant
    D. may increase or decrease, depending on the electrode being used

12. Welding of light gauge metals requires _____ electrodes and _____ voltages.

    A. large; high
    B. large; low
    C. small; high
    D. small; low

13. In straight polarity,

    A. both the electrode and the work are negative
    B. both the electrode and the work are positive
    C. the electrode is negative, the work is positive
    D. the electrode is positive, the work is negative

14. Freezing of the electrode is caused by

    A. insufficient current
    B. electrode being held too long in contact with the work
    C. work not being clean
    D. improper electrode for work being done

15. When welding metal of the same thickness with the same electrode, in the overhead and in the flat position, welding in the overhead position USUALLY requires

    A. less voltage than the flat position
    B. more voltage than the flat position
    C. the same voltage as the flat position
    D. more or less voltage than the flat position depending on the metal being welded

16. Compared with a bare electrode, a shielded electrode produces

    A. more nitrides
    B. more oxidation
    C. a hotter arc
    D. a more stable arc

17. Arc blow is MOST commonly corrected by

    A. welding away from the ground
    B. changing the polarity of the electrode
    C. increasing the voltage
    D. decreasing the current

18. Preheating is MOST commonly used when welding

    A. high manganese-cast steel
    B. chrome-nickel stainless steel
    C. wrought iron
    D. bronze

19. When welding with a shielded electrode, the slag formed

   A. increases the rate of cooling of weld metal
   B. helps prevent warping
   C. slows the speed of welding
   D. removes oxides from the weld

20. When welding with an electric arc, you find that the arc has a hissing and steady sputtering sound.
    The MOST probable cause of this is

   A. low voltage
   B. low current
   C. high voltage
   D. high current

21. When welding in the flat position with 3/8" bare electrodes, the *approximate* range of amperes that would be used is MOST NEARLY

   A. 40 to 60   B. 110 to 150   C. 250 to 300   D. 450 to 550

Questions 22-35.

DIRECTIONS: Questions 22 through 35, inclusive, are to be answered on the basis of welding with an oxy-acetylene flame.

22. The color of the hose used to connect the torch to the acetylene cylinder is

   A. green   B. yellow   C. red   D. black

23. The tool MOST commonly used to clean a torch tip is a

   A. drill   B. file   C. scriber   D. reamer

24. To test for leaks in an oxy-acetylene torch, you should use

   A. a match
   B. #6 fuel oil
   C. soapy water
   D. carbon tetrachloride

25. Of the following statements relative to oxygen or acetylene cylinders, the one that is MOST NEARLY CORRECT is:

   A. Oxygen may be used in place of compressed air in compressed air equipment
   B. A wrench should not be used to open an oxygen cylinder valve
   C. A frozen acetylene cylinder valve should be thawed with boiling water
   D. Oxygen cylinders should be stored lying down

26. Acetylene is USUALLY used at a pressure of less than _____ lbs./sq.in.

   A. 15   B. 30   C. 45   D. 60

27. The hottest part of a neutral oxy-acetylene flame is located APPROXIMATELY

   A. at the outermost tip of the flame
   B. midway between the tip of the flame and the tip of the inner cone
   C. at the tip of the inner cone
   D. at the tip of the torch

28. The number of distinct flame zones in a reducing flame is

    A. 1   B. 2   C. 3   D. 4

29. A reducing flame has

    A. more oxygen by volume than acetylene
    B. more acetylene by volume than oxygen
    C. the same volume of oxygen and acetylene
    D. no acetylene

30. Fusion welding of cast steel is MOST commonly done with a(n) _____ flame.

    A. neutral   B. oxidizing   C. reducing   D. carburizing

31. When welding materials of the same thickness, the one of the following that requires the SMALLEST torch tip is

    A. cast iron
    B. steel
    C. wrought iron
    D. aluminum

32. As compared to fusion welding, brazing of the same thickness of steel requires

    A. a smaller torch tip
    B. a larger torch tip
    C. the same size torch tip
    D. a smaller or larger torch tip depending on the carbon content of the steel

33. Of the following statements relative to hard surfacing, the one that is MOST NEARLY CORRECT is:

    A. Alloys in hard surfacing rods will not oxidize if a neutral flame is used
    B. A smaller torch tip is used for hard surfacing than is used for fusion welding of steel of the same thickness
    C. Hard surfacing rods are least likely to be used when the part must be heat treated after welding
    D. Hard surfacing is usually done with a rod having a low Rockwell C test

34. Of the following metals to be fusion welded, the one for which a flux is USUALLY used is _____ steel.

    A. low carbon
    B. stainless
    C. carbon-molybdenum
    D. nickel alloy

35. A metal, when melted with an oxy-acetylene torch, gives off sparks. This metal MOST likely is

    A. gray cast iron
    B. cast steel
    C. aluminum
    D. monel

KEY (CORRECT ANSWERS)

1.	D	16.	D
2.	C	17.	A
3.	C	18.	D
4.	A	19.	D
5.	C	20.	A
6.	D	21.	D
7.	A	22.	C
8.	D	23.	A
9.	A	24.	C
10.	D	25.	B
11.	B	26.	A
12.	C	27.	C
13.	C	28.	C
14.	B	29.	B
15.	A	30.	A

31. D
32. A
33. C
34. B
35. B

SAFETY EXAMINATION SECTION
TEST 1

DIRECTIONS: Each question or incomplete statement is followed by several suggested answers or completions. Select the one that BEST answers the question or completes the statement. *PRINT THE LETTER OF THE CORRECT ANSWER IN THE SPACE AT THE RIGHT.*

1. Which one of the following is an INCORRECT safety guideline? 1.____

    A. All working conditions and equipment should be considered carefully before beginning an operation.
    B. Aisles should be lighted properly.
    C. Personnel should be provided with protective clothing essential to safe performance of a task.
    D. In manual lifting, the worker must keep his knees straight and lift with the arm muscles.

2. Of the following, the supply item with the GREATEST susceptibility to spontaneous heating is 2.____

    A. alcohol, ethyl   B. kerosene
    C. candles   D. turpentine

Questions 3-7.

DIRECTIONS: Questions 3 through 7 are descriptions of accidents that occurred in a warehouse. For each accident, choose the letter in front of the safety measure that is MOST likely to prevent a repetition of the accident indicated.

SAFETY MEASURE

    A. Posting warning signs
    B. Redesign of layout or facilities
    C. Repairing, improving or replacing supplies, tools or equipment
    D. Training the staff in safe practices

3. After a new all-glass door was installed at the entrance to the warehouse, one of the employees banged his head into the door causing a large lump on his forehead when he failed to realize that the door was closed. 3.____

4. While tieing up a package with manila rope, an employee got several small rope splinters in his right hand and he had to have medical treatment to remove the splinters. 4.____

5. An employee discovered a small fire in a wastepaper basket but was unable to prevent it from spreading because all the nearby fire extinguishers were inaccessible due to skids of material being stacked in front of the extinguishers. 5.____

6. When a laborer attempted to drop the tailgate of a delivery truck while the truck was being backed into the loading dock, he had his fingers crushed when the truck continued to move while he was working on lowering the tailgate. 6.____

7. An employee carrying a carton with both hands tripped over a broom which had been left lying in an aisle by another employee after the latter had swept the aisle. 7.___

8. Safety experts agree that accidents can probably BEST be prevented by 8.___

   A. developing safety consciousness among employees
   B. developing a program which publicizes major accidents
   C. penalizing employees the first time they do not follow safety procedures
   D. giving recognition to employees with accident-free records

9. The accident records of many agencies indicate that most on-the-job injuries are caused by the unsafe acts of their employees. 9.___
   Which one of the following statements pinpoints the MOST probable cause of this safety problem?

   A. Responsibility for preventing on-the-job accidents has not been delegated.
   B. Lack of proper supervision has permitted these unsafe actions to continue.
   C. No consideration has been given to eliminating environmental job hazards.
   D. Penalties for causing on-the-job accidents are not sufficiently severe.

10. Which of the following methods is LEAST essential to the success of an accident prevention program? 10.___

    A. Determining corrective measures by analyzing the causes of accidents and making recommendations to eliminate them
    B. Educating employees as to the importance of safe working conditions and methods
    C. Determining accident causes by seeking out the conditions from which each accident has developed
    D. Holding each supervisor responsible for accidents occurring during the on-the-job performance of his immediate subordinates

11. The effectiveness of a public relations program in a public agency is BEST indicated by the 11.___

    A. amount of mass media publicity favorable to the policies of the agency
    B. morale of those employees who directly serve the patrons of the agency
    C. public's understanding and support of the agency's program and policies
    D. number of complaints received by the agency from patrons using its facilities

12. Buttered bread and coffee dropped on an office floor in a terminal are 12.___

    A. minor hazards which should cause no serious injury
    B. unattractive, but not dangerous
    C. the most dangerous types of office hazards
    D. hazards which should be corrected immediately

13. A laborer was sent upstairs to get a 20-pound sack of rock salt. While going downstairs and reading the printing on the sack, he fell, and the sack of rock salt fell and broke his toe. 13.___
    Which of the following is MOST likely to have been the MOST important cause of the accident?
    The

A. stairs were beginning to become worn
B. laborer was carrying too heavy a sack of rock salt
C. rock salt was in a place that was too inaccessible
D. laborer was not careful about the way he went down the stairs

14. A COMMONLY recommended safe distance between the foot of an extension ladder and the wall against which it is placed is

   A. 3 feet for ladders less than 18 feet in height
   B. between 3 feet and 6 feet for ladders less than 18 feet in length
   C. 1/8 the length of the extended ladder
   D. 1/4 the length of the extended ladder

15. The BEST type of fire extinguisher for electrical fires is the _____ extinguisher.

   A. dry chemical   B. foam
   C. carbon monoxide   D. baking soda-acid

16. A Class A extinguisher should be used for fires in

   A. potassium, magnesium, zinc, sodium
   B. electrical wiring
   C. oil, gasoline
   D. wood, paper, and textiles

17. The one of the following which is NOT a safe practice when lifting heavy objects is:

   A. Keep the back as nearly upright as possible
   B. If the object feels too heavy, keep lifting until you get help
   C. Spread the feet apart
   D. Use the arm and leg muscles

18. In a shop, it would be MOST necessary to provide a fitted cover on the metal container for

   A. old paint brushes   B. oily rags and waste
   C. sand   D. broken glass

19. Safety shoes usually have the unique feature of

   A. extra hard heels and soles to prevent nails from piercing the shoes
   B. special leather to prevent the piercing of the shoes by falling objects
   C. a metal guard over the toes which is built into the shoes
   D. a non-slip tread on the heels and soles

20. Of the following, the MOST important factor contributing to a helper's safety on the job is for him to

   A. work slowly   B. wear gloves
   C. be alert   D. know his job well

21. If it is necessary for you to lift one end of a piece of heavy equipment with a crowbar in order to allow a maintainer to work underneath it, the BEST of the following procedures to follow is to

    A. support the handle of the bar on a box
    B. insert temporary blocks to support the piece
    C. call the supervisor to help you
    D. wear heavy gloves

22. Of the following, the MOST important reason for not letting oily rags accumulate in an open storage bin is that they

    A. may start a fire by spontaneous combustion
    B. will drip oil onto other items in the bin
    C. may cause a foul odor
    D. will make the area messy

23. Of the following, the BEST method to employ in putting out a gasoline fire is to

    A. use a bucket of water
    B. smother it with rags
    C. use a carbon dioxide extinguisher
    D. use a carbon tetrachloride extinguisher

24. When opening an emergency exit door set in the sidewalk, the door should be raised slowly to avoid

    A. a sudden rush of air from the street
    B. making unnecessary noise
    C. damage to the sidewalk
    D. injuring pedestrians

25. The BEST reason to turn off lights when cleaning lampshades on electrical fixtures is to

    A. conserve energy
    B. avoid electrical shock
    C. prevent breakage of lightbulbs
    D. prevent unnecessary eye strain

KEY (CORRECT ANSWERS)

1. D
2. D
3. A
4. D
5. B

6. D
7. D
8. A
9. B
10. D

11. C
12. D
13. D
14. D
15. A

16. D
17. B
18. B
19. C
20. C

21. B
22. A
23. C
24. D
25. B

TEST 2

DIRECTIONS: Each question or incomplete statement is followed by several suggested answers or completions. Select the one that BEST answers the question or completes the statement. *PRINT THE LETTER OF THE CORRECT ANSWER IN THE SPACE AT THE RIGHT.*

1. The MOST important reason for roping off a work area in a terminal is to

   A. protect the public
   B. protect the repair crew
   C. prevent distraction of the crew by the public
   D. prevent delays to the public

   1.____

2. Shoes which have a sponge rubber sole should NOT be worn around a work area because such a sole

   A. will wear quickly
   B. is not waterproof
   C. does not keep the feet warm
   D. is easily punctured by steel objects

   2.____

3. When repair work is being done on an elevated structure, canvas spreads are suspended under the working area MAINLY to

   A. reduce noise   B. discourage crowds
   C. protect the structure D. protect pedestrians

   3.____

4. It is poor practice to hold a piece of wood in the hands or lap when tightening a screw in the wood.
   This is for the reason that

   A. sufficient leverage cannot be obtained
   B. the screwdriver may bend
   C. the wood will probably split
   D. personal injury is likely to result

   4.____

5. Steel helmets give workers the MOST protection from

   A. falling objects   B. eye injuries
   C. fire   D. electric shock

   5.____

6. It is POOR practice to wear goggles

   A. when chipping stone
   B. when using a grinder
   C. while climbing or descending ladders
   D. when handling molten metal

   6.____

7. When using a brace and bit to bore a hole completely through a partition, it is MOST important to

   7.____

74

A. lean heavily on the brace and bit
B. maintain a steady turning speed all through the job
C. have the body in a position that will not be easily thrown off balance
D. reverse the direction of the bit at frequent intervals

8. Gloves should be used when handling 8.____

   A. lanterns B. wooden rules
   C. heavy ropes D. all small tools

Questions 9-16.

DIRECTIONS: Questions 9 through 16, inclusive, are based on the ladder safety rules given below. Read these rules fully before answering these items.

LADDER SAFETY RULES

When a ladder is placed on a slightly uneven supporting surface, use a flat piece of board or small wedge to even up the ladder feet. To secure the proper angle for resting a ladder, it should be placed so that the distance from the base of the ladder to the supporting wall is 1/4 the length of the ladder. To avoid overloading a ladder, only one person should work on a ladder at a time. Do not place a ladder in front of a door. When the top rung of a ladder rests against a pole, the ladder should be lashed securely. Clear loose stones or debris from the ground around the base of a ladder before climbing. While on a ladder, do not attempt to lean so that any part of the body, except arms or hands, extends more than 12 inches beyond the side rail. Always face the ladder when ascending or descending. When carrying ladders through buildings, watch for ceiling globes and lighting fixtures. Avoid the use of rolling ladders as scaffold supports.

9. A small wedge is used to 9.____

   A. even up the feet of a ladder resting on an uneven surface
   B. lock the wheels of a roller ladder
   C. secure the proper resting angle for a ladder
   D. secure a ladder against a pole

10. An 8 foot ladder resting against a wall should be so inclined that the distance between the base of the ladder and the wall is _____ feet. 10.____

   A. 2 B. 5 C. 7 D. 9

11. A ladder should be lashed securely when 11.____

   A. it is placed in front of a door
   B. loose stones are on the ground near the base of the ladder
   C. the top rung rests against a pole
   D. two people are working from the same ladder

12. Rolling ladders 12.____

   A. should be used for scaffold supports
   B. should not be used for scaffold supports
   C. are useful on uneven ground
   D. should be used against a pole

13. When carrying a ladder through a building, it is necessary to

    A. have two men to carry it
    B. carry the ladder vertically
    C. watch for ceiling globes
    D. face the ladder while carrying it

14. It is POOR practice to

    A. lash a ladder securely at any time
    B. clear debris from the base of a ladder before climbing
    C. even up the feet of a ladder resting on slightly uneven ground
    D. place a ladder in front of a door

15. A person on a ladder should NOT extend his head beyond the side rail by more than _____ inches.

    A. 12   B. 9   C. 7   D. 5

16. The MOST important reason for permitting only one person to work on a ladder at a time is that

    A. both could not face the ladder at one time
    B. the ladder will be overloaded
    C. time would be lost going up and down the ladder
    D. they would obstruct each other

17. Many portable electric power tools, such as electric drills, have a third conductor in the power lead which is used to connect the case of the tool to a grounded part of the electric outlet.
    The reason for this extra conductor is to

    A. have a spare wire in case one power wire should break
    B. strengthen the power lead so it cannot easily be damaged
    C. prevent the user of the tool from being shocked
    D. enable the tool to be used for long periods of time without overheating

18. Protective goggles should NOT be worn when

    A. standing on a ladder drilling a steel beam
    B. descending a ladder after completing a job
    C. chipping concrete near a third rail
    D. sharpening a cold chisel on a grinding stone

19. When the foot of an extension ladder, placed against a high wall, rests on a sidewalk or another such similar surface, it is advisable to tie a rope between the bottom rung of the ladder and a point on the wall opposite this rung.
    This is done to prevent

    A. people from walking under the ladder
    B. another worker from removing the ladder
    C. the ladder from vibrating when ascending or descending
    D. the foot of the ladder from slipping

20. In construction work, practically all accidents can be blamed on the

   A. failure of an individual to give close attention to the job assigned to him
   B. use of improper tools
   C. lack of cooperation among the men in a gang
   D. fact that an incompetent man was placed in a key position

21. If it is necessary for you to do some work with your hands under a piece of heavy equipment while a fellow worker lifts up and holds one end of it by means of a pinch bar, one important precaution you should take is to

   A. wear gloves
   B. watch the bar to be ready if it slips
   C. insert a temporary block to support the piece
   D. work as fast as possible

22. Employees of the transit system whose work requires them to enter upon the tracks in the subway are cautioned not to wear loose fitting clothing.
    The MOST important reason for this caution is that loose fitting clothing may

   A. interfere when men are using heavy tools
   B. catch on some projection of a passing train
   C. tear more easily than snug fitting clothing
   D. give insufficient protection against subway dust

23. The MOST important reason for insisting on neatness in maintenance quarters is that it

   A. keeps the men busy in slack periods
   B. prevents tools from becoming rusty
   C. makes a good impression on visitors and officials
   D. decreases the chances of accidents to employees

24. Maintenance workers whose duties require them to do certain types of work generally work in pairs.
    The LEAST likely of the following possible reasons for this practice is that

   A. some of the work requires two men
   B. the men can help each other in case of accident
   C. there is too much equipment for one man to carry
   D. it protects against vandalism

25. A foreman reprimands a helper for actions in violation of the rules and regulations.
    The BEST reaction of the helper in this situation is to

   A. tell the foreman that he was careful and that he did not take any chances
   B. explain that he took this action to save time
   C. keep quiet and accept the criticism
   D. demand that the foreman show him the rule he violated

KEY (CORRECT ANSWERS)

1. A
2. D
3. D
4. D
5. A

6. C
7. C
8. C
9. A
10. A

11. C
12. B
13. C
14. D
15. A

16. B
17. C
18. B
19. D
20. A

21. C
22. B
23. D
24. D
25. C

ARITHMETICAL REASONING
EXAMINATION SECTION
TEST 1

DIRECTIONS: Each question or incomplete statement is followed by several suggested answers or completions. Select the one that BEST answers the question or completes the statement. *PRINT THE LETTER OF THE CORRECT ANSWER IN THE SPACE AT THE RIGHT.*

1. A supplier quotes a list price of $172.00 less 15 and 10 percent for twelve tools. The actual cost for these twelve tools is MOST NEARLY   1.____

    A. $146   B. $132   C. $129   D. $112

2. If the diameter of a circular piece of sheet metal is 1 1/2 feet, the area, in square inches, is MOST NEARLY   2.____

    A. 1.77   B. 2.36   C. 254   D. 324

3. The sum of 5'6", 7'3", 9'3 1/2", and 3'7 1/4" is   3.____

    A. 19'8 1/2"   B. 22' 1/2"   C. 25'7 3/4"   D. 28'8 3/4"

4. If the floor area of one shop is 15' by 21'3" and the size of an adjacent shop is 18' by 30'6", then the TOTAL floor area of these two shops is _____ square feet.   4.____

    A. 1127.75   B. 867.75   C. 549.0   D. 318.75

5. The fraction which is equal to 0.875 is   5.____

    A. 7/16   B. 5/8   C. 3/4   D. 7/8

6. The sum of 1/2, 2 1/32, 4 3/16, and 1 7/8 is MOST NEARLY   6.____

    A. 9.593   B. 9.625   C. 9.687   D. 10.593

7. If the base of a right triangle is 9" and the altitude is 12", the length of the third side will be   7.____

    A. 13"   B. 14"   C. 15"   D. 16"

8. If a steel bar 1" in diameter and 12' long weighs 32 lbs., then the weight of a piece of this bar 5'9" long is MOST NEARLY _____ lbs.   8.____

    A. 15.33   B. 15.26   C. 16.33   D. 15.06

9. The diameter of a circle whose circumference is 12" is MOST NEARLY   9.____

    A. 3.82"   B. 3.72"   C. 3.62"   D. 3.52"

10. A dimension of 39/64 inches converted to decimals is MOST NEARLY   10.____

    A. .600"   B. .609"   C. .607"   D. .611"

11. A farm worker was paid a weekly wage of $415.20 for a 44-hour work week. As a result of a new labor contract, he is paid $431.40 a week for a 40-hour work week with time and one-half pay for time worked in excess of 40 hours in any work week.
    If he continues to work 44 hours weekly under the new contract, the amount by which his average hourly rate for a 44-hour work week under the new contract exceeds the hourly rate previously paid him lies between _____ and _____, inclusive.

    A. 80¢; $1.00 B. $1.00; $1.20
    C. $1.25; $1.45 D. $1.50; $1.70

12. The sum of 4 feet 3 1/4 inches, 7 feet 2 1/2 inches, and 11 feet 1/4 inch is _____ feet _____ inches.

    A. 21; 6 1/4   B. 22; 6   C. 23; 5   D. 24; 5 3/4

13. The number 0.038 is read as

    A. 38 tenths   B. 38 hundredths
    C. 38 thousandths   D. 38 ten-thousandths

14. Assume that an employee is paid at the rate of $10.86 per hour with time and a half for overtime past 40 hours in a week.
    If he works 43 hours in a week, his gross weekly pay is

    A. $434.40   B. $438.40   C. $459.18   D. $483.27

15. The sum of the following dimensions: 3'2 1/4", 8 7/8", 2'6 3/8", 2'9 3/4", and 1'0" is

    A. 16'7 1/4"   B. 10'7 1/4"   C. 10'3 1/4"   D. 9'3 1/4"

16. Two gears are meshed together and have a gear ratio of 6 to 1.
    If the small gear rotates 120 revolutions per minute, the large gear rotates at

    A. 20   B. 40   C. 60   D. 720

17. The vacuum side of a compound gage reads 14 inches of vacuum. The barometer reading is 29.76 inches of mercury. The equivalent absolute pressure of the compound gage reading, in inches of mercury, is MOST likely

    A. 15.06   B. 15.76   C. 43.06   D. 43.76

18. The fraction 5/8 expressed as a decimal is

    A. 0.125   B. 0.412   C. 0.625   D. 0.875

19. If 300 feet of a certain size pipe weighs 450 pounds, the number of pounds that 100 feet will weigh is

    A. 1,350   B. 150   C. 300   D. 250

20. As an oiler, you work for a facility that has automobiles that use, on the average, 600 quarts of one grade of lubricating oil every month.
    The number of one-gallon cans of the above oil that should be ordered each month to meet this requirement is

    A. 100   B. 125   C. 140   D. 150

21. The inside dimensions of a rectangular oil gravity tank are: height 15", width 9", length 10".
    The amount of oil in the tank, in gallons, (231 cu.in. = 1 gallon), when the oil level is 9" high, is MOST NEARLY

    A. 2.3   B. 3.5   C. 5.2   D. 5.8

22. If 30 gallons of oil cost $76.80, 45 gallons of oil at the same rate will cost

    A. $91.20   B. $115.20   C. $123.20   D. $131.20

23. If an oiler earns $18,000 in the first six months of a year and receives a 10% raise in salary for the next six months of the same year, his TOTAL earnings for the year will be

    A. $36,000   B. $37,500   C. $37,800   D. $39,600

24. If the cost of lubricating oil increases 15%, then a gallon of oil which used to cost $10.00 will now cost MOST NEARLY

    A. $10.50   B. $11.00   C. $11.50   D. $12.00

25. The sum of 7/8", 3/4", 1/2", and 3/8" is

    A. 2 1/8"   B. 2 1/4"   C. 2 3/8"   D. 2 1/2"

KEY (CORRECT ANSWERS)

1. B		11. A	
2. C		12. B	
3. C		13. C	
4. B		14. D	
5. D		15. C	
6. A		16. A	
7. C		17. B	
8. A		18. C	
9. A		19. B	
10. B		20. D	

21. B
22. B
23. C
24. C
25. D

SOLUTIONS TO PROBLEMS

1. Actual cost = ($172)(.85)(.90) = $131.58 ≈ $132

2. Radius = .75', then area = $(3.14)(.75)^2$ ≈ 1.77 sq.ft.
   Since 1 sq.ft. = 144 sq.in., the area ≈ 254 sq.in.

3. 5'6" + 7'3" + 9'3 1/2" + 3'7 1/4" = 24'19 3/4" = 25'7 3/4"

4. Total area = (15)(21.25) + (18)(30.5) = 867.75 sq.ft.

5. .875 = 875/1000 = 7/8

6. 1 1/2 + 2 1/32 + 4 3/16 + 1 7/8 = 8 51/32 = 9 19/32 = 9.593

7. Third side = $\sqrt{9^2+12^2} = \sqrt{225} = 15$"

8. Let x = weight. Then, 12/32 = 5.75/x . Solving, x ≈ 15.33 lbs.

9. 12" = (3.14)(diameter), so diameter ≈ 3.82"

10. $\frac{39}{64}$" = .609375" ≈ .609"

11. Under his new contract, the weekly wage for 44 hours can be found by first determining his hourly rate for the first 40 hours = $431.40 ÷ 40 ≈ $10.80. Now, his time and one-half pay will = ($10.80)(1.5) = $16.20. His weekly wage for the new contract = $431.40 + (4)($16.20) = $496.20. His new hourly rate for 44 hours = $496.20 ÷ 44 ≈ $10.34. Under the old contract, his hourly rate for 44 hours was $415.20 ÷ 44 = $9.44. His hourly rate increase = $10.34 - $9.44 = $0.90. (Answer key: between $0.80 and $1.00)

12. 4'3 1/4" + 7'2 1/2" + 11' 1/4" = 22'6"

13. .038 = 38 thousandths

14. ($10.86)(40) + ($16.29)(3) = $483.27

15. 3'2 1/4" + 8 7/8" + 2'6 3/8" + 2'9 3/4" + 1'0" = 8'25 18/8" = 10'3 1/4"

16. The gear ratio is inversely proportional to the gear size. Let x = large gear's rpm. Then, 6/1 = 120/x . Solving, x = 20

17. Subtract 14 from 29.76

18. 5/8 = .625

19. Let x = number of pounds. Then, 300/450 = 100/x . Solving, x = 150

20. 600 quarts = 150 gallons, since 4 quarts = 1 gallon

21. (9")(9")(10") = 810 cu.in. Then, 810 ÷ 231 ≈ 3.5

22. Let x = unknown cost. Then, 30/$76.80 = 45/x. Solving, x = $115.20

23. $18,000 + ($18,000)(1.10) = $37,800

24. ($10.00)(1.15) = $11.50

25. 7/8" + 3/4" + 1/2" + 3/8" = 20/8" = 2 1/2"

TEST 2

DIRECTIONS: Each question or incomplete statement is followed by several suggested answers or completions. Select the one that BEST answers the question or completes the statement. *PRINT THE LETTER OF THE CORRECT ANSWER IN THE SPACE AT THE RIGHT.*

1. A sheet metal plate has been cut in the form of a right triangle with sides of 5, 12, and 13 inches.
   The area of this plate, in square inches, is

   A. 30   B. 32 1/2   C. 60   D. 78

   1.____

2. If steel weighs 480 lbs. per cubic foot, the weight of an 18" x 18" x 2" steel base plate is _____ lbs.

   A. 180   B. 216   C. 427   D. 648

   2.____

3. By trial, it is found that by using 2 cubic feet of sand, a 5 cubic foot batch of concrete is produced.
   Using the same proportions, the amount of sand, in cubic feet, required to produce 2 cubic yards of concrete is MOST NEARLY

   A. 7   B. 22   C. 27   D. 45

   3.____

4. The total number of cubic yards of earth to be removed to make a trench 3'9" wide, 25'0" long, and 4'3" deep is MOST NEARLY

   A. 53.1   B. 35.4   C. 26.6   D. 14.8

   4.____

5. A large number of 2 x 4 studs, some 10'5" long and some 6'5 1/2" long, are required for a job.
   To minimize waste, it would be PREFERABLE to order lengths of _____ feet.

   A. 16   B. 17   C. 18   D. 19

   5.____

6. A 6" pipe is connected to a 4" pipe through a reducer. If 100 cubic feet of water is flowing through the 6" pipe per minute, the flow, in cubic feet, per minute through the 4" pipe is

   A. 225   B. 100   C. 66.6   D. 44.4

   6.____

7. If steel weighs 0.28 pounds per cubic inch, then the weight, in pounds, of a 2" square steel bar 120" long is MOST NEARLY

   A. 115   B. 125   C. 135   D. 155

   7.____

8. A three-inch diameter steel bar two feet long weighs MOST NEARLY (assume steel weighs 480 lbs./cu.ft.) _____ lbs.

   A. 48   B. 58   C. 68   D. 78

   8.____

9. The area of a circular plate will be reduced by 5% if a sector removed from it has an angle of _____ degrees.

   A. 18   B. 24   C. 32   D. 60

   9.____

10. If a 4 1/16 inch shaft wears six thousandths of an inch, the NEW diameter will be _____ inches.

    A. 4.0031   B. 4.0565   C. 4.0578   D. 4.0605

11. A set of mechanical plan drawings is drawn to a scale of 1/8" = 1 foot.
    If a length of pipe measures 15 7/16" on the drawing, the ACTUAL length of the pipe is _____ feet.

    A. 121.5   B. 122.5   C. 123.5   D. 124.5

12. An electrical drawing is drawn to a scale of 1/4" = 1'. If a length of conduit on the drawing measures 7 3/8", the actual length of the conduit, in feet, is

    A. 7.5   B. 15.5   C. 22.5   D. 29.5

13. Assume that you have assigned 6 mechanics to do a job that must be finished in 4 days. At the end of 3 days, your men have completed only two-thirds of the job. In order to complete the job on time and because the job is such that it cannot be speeded up, you should assign a MINIMUM of _____ extra men.

    A. 3   B. 4   C. 5   D. 6

14. Assume that a trench is 42" wide, 5' deep, and 100' long. If the unit price of excavating the trench is $105 per cubic yard, the cost of excavating the trench is MOST NEARLY

    A. $6,805   B. $15,330   C. $21,000   D. $63,000

15. If the scale on a shop drawing is 1/4 inch to the foot, then the length of a part which measures 2 3/8 inches long on the drawing is ACTUALLY _____ feet.

    A. 9 1/2   B. 8 1/2   C. 7 1/4   D. 4 1/4

16. It is necessary to pour a new concrete floor for a shop. If the dimensions of the concrete slab for the floor are to be 27' x 18' x 6", then the number of cubic yards of concrete that must be poured is

    A. 9   B. 16   C. 54   D. 243

17. The jaws of a vise move 1/4" for each complete turn of the handle.
    The number of complete turns necessary to open the jaws 2 3/4" is

    A. 9   B. 10   C. 11   D. 12

18. Assume that a jobbing shop is to submit a price for a contract involving 300 pieces of work. Assume that material costs 50 cents per piece, labor costs $7.50 an hour, and a lathe operator can complete 5 pieces in an hour.
    If overhead is 40% of material and labor costs and the profit is 10% of all costs, the submitted price for the entire job will be

    A. $630.24   B. $872.80   C. $900.00   D. $924.00

19. The following formula is used in connection with the three-wire method of measuring pitch diameters of screw threads: $G=\dfrac{0.57735}{N}$, where G = wire size and N = number of threads per inch.
According to this formula, the proper size of wire for a 1"-8NC thread is MOST NEARLY

   A. .0722"   B. .7217"   C. .0072"   D. .0074"

20. A millimeter is 1/25.4 of an inch and there are 10 millimeters to a centimeter.
If a piece of stock measures 127 centimeters long, the length of the stock, in feet and inches, would be MOST NEARLY

   A. 2'1"   B. 4'2"   C. 8'4"   D. 41'8"

21. For a certain job, you will need 25 steel bars 1 inch in diameter and 4"6" long.
If these bars weigh 3 pounds per foot of length, then the TOTAL weight for all 25 bars is _____ pounds.

   A. 13.5   B. 75.0   C. 112.5   D. 337.5

22. If steel weighs 0.30 pounds per cubic inch, then the weight of a 2 inch square steel bar 90 inches long is _____ pounds.

   A. 27   B. 54   C. 108   D. 360

23. A concrete wall is 36' long, 9' high, and 1 1/2' thick. The number of cubic yards of concrete that were needed to make this wall is

   A. 14   B. 18   C. 27   D. 36

24. If the scale on a shop drawing is 1/2 inch to the foot, then the length of a part which measures 41/4 inches long on the drawing has a length of APPROXIMATELY _____ feet.

   A. 2 1/8   B. 4 1/4   C. 8 1/2   D. 10 3/4

25. If the allowable load on a wooden scaffold is 60 pounds per square foot and the scaffold surface area is 3 feet by 12 feet, then the MAXIMUM total distributed load that is permitted on the scaffold is _____ pounds.

   A. 720   B. 1,800   C. 2,160   D. 2,400

KEY (CORRECT ANSWERS)

1. A
2. A
3. B
4. D
5. B

6. B
7. C
8. A
9. A
10. B

11. C
12. D
13. A
14. A
15. A

16. A
17. C
18. D
19. A
20. B

21. D
22. C
23. B
24. C
25. C

SOLUTIONS TO PROBLEMS

1. Area = (1/2)(base)(height) = (1/2)(5")(12") = 30 sq.in.

2. Volume = (18") (18") (2") = 648 cu.in. = 648/1720 cu.ft.
   Then, (480)(648/1720) = ≈ 180 lbs.

3. 2 cu.yds. = 54 cu.ft. Let x = required cubic feet of sand. Then, 2/5 = x/54. Solving, x = 21.6 (or about 22)

4. (3.75')(25')(4.25') = 398.4375 cu.ft. ≈ 14.8 cu.yds.

5. 10'5" + 6'5 1/2" = 16'10 1/2", so lengths of 17 feet are needed

6. The amount of water flowing through each pipe must be equal.

7. (2")(2")(120") = 480 cu. in. Then, (480)(.28) ≈ 135 lbs.

8. Volume = (π) (.125 ')^2 (2) ≈ .1 cu.ft. Then, (.1)(480) = 48 lbs.

9. (360°)(.05) - 18°

10. 4 1/16 - .006 = 4.0625 - .006 = 4.0565

11. 15 7/16" ÷ 1/8" = 247/16 . 8/1 = 123.5. Then, (123.5)(1 ft.) = 123.5 ft.

12. 7 3/8" ÷ 1/4" = 59/8 . 4/1 = 29.5 Then, (29.5)(1 ft.) = 29.5 ft.

13. (6)(4) = 24 man-days normally required. Since after 3 days only the equivalent of (2/3)(24) = 16 man-days of work has been 1 done, 8 man-days of work is still left. 16 ÷ 3 = 5 1/3, which means the crew is equivalent to only 5 1/3 men. To do the 8 man-days of work, it will require at least 8 - 5 1/3 = 2 2/3 = 3 additional men.

14. (3.5')(5')(100') = 1750 cu.ft. ≈ 64.8 cu.yds. Then, (64.8)($105) ≈ $6805

15. 2 3/8" ÷ 1/4" = 19/8 . 4/1 = 9 1/2 Then, (9 1/2)(1 ft.) = 9 1/2 feet

16. (27')(18')(1/2') = 243 cu.ft. = 9 cu.yds. (1 cu.yd. = 27 cu.ft.)

17. 2 3/4" ÷ 1/4" = 11/4 . 4/1 = 11

18. Material cost = (300)($.50) = $150. Labor cost = ($7.50)(300/5) = $450. Overhead = (.40)($150+$450) = $240. Profit = .10($150+$450+$240) = $84. Submitted price = $150 + $450 + $240 + $84 = $924

19. 6 = .57735" ÷ 8 = .0722"

20. 127 cm = 1270 mm = 1270/25.4" ≈ 50" = 4.2"

21. (25)(4.5') = 112.5' Then, (112.5X3) = 337.5 lbs.

22. (2")(2")(90") = 360 cu.in. Then, (360)(30) = 108 lbs.

23. (36')(9')(1 1/2') = 486 cu.ft. = 18 cu.yds. (1 cu.yd. = 27 cu.ft.)

24. 4 1/4" ÷ 1/2" = 17/4 . 2/1 = 8 1/2. Then, (8 1/2)(1 ft.) = 8 1/2 ft.

25. (12')(3') = 36 sq.ft. Then, (36)(60) = 2160 lbs.

TEST 3

DIRECTIONS: Each question or incomplete statement is followed by several suggested answers or completions. Select the one that BEST answers the question or completes the statement. *PRINT THE LETTER OF THE CORRECT ANSWER IN THE SPACE AT THE RIGHT.*

1. A right triangular metal sheet for a roofing job has sides of 36 inches and 4 feet. The length of the remaining side is

    A. 7 feet
    B. 6 feet
    C. 60 inches
    D. 90 inches

2. A U.S. Standard Gauge thickness is given as 0.15625. This thickness, in fractions of an inch, is MOST NEARLY _____ inches.

    A. 1/8 B. 4/32 C. 5/32 D. 3/64

3. The weight per 100 of sheet metal fasteners is given as 2/3 pound. The APPROXIMATE number of fasteners in a 2-pound package is

    A. 166 B. 200 C. 300 D. 266

4. The decimal equivalent of 27/32 is MOST NEARLY

    A. 0.813 B. 0.828 C. 0.844 D. 0.859

5. If a scaled measurement of 1'3" on the drawing of a sheet metal layout represents an actual length of 10"0", then the drawing has been made to a scale of _____ inch to the foot.

    A. 3/4 B. 1 1/4 C. 1 1/2 D. 1 3/4

6. Two and two-thirds tees can be made from one sheet of steel. If 24 tees must be made, then the number of sheets required is

    A. 6 B. 7 C. 8 D. 9

7. A main duct 20 inches in diameter discharges into two branch ducts. The sum of the areas of the branches is to be equal to the area of the main duct. One branch is 12 inches in diameter.
   The diameter of the other branch is _____ inches.

    A. 16 B. 12 C. 10 D. 8

8. If steel weighs 480 lbs. per cubic foot, the weight of 10 sheets, each 6 feet by 3 feet by 1/32 inch, is _____ lbs.

    A. 2,700 B. 1,237 C. 270 D. 225

9. The area, in square inches, of a right triangle that has sides of 12 1/2, 10, and 7 1/2 inches is

    A. 18 1/4 B. 37 1/2 C. 75 D. 60

10. In making a container to hold 1 gallon (231 cu.in.) and to be 6 inches in diameter at the top and 8 inches in diameter at the bottom, the height must be, in inches,

    A. 10.0 B. 8.2 C. 4.6 D. 6

11. A sheet metal worker is given a job to make a transition piece from a 8 1/2" diameter duct to an 11 1/4" diameter duct. If the length of the transition piece is 5 1/2" for each inch change in diameter, then the length of the transition piece is

    A. 14 7/8" B. 15" C. 15 1/8" D. 15 1/4"

12. A duct layout is drawn to a scale of 3/8" to a foot. If the length of a run shown on the drawing scales 7 1/2", then the ACTUAL length of the run is

    A. 19'6" B. 19'9" C. 20'0" D. 20'3"

13. An 18" x 24" duct is to be connected to a 24" x 24" duct by means of an eccentric transition piece (3 sides flush). If the taper is to be 1" in 4", then the length of the transition piece is

    A. 6" B. 12" C. 18" D. 24"

14. Twenty-seven pairs of 3/8" diameter rods each 3'3 1/2" long are needed to support a duct.
    If the available rods are ten feet long, then the MINIMUM number of rods that will be needed to make the twenty-seven sets is

    A. 9 B. 12 C. 15 D. 18

15. A rectangular sheet metal air duct with open ends is 12 feet long and 15" x 20" in cross-section. If one square foot of the sheet metal weighs 1/2 pound, then the TOTAL weight of the duct is _____ lbs.

    A. 10 B. 17 1/2 C. 35 D. 150

16. The sum of 1/12 and 1/4 is

    A. 1/3 B. 5/12 C. 7/12 D. 3/8

17. The product of 12 and 2 1/3 is

    A. 27 B. 28 C. 29 D. 30

18. If 4 1/2 is subtracted from 7 1/5, the remainder is

    A. 3 7/10 B. 2 7/10 C. 3 3/10 D. 2 3/10

19. The number of cubic yards in 47 cubic feet is MOST NEARLY

    A. 1.70 B. 1.74 C. 1.78 D. 1.82

20. A wall 8'0" high by 12'6" long has a window opening 4'0" high by 3'6" wide.
    The net area of the wall (allowing for the window opening) is, in square feet,

    A. 86 B. 87 C. 88 D. 89

21. A worker's hourly rate is $11.36. 21.____
    If he works 11 1/2 hours, he should receive

    A. $129.84   B. $130.64   C. $131.48   D. $132.24

22. The number of cubic feet in 3 cubic yards is 22.____

    A. 81   B. 82   C. 83   D. 84

23. At an annual rate of $.40 per $100, what is the fire insurance premium for one year on a 23.____
    house that is insured for $80,000?

    A. $120   B. $160   C. $240   D. $320

24. A meter equals approximately 1.09 yards. 24.____
    How much longer, in yards, is a 100-meter dash than a 100-yard dash?

    A. 6   B. 8   C. 9   D. 12

25. A train leaves New York City at 8:10 A.M. and arrives in Buffalo at 4:45 P.M. on the same 25.____
    day. How long, in hours and minutes, does it take the train to make the trip?
    _____ hours, _____ minutes.

    A. 6; 22   B. 7; 16   C. 7; 28   D. 8; 35

KEY (CORRECT ANSWERS)

1. C	11. C
2. C	12. C
3. C	13. D
4. C	14. D
5. C	15. C
6. D	16. A
7. A	17. B
8. D	18. B
9. B	19. B
10. D	20. A

21. B
22. A
23. D
24. C
25. D

SOLUTIONS TO PROBLEMS

1. Let x = remaining side. Converting to inches, $x^2 = 36^2 + 48^2$ So, $x^2 = 3600$. Solving, x = 60 inches.

2. $.15625 = \dfrac{15,625}{100,000} = \dfrac{5}{32}$

3. 2 ÷ 2/3 = 3. Then, (3)(100) = 300 fasteners

4. 27/32 = .84375 ≈ .844

5. 1'3" ÷ 10 = 15" ÷ 10 = 1 1/2"

6. 24 ÷ 2 2/3 = 24/1.3/8 = 9

7. Area of main duct = $(\pi)(10^2) = 100\pi$. One of the branches has an area of $(\pi)(6^2) = 36\pi$. Thus, the area of the 2nd branch = $100\pi - 36\pi = 64\pi$. The 2nd branch's radius must be 8" and its diameter must be 16".

8. Volume = (1/384')(6')(3') = .046875 cu.ft. Then, 10 sheets have a volume of .46875 cu.ft. Now, (.46875)(480) = 225 lbs.

9. Note that $(7\ 1/2)^2 + (10)^2 = (12\ 1/2)^2$, so that this is a right triangle. Area = (1/2)(10")(7 1/2") = 371/2 sq.in.

10. $231 = \dfrac{h}{3}[(\pi)(3)^2 + (\pi)(4)^2 + \sqrt{(9\pi)(16\pi)}]$, where h = required height. Then,

    $231 = \dfrac{h}{3}(9\pi + 16\pi + 12\pi)$. Simplifying, $231 = 37\pi h/3$.
    Solving, h ~ 5.96" or 6"

11. 11 1/4 - 8 1/2 = 2 3/4. Then, (2 3/4)(5 1/2) = 11/4 .11/2 = 15 1/8

12. 7 1/2 " ÷ 3/8" = 15/2 .8/3 = 20 Then, (20)(1 ft.) = 20 feet

13. 24" - 18" = 6" Then, (6")(4) = 24"

14. 3'3 1/2" = 39.5". Now, (27)(2)(39.5") = 2133". 10 ft. = 120". Finally, 2133 ÷ 120 = 17.775, so 18 rods are needed.

15. Surface area = (2)(12')(1 1/4') + (2)(12')(1 2/3') = 70 sq.ft. Then, (70)(1/2 lb.) - 35 lbs.

16. 1/12 + 1/4 = 4/12 = 1/3

17. $(12)(2\ 1/3) = 12/1 \cdot 7/3 = 28$

18. $7\ 1/5 - 4\ 1/2 = 7\ 2/10 - 4\ 5/10 = 6\ 12/10 - 4\ 5/10 = 2\ 7/10$

19. 47 cu.ft. = 47/27 cu.yds. = 1.74 cu.yds.

20. (8')(12.5') - (4')(3.5') = 86 sq.ft.

21. ($11.36)(11.5) = $130.64

22. 1 cu.yd. = 27 cu.ft., so 3 cu.yds. = 81 cu.ft.

23. $80,000 ÷ $100 = 800. Then, (800)($.40) = $320

24. 100 meters = 109 yds. Then, 109 - 100 = 9 yds.

25. 4:45 P.M. - 8:10 A.M. = 8 hrs. 35 min.

BASIC FUNDAMENTALS OF BLACKSMITHING

CONTENTS

	Page
INTRODUCTION TO BLACKSMITHING	1
BLACKSMITH'S TOOLS	1
ANVIL	2
HAND FORMING TOOLS	4
HAMMERS	5
FORGE	6
FORGE OPERATION	7
FLUXES	7
WELDING STEEL	7
TEMPER OF STEEL	8
HARDENING AND TEMPERING	9
THERMAL CRITICAL POINTS OF STEEL	11

BASIC FUNDAMENTAL OF BLACKSMITHING

By definition, a blacksmith is a smith who works in or welds wrought iron, as by bearing upon an anvil, and makes or shapes small utensils or parts of machines, horse shoes, etc., one who forges or welds iron on an anvil.

Formerly, a blacksmith was a smith who worked in black metal or iron, as distinguished from a white smith, who worked on white metal or tin.

BLACKSMITH'S TOOLS

The sections of metal worked by the blacksmith are few and simple. The sections of iron and steel dealt with by the smith are either round, square or a rectangular bar; hence, no complicated tools are necessary. The only cutting tools used by the blacksmith are those actually employed to sever the forging from the stock or to remove extraneous metal, the chief art of smithing consisting in reducing the sectional bar to the desired form or drawing it out.

Tongs

Next to the anvil and hammer in importance are the tongs, of which there is a great variety. Tongs are used for holding metal that is at too high a temperature to be held in the bare hands; for placing iron in and removing it from the fire, and work of a similar character. As the hand should be free to manipulate and turn the metal, the tongs are held in position by a link driven on over the handles. The elasticity of the handles serves to hold the work securely.

Following is a list of tongs used in blacksmithing:
1. Straight lip
2. Single pick up
3. Double pick up
4. Rivet
5. Lathe tool
6. Pick
7. Curved lip or bolt; fluted jaw
8. Gad
9. Bolt
10. Round jaw
11. Angle jaw
12. Clip
13. Modified pincer
14. Box
15. Single gooseneck
16. Farrier's pincer
17. Cutting nipper
18. Hoop parer
19. Hoop tester
20. Clincher
21. Horseshoe nail puller or cotter pin puller
22. V shape

The simplest form of tongs is called a *flat tong*, from the shape of the jaws. They are used for holding flat pieces of metal, and vary in size according to the work in hand.

The *single and double pick up tongs* are used for picking up hot pieces of metal that may have fallen upon the floor. They are usually light and have long handles so that objects on the ground may be reached without stooping.

Round bit tongs are used for holding cylindrical objects. The jaws are concave and are suited for holding such objects. Tongs of this kind are frequently made of great strength and weight and are adapted to the handling of heavy shafts and axles. Similar tongs are used for holding square pieces. In such, the jaws have a rectangular recess instead of a circular one. A square piece can thus be held more securely by gripping on the corners than when it is seized on the flat surface.

ANVIL

By definition, an anvil is a heavy block of iron and steel upon the surfaces of which the smith beats heated plastic metal t the desired shape.

Typical blacksmith's anvil with first class construction is made of best wrought iron and faced with best crucible cast steel. Top and bottom are each one solid piece and welded at waist.

Following are important parts of an anvil:
1. Face
2. Rounded corner
3. Hardy hole
4. Punch or slug hole
5. Cutting block
6. Horn
7. Heel
8. Body
9. Feet

The *face* of a good anvil is of hardened and tempered steel. The smith is very particular about its condition. Care must be exercised to prevent cutting into the face of the anvil or marring it with the edge of the sledge or hammer.

The edges of the anvil should not be chipped from careless operations.

The *rounded corner* provides a working surface of very short radiums.

The *hardy hole* is a square opening in the face of the anvil at the heel end, into which the tangs of the anvil tools fit.

The *punch or slug hole* is used in punching to provide a space through which the slugs may pass.

The *cutting block*, which is not hardened, is used for placing stock to be cut with a chisel.

The *horn or beak* serves as a mould for bending curved portions of the work. The horn should be well-dressed, smooth, and drawn to a small round point.

The *heel* presents a flat working surface, and its corners and edges should be comparatively sharp.

The *body* should be amply large to quickly absorb the heaviest blows.

The *feet* (four in number) serve to increase the base upon which the anvil rests as well as to afford the means for clamping it down into position.

The anvil should be placed at the end of a heavy block of wood sunk into the ground to a depth of at least two feet, so that it may rest upon a firm but elastic foundation. As the anvil is subjected to constant vibrations, by nature of the work, it is necessary that it should be firmly fastened to the block. In doing this, avoid spiking, as the spikes will soon work loose and the block be spoiled. There are two iron rods about $3/8$" in diameter passing over the feet of the anvil and running through a 1 in. round or square bar extending through the block. Nuts on these rods make it possible to draw them very tight and thus hold the anvil firmly.

Anvil Tools

Under this heading is included all the tools provided with a tang, so that they may be held in the hardy hole of the anvil as distinguished from the tools erroneously called *anvil tools*, held in the smith's hand and used in combination with the anvil tools; they are properly called hand forming tools. The anvil tools ordinarily used for general work, and which should always be included in any blacksmith's shop equipment are:

1. Bottom hardies
    a. Cold cut
    b. Hot cut
2. Bending fork
3. Bottom fuller
4. Bottom swage
5. Cutting block
6. Punching block

Hardies are bottom cutting chisels used to cut off lengths from bars, or crop ends from forgings. They are called *cold* or *hot* according to as they are shaped and tempered for cutting cold or hot iron.

Bending fork is made with square, flat or round fingers and is used extensively in a variety of bending operations.

Bottom fuller is simply an inverted wedge with a blunt nose or working edge. It is used for spreading or notching the work.

Bottom swage, the most common form of swage, has a concave face and is accordingly used to smooth off a round bar. It is also used for drawing metal down to the required diameter.

Cutting block is a flat plate of mild steel that is used for cutting operations, which because of the shape of the work, cannot be conveniently performed on the cutting face of the anvil.

Punching block is a block similar to the cutting block, but provided with a series of holes of various sizes. The holes provide a space through which slugs punched from the work may pass.

It should be understood that in addition to the standard anvil tools just described there are numerous special tools occasionally used.

HAND FORMING TOOLS

These are virtually counterparts of the anvil tools and are used in combination with the anvil tools. They are called hand forming tools because they are provided with a handle so that they may be held by the smith's hand in forming or shaping the work, the corresponding anvil tool used at the same time being held by the anvil by inserting the tang into the hardy hole of the anvil.

Following is a list of hand forming tools that are ordinarily used:
1. Top hardies
    a. Cold cut
    b. Hot cut
2. Top fuller
3. Top swage
4. Flatters
    a. Plain
    b. Offset
5. Punches
6. Cutting tool
7. Bucking bar
8. Heading tool
9. Shearing tool

The smith, in forming his metals, holds these tools in position by the handle, while the helper strikes the head of the placed tool in a sledge.

Below follows a description of the hand forming tools.

Cold cut top hardy is a stout bladed tool used to cut cold metals.

Hot cut top hardy is a thin bladed tool. This tool should never be used to cut cold metal.

Top fuller is a tool having a rounded nose, and is used for spreading and notching metals.

Top swage is a tool having a grooved face and is used to swage or form metals to the shape of the groove, or for drawing metal down to a required diameter.

Flatters is used to smooth off and finish small flat surfaces. Its principal use is for striking blows in a definite spot or inaccessible place. A regular flatter is a flat faced tool used to smooth and finish the surface of forgings. To get the best smooth finish, do not have the temperature of the forging too high, dip the face of the flatter in water, have water on the face of the anvil, and do not strike the flatter too heavily.

Punches are used for making large holes in hot metal. The working end is shaped according to the kind of hole desired, as round, square, oblong, etc. The size depends upon the hole to be punched. They are invariably used for making holes through hot metal. The ordinary method is to punch partway through from one side; then turn the piece and drive through from the opposite direction. This avoids tearing the metal on the surface, and leaves a smooth hole at each end.

Cupping tool is a tool with a rounded cavity and is used for finishing the heads of rivets.

Bucking bar is called an inertia tool; and to possess that property in sufficiently marked degree, it is made heavy. The bar has a suitable cavity in its working face and is used to *buck* or back up a rivet while it is being headed.

Heading tool is used for making up bolt heads. It has a hole, about $2/32$" larger than the diameter of the stock that is being used, the face end of the hole being beveled.

Shearing tool which has a cutting end that is ground to the proper angle to adapt it to the work for which it is intended.

Swage Block

In connection with the use of the swage, which is used for drawing metal down to a required diameter, a swage block is very convenient. It takes the place of both the anvil and the bottom swage. It is usually made of cast iron of an approximately square shape, with a number of grooves of different dimensions cut on the face. These grooves are used according to the diameter shape of the piece being worked. It is called a swage block. The grooves are semi-elliptical, which should also be the shape of the curve of the top swage. The angular grooves are right-angled and are adapted to receive different sizes of square iron. The holes through the casting are available for punching, drifting, etc.

HAMMERS

Ordinarily, five kinds of hammers are used in a blacksmith's shop and they are known as:
1. Ball peen
2. Cross peen
3. Straight peen
4. Riveting
5. Sledge

By definition, the word *peen* (also spelled *pein*) means the end of a hammer head opposite the face when adapted for striking; usually shaped for indenting, as when pointed, conical, hemispherical, or wedge-shaped.

All hammers used directly upon hot iron or steel should have the centers of their faces slightly crowning or convex, and the edges well-rounded off to prevent their leaving sharp and unsightly marks upon the work, which is very apt to be the case when a hammer with a perfectly level face and sharp edges is used even by experienced workmen.

Sledge hammers are used by the blacksmith's assistant or helper, for making forgings heavier than could be successfully made by hand hammering. The sledge hammer is used both directly upon the hot metal in roughly blocking it to shape, and in finishing it by means of other tools which are placed upon the work and struck with the sledge.

The corners between the face and the eye are worked into octagonal shape, and the peen which is circular on the top stands straight with the handle. The weight of sledge hammers varies according to the size and weight of the work for which they are used; some hammers only weigh 8 lbs., while others weigh 20 lbs. or over.

Smaller hammers of the same pattern, weighing less than 8 lbs., are called *quarter hammers*, and those used for the very lightest work, generally made with a ball peen like a hand hammer, are called *backing hammers*.

FORGE

This consists of an open fireplace or hearth arranged for forced draft. The smith heats his metal to the working temperature in the forge.

The principle parts of a forge are:
1. Fire pot
2. Hearth
3. Tuyere
4. Blower
5. Hood

The *fire pot* consists of an inverted conical-shaped vessel. The fire is built in the fire pot. At the lower end of the fire pot is the *tuyere*, which is simply a pipe, one end of which projects into the bottom of the fire pot and through which a blast of air obtained by a *blower* (or bellows) is used for forced draft. Surrounding the fire pot is a large box like casing or *hearth* filled with cinders and on which coal is tamped around the fire on which the metal to be heated is rested.

The small circular type forge, owing to its portability, can be carried into the field for such purposes as tool dressing and the like. The best type of portable forge may be taken apart into three pieces by the disconnection of the wing nuts, fan, pan, and legs, packing separately for transportation. Whenever more than rivet heating or chisel dressing is intended, it is advisable to use a large square pan forge of a more substantial type.

As bellows are undesirable, a forge 28 x 40 in. may be recommended with a 14 in. fan; the latter will be driven by means of a lever through a sort of sun and planet motion, or by the intervention of a chain like the gear chain of a bicycle, from a large sprocket wheel. In either case, the final multiplying power is transmitted to the fan pulley by a belt, as a plain flat leather or textile one.

FORGE OPERATION

The fuel used on the forge is bituminous coal. It should contain as little sulphur and earthly matter as possible. The best quality coal is called smithing coal, although charcoal or coke may be used. In building a fire, place a block or brick over the tuyere opening and back the coal in the fire pot; then remove the block or brick and insert shavings to the opening. When the shavings are well-ignited, place some coke on them and accelerate the fire with the blower. Add a quantity of smithing coal well-dampened with water and partial burn out the gases.

The depth of the fire should always be liberal, because with a shallow fire the blast will blow through the fire, and the excess air will rapidly oxidize the metal being heated. The fire should be limited to as small a space as is necessary to heat the metal. It is regulated by quenching around its exterior portion. Only use the blast when heating the metal; and if it be desired to keep the fire for any length of time, it should be well-banked.

FLUXES

A flux is a substance, such as borax, which promotes the fusing of metals; thus, in soldering tin ware, rosin is used as a flux; the flux forms a skin on the surface of the heated metal and protects it from the attack of the oxygen in the atmosphere. The light blows given in the first stage of welding expel both flux and scale from the joint.

In practical operation, the smith often uses a little fine sand to sprinkler over the portions of the iron; ordinary borax is often applied for the same purpose, especially with mild steel.

WELDING STEEL

In welding cast or tool steel, the following points deserve careful study:

1. Do not use coal, as it may contain sulphur, but use coke, charcoal, or what is known as breeze, namely, washed and sorted cinders of partly burnt coal.

2. Keep the cast steel covered up while heating, and bring it to its heat as quickly as possible, with a view to prevent oxidation.

3. As cast steel requires but a low welding heat, it must not be made too hot; in that case, it will either burn or break into pieces while being hammered.

4. Apply some flux before putting the work into the fire, to protect the surface from the formation of scale or oxide, and add more at discretion.

5. When welding steel and iron, the iron must be hotter than the steel.

6. Clean off both surfaces with a short besom or hand broom before putting the parts together, and sprinkle flux at the last moment.

7. Strike light blows and quick at first, and then increase to heavy blows at completion.

TEMPER OF STEEL

This term, as used by steel makers, denotes the amount of carbon which is present in steel and its consequent hardness. The chief classifications are enunciated below:

Razor Temper: This has 1½% of carbon, and is so easily overheated that its manipulation can only be entrusted to a person accustomed to working with it. When property treated, it will do twice the work of ordinary tool steel in turning chilled rolls, etc.

Varieties of Temper in Steel: The following are some of the ordinary tempers which the blacksmith should understand. In this case, tempering relates to the degree of hardness obtained by plunging the steel when heated to a cherry red into cold water.

   Saw File Temper: Contains 1¾% carbon and demands careful treatment. Although it will stand the fire better, it must not be heated above a cherry red.

   Tool Temper: This possesses 1¼% carbon and is the quality recommended for machine tools. This steel may be welded, but the operation demands skill and experience.

   Spindle Temper: With $1\frac{1}{8}$% carbon, this furnishes the best results for very large turning tools, milling cutters, taps and screwing tackle. Considerable care is required in welding it, the flux previously referred to (composed of borax, sal-ammoniac, and yellow prussiate of potash) having been used with success.

   Chisel Temper: This useful temper has 1% of carbon and possesses great toughness in its soft state. It hardens at a low heat and may be welded without difficulty, being thus adapted for providing a cutting tip to tools and instruments which have to stand blows and jarring.

   Set Temper. Containing $\frac{7}{8}$ of 1% of carbon, this quality is well-adapted for tools such as drifts, cold sets, etc. which have to stand their principal punishment on the unhardened parts. Can be welded easily by a toolsmith.

   Die Temper: This has only ¾ of 1% carbon and is the most suitable temper for such tools as dies for presses, rivet snaps, etc., where hardness is required only upon the surface, and the capacity of withstanding great pressure is of the utmost importance. This quality welds with freedom.

In the following table, tempering relates to the degree of hardness obtained by plunging the steel when heated to a cherry red into cold water.

Table of Colors of Tempered Steel		
Colors	Temperature (°F)	Class of Tools for Which Used
Very pale yellow	430	Scrapers for brass Light turning tools Hammer faces
Light straw	450	Plaining tools Drills
Medium straw	460	Milling cutters
Full straw	470	Boring cutters Screwing dies
Dark yellow	490	Taps Chasing combs Punches and dies
Yellow brown	500	Reamers Gouges
Purple orange	520	Twist drills Flat drills for brass
Light purple	530	Augers Chipping chisels for steel Axes and adzes
Dark purple	550	Chipping chisels for cast iron Firmer chisels Cold sets
Dark blue	570	Springs Circular saws for metal Screwdrivers
Middle blue	590	Saws for wood
Light blue	610	Saws for wood
Greenish pale blue	630	Saws for wood

HARDENING AND TEMPERING

By definition, *tempering* means the giving of any required degree of hardness to a piece of steel; properly speaking, there are two distinct processes implied in the term, one being *hardening*, in which the steel is heated to a cherry red, corresponding to about 1650°F, and plunged into cold water, making the steel hard enough to scratch glass. Next follows the second process of tempering, which must be performed *to draw the temper* to the proper degree.

In this, the steel is reheated after hardening until it attains the proper color, corresponding to its temperature, as seen in the preceding table. The steel is then plunged into water for the second and final time. The colors upon the surface of the steel are due to films of oxide of varying thickness, formed by the action of the air upon the metal. When the quenching medium is water, the preliminary process of hardening must be carried out, or else the act of tempering would be without effect.

The heating is best carried out in a clear coke or charcoal fire, or, if the articles be small, they may be placed within a D-shaped muffle, or shallow sheet-iron box placed over the fire, to avoid formation of scale, unequal heating or discoloration of polished work; tool should be protected from the blast or draughts while heating or annealing, and the heat should be as uniform as possible over the whole of the article. This is effected by moving it about through the fire, or, when the muffle is used, by turning the pieces around and over with the tongs.

If steel is exposed to too great a heat, it becomes *burnt*, and its quality is deteriorated. In view of this, until the quality of any particular steel becomes well-known, it is wise to be even overcautious in the amount of heat applied. At the worst, the piece need only be rehardened at a high temperature, whereas, if overheated, its quality will be permanently injured.

Tool steel showing a bright and granular fracture has probably been overheated; if not, it will be dark and even.

When an article is heated in a bath of molten lead, the surface of the latter being strewn with powdered charcoal to prevent oxidation, and then tempered, the interior will be softer than the outside; this result is desirable for taps, reamers, etc.

The cooling medium used, it is well to bear in mind, influences the hardness of the temper; with oil, a species of tempering can take place without preliminary hardening, which is especially useful in dealing with large pieces, as not only does it harden the material, but may increase its strength while the uniformity of the process is assured. The articles are heated all over to a dull red heat, and then immersed in the oil, generally olive oil. Only one degree of hardness, that of a very dark straw color, can be obtained in this way; but there is a more equable temper imparted for the same color than with water quenching, on account of slower cooling.

Plain water makes the best bath for all general purposes; the most favorable results have been attained with it at a temperature of about 40°F. Many toolsmiths prefer to use the same water over and over again instead of changing it, but it is as well to keep it in circulation in the bath. A good plan is to admit a copious supply through a perforated false bottom, the excess of heated water escaping by a waste pipe near the top.

An oily film on the surface of the water will often save small articles from cracking, and will also take the chill off the water. First hardening in water and then tempering in oil gives a superior softness to tools.

For harder materials, brine may be used, composed of fresh water with enough salt added to float an egg, or half a pint of salt to a gallon of soft water. A mercury bath is supposed by many to make the hardest grade of steel, but if the very hardest possible point is wanted on a steel tool, its point should be brought to a cherry red and then be thrust into a solid block of lead until cooled.

In tempering tools, it is always advisable that the parts should be ground or machined to a surface beforehand, as the natural skin of the metal gives false colors.

Unequal heating is as much responsible for the cracking of milling cutters, pipe cutter wheels, etc., as unequal cooling, and to avoid this the process of heating in a bath of molten lead maintained at a high temperature has been successfully tried.

When dipping these articles, it is wise to sling them from a wire threaded through the holes and having its ends twisted over a small rod to carry or suspend it, the hole being filled with fire clay. This prevents cracking at the central hole.

Toothed drifts for cutting out long narrow holes should be tempered all over to a purple blue; those of stouter proportions can be made of a brown purple.

Taps require to be softer at the shank than at the teeth to avoid breaking off in use. A neat way of effecting this is to procure a piece of iron tube just a shade larger than the tap, and a pair of round bit tongs. After the tool is made and polished, it is first hardened, and then the temper is lowered in the following manner: The preliminary heating being done in a muffle or on a plate, to avoid discoloration, the tongs, which have been made bright red in the fire, are used to grip the tap by the shank, to bring the color down. Meanwhile, the piece of pipe has been brought to a dull red. As soon as the first signs of straw color appear on the shank, from the heat of the tongs, the tap is thrust into the tube up to the end of the threads. This keeps the color back on the screwed portion, and the shank will be dark blue by the time the threads have reached dark straw, when the whole can be plunged into the water. It is, of course, necessary to employ long-nosed tongs to heat the whole of the shank.

The countersink is used for enlarging orifices, such as are employed for rivet holes requiring to be flush or even with the surface of the riveted plate. In tempering these tools or any others having a pin or projection to serve as a guide in the hole, it is necessary that the pin or teat working in the hole should be much harder than the cutting edge. It is, therefore, customary first to harden the tool fully, dipping it gradually into clean water to avoid cracking, and then lower the hardness to the requisite temper by heating the tool upon a bar of red hot iron.

As soon as the pale straw color has come down to the pin, it must be kept in that state by directing a little stream of oil upon it, while the color *comes down* to the required shade on the main part of the tool, plunging it into clean water as soon as that stage has been reached.

THERMAL CRITICAL POINTS OF STEEL

If one should watch the slow heating of a piece of steel in a furnace, it would be noted that the temperature of the steel gradually increases with the increasing heat of the furnace until a temperature is reached when the steel may become slightly darker and cooler than the furnace.

As the heating is continued, the piece will again assume the temperature of the furnace. In the rising heat, the darkening of the piece of steel is due to the absorption of heat to convert ferrite and pearlite into austenite. Now, if the furnace be permitted to cool slowly during some point in the process, the steel may become brighter or visibly hotter than the furnace, after which it assumes its normal rate of cooling which continues on down to atmospheric temperatures. Such a rise in temperature in a slow cooling indicates a giving off of heat during the conversion of the austenite back to ferrite and pearlite.

A transforming of the constituents composing the steel accompanies these thermal changes as, for example, on heating, the decomposition of ferrite and pearlite.

To form austenite as mentioned above or vice versa, the decomposition of the austenite into its constituents, ferrite and pearlite, as the case may be, during slow cooling. The temperatures or points where these changes take place during the heating and cooling are called the critical points of steel.

To distinguish these two points, or ranges as is actually the case, those occurring on the heating are termed *decalescence*, and those on the cooling *recalescence* points. These terms are usually noted by the symbols Ac for *decalescence* and Ar for *recalescence*. When the various critical points occurring in steel are considered collectively, the range of temperature that they cover is called the critical range. The meaning of the expression *critical range on heating* and *critical range on cooling* is obvious.

BLACKSMITH'S ANVILS AND IRON WORKING TOOLS

I. Purpose of Blacksmith's Anvils and Iron Working Tools
(figs. 1 and 2)

Blacksmith's anvils are designed to provide a working surface when punching holes through metal and for supporting the metal when it is being forged and shaped. Iron working tools such as flatters, fullers, swages, hardies, and set hammers are used to form or shape forgings. Heading tools are used to shape bolts.

II. Types of Blacksmith's Anvils

The blacksmith's anvil (fig. 1) has a flat face with a horn on one end and two holes in the flat face opposite the horn. The round hole is called a spud or pritchet hole and permits slugs of metal to drop through it when holes are punched. The square hole is designed to hold hardies and bottom fullers and swages.

The cone-shaped horn is used to form curved shapes from bars and rods. The flat or top face is used to support the metal being worked on. Blacksmith's anvils are made of steel and weigh anywhere from 25 to 250 pounds. They have two mounting flanges which may be used to secure the anvil on a bench or on a concrete base.

III. Types of Blacksmith's Iron Working Tools

a. Flatter. A flatter (fig. 2) is a hammerlike tool with a flat face. It is used for smoothing and finishing flat forgings.

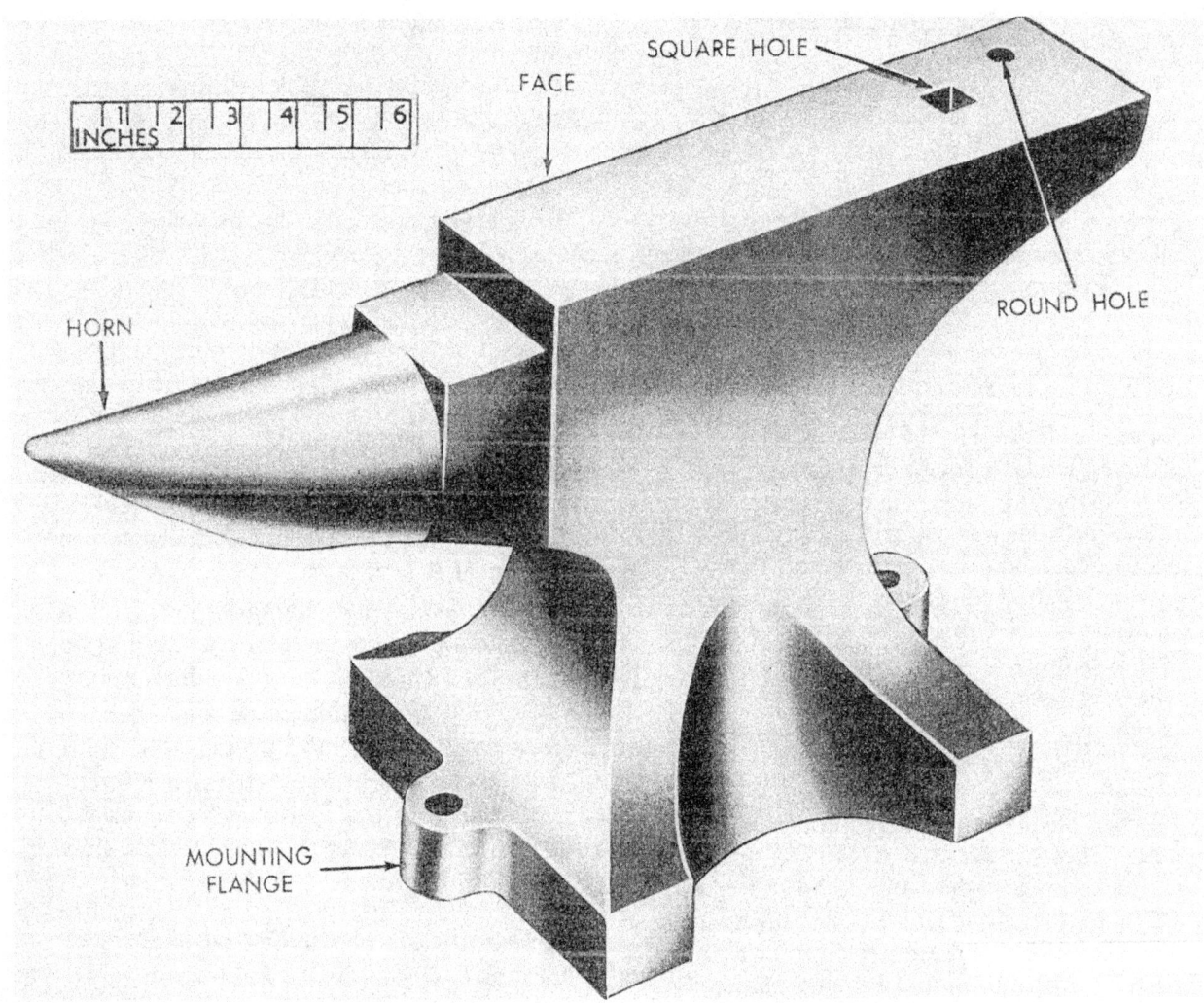

Figure 1 Blacksmith's anvil.

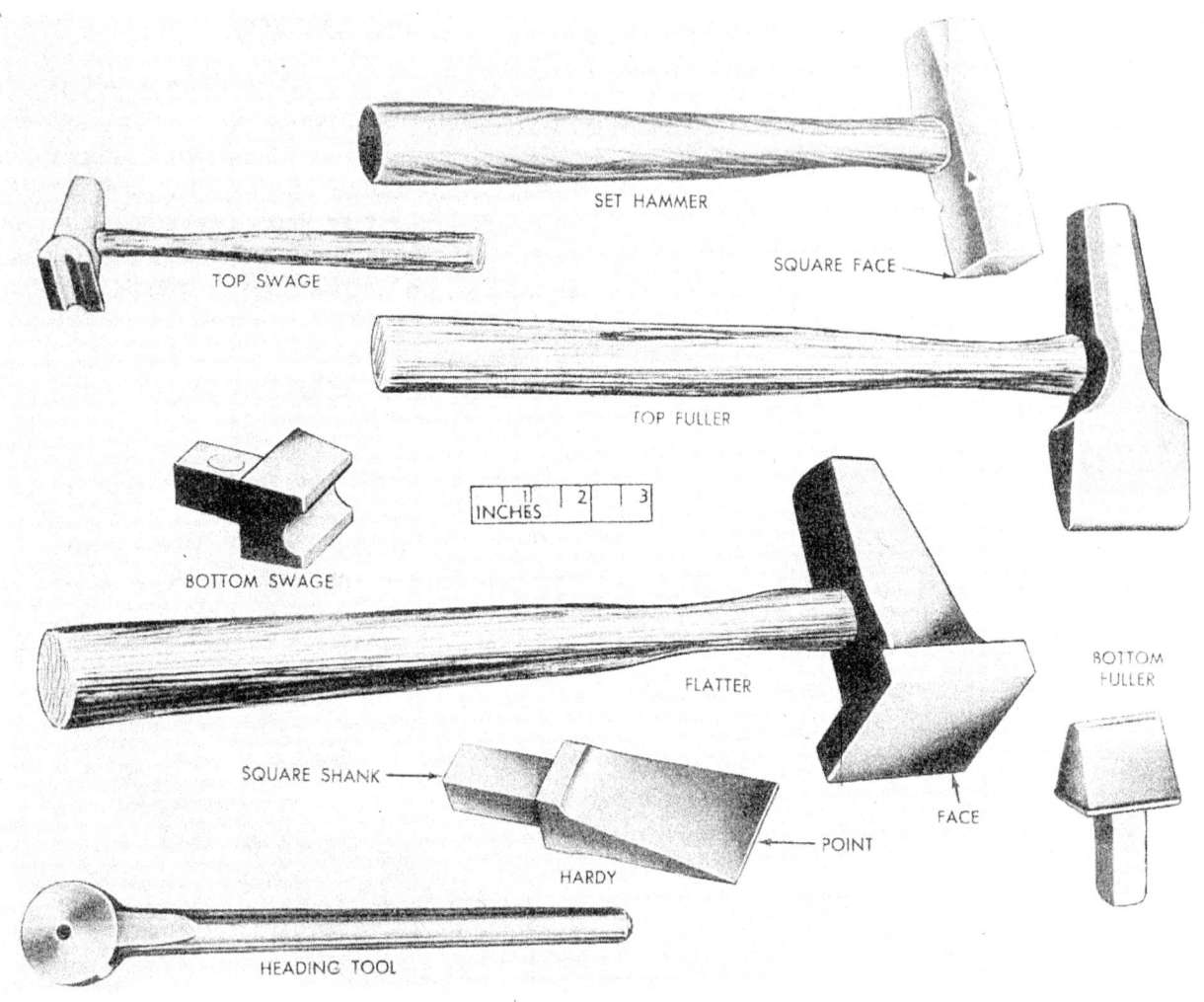

Figure 2 Blacksmith's tools.

b. *Fuller.* Fullers (fig. 2) are used for necking and grooving forgings and for drawing down a forging to a smaller size. Top fullers have handles and range in size from ¼ to 2 inches across the face and weigh from 2 to 4½ pounds. Bottom fullers have a square shank and are sized from ½ to 1 inch, weighing 2½ to 3 pounds.

c. *Swages.* Swages (fig. 2) are used for shaping, sizing, and smoothing round forgings. They are issued in sets of 6 swags, sized for ¼-, ⅜-, ½-, ⅝-, ¾-, and 1-inch round forgings. Swage blocks are also available for special jobs. These block are usually 4 inches thick, 11 or 13 inches wide, and 15 or 18 inches long. The bottom swage blocks have various shaped perforations and grooves for swaging and upsetting forgings and are square shanked. Top swages have handles and are shaped to work with bottom swages.

d. *Hardy.* A hardy (fig. 2) has a chisel-like point and a square shank. It fits into the square hole in the anvil. Metal to be cut is placed over the point and struck with a hammer or sledge until it separates.

e. *Set Hammer.* A set hammer (fig. 2) is used for setting down metal in a forging to form a square corner. It has a 1½-inch square face and weighs 3¼ pounds.

f. *Heading Tool.* A heading tool (fig. 2) is used to form bolt heads. It has a circular head with a hole in the center. Six heads are available with a different size hole. Hole sizes are ¼, ⅜, ½, ⅝, ¾, and 1 inch.

IV. Use and Care of Anvils and Tools

The top face of the anvil, as well as the horn, must be kept smooth and clean so as not to damage the work placed upon them. The flatters, fullers, swages, and set hammer must be kept properly ground, shaped, and clean. Hammers must be kept in good condition. Handles are repaired and replaced in the same manner as hammer handles. Shaping of tools is performed by grinding in the same manner as hammer heads. The hardy must be kept sharp and is ground as you would grind a chisel. To prevent rusting, cover tools and anvil with a thin film of oil after use.

V. Safety Precautions

Use extreme care when using tools to prevent metal chips from flying around and to prevent hot sparks from causing personal injury or fires. When heating metal to be forged, wear goggles to protect the eyes, particularly when shaping and cutting.

BLACKSMITHING

CONTENTS

		Page
I.	IRON AND STEEL	1
II.	THE FARM SHOP	2
	Location and Plan	2
	Equipment and Tools: The Forge	3
	The Anvil	4
	The Vise	5
	The Work Bench	5
	The Tool Table	5
	Water Tank	5
	Rack for Iron and Steel	6
	Necessary Tools	6
	Other Tools	7
	Two Useful Anvil Tools	8
III.	THE FORGE FIRE	9
	Smithing Coal	9
	Managing the Fire	9
IV.	FORGING IRON AND STEEL	10
	Drawing	10
	Upsetting	11
	Bending	11
	Scarfing	11
	Welding	12
	Punching	13
	Riveting	13
V.	SIMPLE EXERCISES IN BLACKSMITHING	14
	A Fire Poker	14
	Staple Puller	14
	Hook and Staple	15
	Chain Links	16
	Cold Shut Links	17
	Chain Hook	18
	Swivel	19
	Ring	20
	Clevis	20
	Pin or Bolt for Clevis	21
	Heading Tool for Bolts	21
	Bolts and Nuts	22
	Welding Separate Irons	23
	Welding Iron and Steel	25

VI.	FORGING AND TEMPERING STEEL TOOLS	27
	Making a Cold Chisel	27
	Forging and Tempering Drills	29
	Stone Drills	30
	Knife Blades	30
	Tempering a Hammer	31
	Blacksmith's Tongs	31
	Files	33
VII.	PLOW WORK	34
	Sharpening Plowshares	34
	New Points	34
	Handy Tools	36
VIII.	WAGON WORK	37
	Setting Tires	37
	Making New Tires	40
	Whiffletree Irons	41
IX.	HORSE SHOEING	42
X.	SOLDERING AND BRAZING	46
	Soldering	46
	Brazing	47
	APPENDIX	48
	Decimal Equivalents	49
	Rules Relative to the Circle	50
	Circumferences of Circles	51
	Weight of Round Mild Steel	51
	Weight of Square Mild Steel	51
	Weight of Flat Mild Steel	
	Sizes of Wire	

BLACKSMITHING

I. IRON AND STEEL

IRON

What we know as cast iron is made by melting pig iron and running it into molds of whatever form we wish to have. Cast iron is very hard and quite brittle. It is not pure iron, but contains several other elements, the most important of which is carbon. It is the carbon in the iron which makes it hard and brittle. If cast iron is kept at a high temperature for a long time, the carbon is burned out of it and it becomes softer and tougher. To make what is known as malleable cast iron, the articles to be made are first fast from pig iron, then placed in ovens where they are kept at a white heat for about a week. This high heat burns out most of the carbon, and the castings become tough enough to stand some bending without danger of breaking. Malleable castings can, therefore, be used for many purposes where ordinary cast iron would be too brittle.

Swedish iron, known also as "Norway iron," is a kind of wrought iron which is still to be found in the market. It is used where very soft and very tough iron is required, as, for example, in the making of rivets and clinch nails. It is so soft that shavings may be cut from it with a good jackknife. It is soft and tough because it is made from the purest iron ore to be found, and in smelting it only charcoal is used. Charcoal contains none of the injurious chemicals found in other coal.

STEEL

Mild steel, also called soft steel or machinery steel, which has almost entirely taken the place of the old-fashioned wrought iron, is made from pig iron by a process which removes almost all the carbon. There are several methods of making mild steel, the most common of which is known as the Bessemer process. This consists of melting the pig iron in large furnaces and holding it at a high heat while air is forced through the molten mass to burn out the carbon. From the furnace the molten steel is poured into molds about the size of a man's body, forming what are known as ingots. These ingots are heated to welding heat and rolled out into bars or beams or railroad rails, or into any shape required. One ingot will make two lengths of railroad rail.

Tool steel is simply pure iron to which a very small percentage of carbon has been added. It is one of the wonders of chemistry that the addition of a small part of one percent of carbon will change soft iron to stiff steel and give it the property known as temper. If we heat a bar of pure iron to a yellow heat, then suddenly cool it in water, no change is made in it. It may be bent the same as before the heating. If we do the same thing with a bar of steel, it will break when we try to bend it. Yet the only difference between the two bars is that the steel contains a part of one percent of carbon.

In making tool steel, rods of pure iron are packed in charcoal in a furnace which may be sealed so that it is practically airtight. The whole mass of iron and charcoal is heated to near a welding heat and kept at that temperature for some time. The iron is not allowed to melt but is kept near the melting point. During this process, a small amount of carbon from the charcoal unites with the iron. A rod is occasionally drawn out of the furnace and tested to determine the amount of carbon absorbed by the iron. When the right percentage of carbon has been absorbed, the furnace is allowed to cool. We now have what is known as blister steel; so called because the surface of the rods is covered with blisters.

It is easy to understand that rods so treated will have very much less carbon in the middle than toward the outside; and any tool made from such steel would be unsatisfactory. What is known to the trade as shear steel is made by welding together rods of blister steel. This welding together and drawing out of the rods makes a somewhat better grade of steel than the blister steel, and some kinds of cheap tools are made of it.

To get a tool steel which is of even carbon content throughout, blister steel is melted in crucibles and then drawn out into bars of any required size. This is called crucible steel and is the kind of steel from which all the best tools are made.

II. THE FARM SHOP

The farm shop and its use should fill an important place in the planning of the farm work and should be given careful thought. The repairs that may be made and the work that may be done year after year in a well-planned, well-lighted, properly equipped workshop, will repay the first cost many times over, in addition to providing pleasant and profitable occupation when the weather or other conditions prevent outside work.

LOCATION AND PLAN

The question of whether the shop is to be a separate building, or is to be combined with a garage or farm machinery building, or other structure, will depend upon what buildings are already in existence on the farm. Each farmstead will have its own problem along this line.

Possible fire hazard should be taken into consideration in connection with combining the forge shop with any other building. In any case, it would be desirable to have the shop some little distance from the barns.

The foundation for the shop should be laid deep enough to rest upon solid subsoil, and should extend at least 6 inches above ground level. This will protect the sills from decay, and allow the floor to be far enough above the outside ground surface to insure dryness, in case a gravel or earthen floor is decided upon.

A concrete floor is to be preferred if it can be afforded; but a very good floor may be made of a mixture of clay and cinders, or clay and fine gravel and sand properly rammed down to make it solid.

In case the forge is to be placed in a shop which is already built, and which has a wooden floor, the space for some distance around the forge and anvil should be covered with sheet iron so as to avoid danger from fire and the annoyance of having to pick up every piece of hot iron that happens to fall on the floor.

The floor space in the shop should be large enough, and the doorway wide enough and high enough so that a wagon, or automobile or tractor or truck in need of repairs could be accommodated. The doorway should be at least 8 feet wide and 7 feet 6 inches high, and there should be a ramp, preferably of concrete, leading up to the doorway and over the sill. It is considered better practice to use double doors for so wide a space rather than one wide door. Most sliding doors or doors hung on rollers, especially if very wide, are likely to warp out of shape and cause trouble. Hinged doors are easier to work, and may be closed more tightly.

Figure 1 shows a floor plan and a desirable arrangement of the equipment in a farm shop. Notice the wide doors, floor space for large machines, and the convenient arrangement of forge, anvil, drill, vise, and tool table with reference to each other. This plan shows a building of about 18 by 24 feet. The roof should be so constructed that no supporting posts will be necessary: thus leaving the entire floor space free of obstruction.

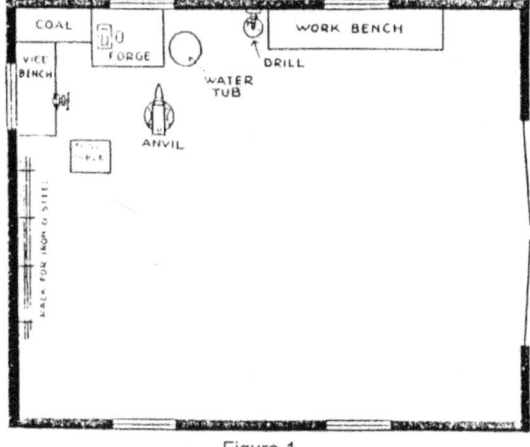

Figure 1

EQUIPMENT AND TOOLS

The Forge

The kind of forge to be used in the farm shop will depend somewhat on the amount of money the owner wishes to invest. A good steel forge suitable for farm work can be purchased for about $200. The only advantage such a forge will have over one that may be built by the farmer is that it is portable, and under some circumstances it may be convenient to move it about from place to place. For a permanent forge, the ideal arrangement would be a brick forge and chimney built in one piece; the forge to be about 2½ by 3½ feet in size and 30 inches high, and the chimney extending up above the comb of the roof at least 2 feet so as to insure a good draft. Figure 2 shows such a brick forge.

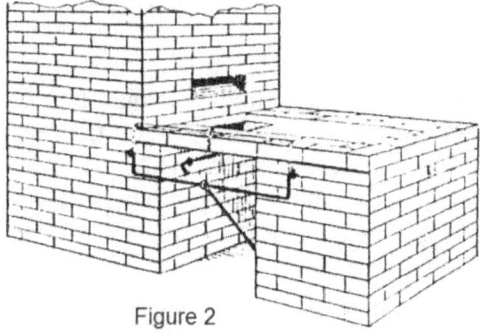

Figure 2

A very good forge may be made of ordinary lumber. If such a forge is decided upon, the box should be about 8 inches deep and of the same size as the brick forge mentioned above. It should be set up on legs of the proper length to bring the top of the box to about 30 inches above the floor. Whether the forge is of brick or of wood, it should have a tuyere iron or air nozzle that can be cleaned out from the bottom; and an ash pit or some sort of container for the ashes should be provided.

Blast for the forge is best provided by a fan blower. A good blower of this type can be had for about $100. A tuyere iron and the necessary pipe for connection with the blower are included for this price. Figure 3 shows blower and tuyere.

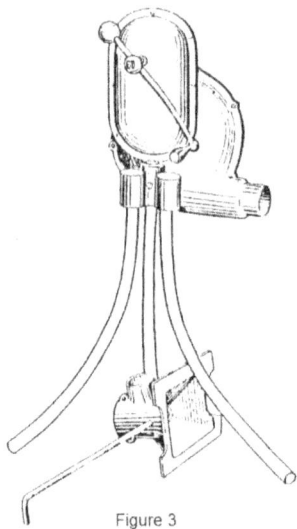

Figure 3

In the case of either the brick or the wooden forge, the tuyere should be so placed that its top is 4 inches below the top of the box; then the box is to be filled with damp clay, well packed, leaving a hollow space around the tuyere about the size and shape of a small hen's nest. The clay should be allowed to dry out slowly to avoid cracking, and should be thoroughly dry before a fire is built in the forge.

In locating the forge, it is well to remember that it is sometimes necessary to heat long rods in the fire, and therefore it is not wise to have the forge in a corner of the shop. The writer once knew a smith who was obliged to cut a hole through the outside wall of his shop in order to be able to handle some long bridge rods that he was hired to weld.

Some thought must be given to taking care of the smoke which seems to be a necessary product of every blacksmith shop. Do not make the mistake of trying to cover the whole forge with a large hood. Such a hood is a nuisance, for it is in the way for many kinds of work, and it does not carry off the smoke as well as a small hood located back of, and close to the fire. If a chimney or pipe with a large flue, the larger the better, is located just back of the forge, and the opening into it is made as it should be, within a few inches of the height of the fire, it will carry off most of the smoke.

In any chimney flue there is, under ordinary conditions, an upward draft of air. The larger the chimney flue the more air is constantly going upward. If the opening into the chimney is throttled down to a narrow slit, there will be a strong current of air entering this slit. If this opening is close to the fire, as shown in Figure 2, the smoke will be drawn into it before it has time to roll out into the air of the room.

The Anvil

Next in importance to the forge, in the furnishing of the shop, is the anvil. This should be of solid steel, with a hardened face. For the farm shop an anvil weighing 100 pounds will be found none too large. In selection an anvil, one should be sure that the face is level and smooth, and the edges of the face sharp and square, except that 5 or 6 inches of the edge of the face next to the horn and on the further side from the smith should be rounding instead of sharp. The reason for this is explained on Page 10 under "Drawing." Figure 27 gives a good idea of the proper shape of an anvil.

The anvil should be located about 6 feet from the fire, and if it is to be used by a right-handed man, should have the horn pointing to the left. It should rest on a block of wood not much larger than its own base, which should be set at least 2 feet into the earth, and be high enough so that the face of the anvil will be of the proper height. This height, for general work, should be on a level with the smith's knuckles as he stands beside the anvil. The anvil block may be a section of timber a foot square, or a section of a tree trunk of the proper size. It should be of seasoned wood, and years may be added to its term of usefulness if the ground end is soaked in creosote before being set in place.

An anvil is so likely to be abused by the amateur smith, that it seems advisable at this point to give a few words of warning.

We are too apt to think of an anvil as simply something to pound on, and it often gets more abuse than is good for it. The face of a good anvil is hardened steel. Any very hard steel is always more or less brittle. The face of a blacksmith's hammer is also of hardened steel and consequently more or less brittle. Remembering these two facts, let us make it a rule always to keep these two brittle things separated by having something between them. This something will generally be a piece of hot iron or steel. No amount of pounding on the iron or steel can harm either anvil or hammer; but the hammer must not hit the anvil. Student blacksmiths often ruin the edge of the anvil by using it to cut off the end of a piece of iron or steel. It is all right to do this if the blows of the hammer are stopped just before the steel is cut in two; but if the hammer reaches the edge of the anvil, two brittle things come in contact and something has to happen.

The Vise

The vise for the farm shop should be what is known as a leg vise, that is, one with a leg extending to the level of the floor. The vise itself is of wrought iron with steel jaws, and should be fastened to a solid post firmly set into the ground. The bottom of the leg should rest on a block which is firmly fastened to the post. This post may be made a part of the work bench, and should be, if possible, located in a good light and near enough to the anvil to allow the smith to reach it without moving more than a step from his place at the fire. Leg vises may now be had with extra jaws for holding pipe or other round objects.

The Work Bench

The work bench should be about 3 feet high and should be provided with racks and shelves for all the tools, such as files, chisels, wrenches, etc., that the smith would naturally use at the vise. It should contain drawers and shelves for stocks and dies and such supplies as rivets, small bolts, washers, and miscellaneous small hardware. If possible, it should be located near a window.

The Tool Table

A tool table, while not an absolute necessity in a farm shop, is a great convenience. It is usually made about 2 feet square, with a rail around the top and a shelf below. The purpose of the table is to hold all the anvil tools, such as top and bottom swages and fullers, hot and cold chisels, extra tongs and extra hammers. It is usually placed near, and at the right hand or tail end of, the anvil.

Water Tank or Tub

Factory made forges are generally provided with a vast iron water tank or box hung to the side of the fire pan, as shown in Figure 4. The usual container for water in the ordinary forge shop is a tub made from a barrel. An ordinary wooden kerosene or vinegar barrel with about a third of the top sawed off makes a very good tub. Just why old blacksmiths call this a "slack tub" is not easy to explain. The word is not to be found in the dictionary. This tub should be placed at the right of the forge within easy reach of the smith as he stands by the fire, and should be filled with water to within a few inches of the top.

Figure 4

Rack for Iron and Steel

Some kind of a rack, so made that rods of iron and steel stock may be laid up on pegs, off the floor, and sorted as to sizes and lengths, is a great convenience. Such a rack may be built close to the wall of the shop and takes up little room.

Necessary Tools

Having a shop provided with the equipment above described, the only absolutely necessary tools needed to begin work are a fire poker, a hammer, a hardy, and two pairs of tongs. The hammer should be what is known as a blacksmith's hand hammer of about 2 pounds weight. The tongs should be of the two kinds shown in Figure 5; one for handling flat or round iron, the other for making bolts. All other tongs needed may be made by the smith as described in Chapter VI.

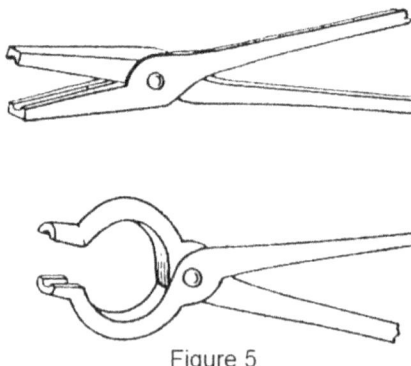

Figure 5

Other Tools

In addition to hammer and tongs, the tools next in order of importance will be a sledge of about 8 pounds in weight, and a set of what English blacksmiths call flogging tools: hot and cold chisels, swages, fullers, set hammer and flatter to be used for heavy work when the smith can have the help of a striker to use the sledge. These tools are shown in Figure 6.

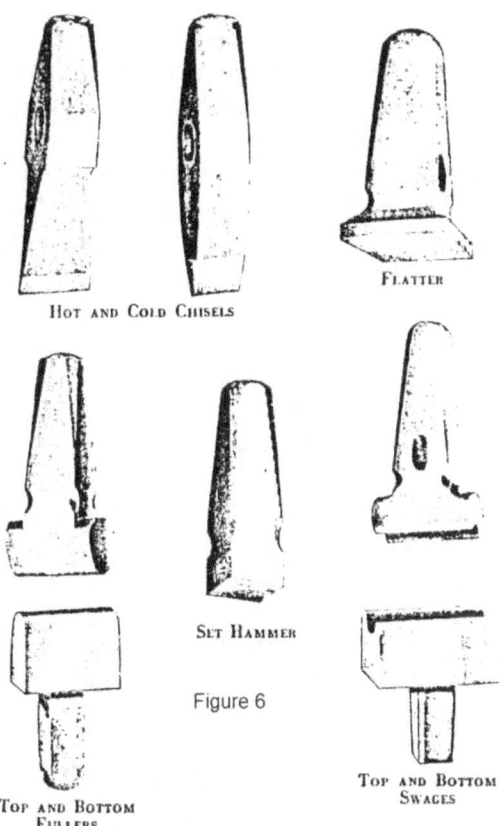

Figure 6

For the work bench there will be needed wrenches, files, punches of different sizes, cold chisels, screw drivers, brace and set of twist drills, stocks, and dies for threading bolts and burrs, hack saw, and blades. If horseshoeing is to be done, a shoeing hammer, hoof nippers, and horse rasp will be needed.

A post drill is such a convenience that it almost comes under the head of necessary equipment.

Some of the above-named tools can be made by the smith in spare time. Others it may be cheaper to buy.

Let us see what the tools and equipment so far mentioned will cost:

```
Anvil (100 pounds) ...................................................$140.00
Blower ..................................................................100.00
Vise .......................................................................55.00
Hardy ......................................................................5.00
Sledge (8 pounds) .....................................................12.50
Flogging tools ..........................................................50.00
Bolt tongs ................................................................7.50
```

```
Flat tongs..................................................................7.50
Hand hammer.............................................................9.00
Horseshoeing tools....................................................25.00
Hack saw and blades ..................................................8.50
Stocks and dies.........................................................50.00
Brace and drills.........................................................40.00
    Total..................................................................$500.00
```

A word should be said about the hardy shown in Figure 7. This is a tool which is much used, and often abused. It is a chisel with a shank made to fit the square hole in the anvil. It should be made of tool steel of about the same grade as that used in making cold chisels. As it is used to cut hot metal, there is no use in tempering it, as the temper would be drawn out of it by the hot metal; but in other respects it is like a chisel. It should have a rather thin edge and be kept sharp. This can be easily done if the smith will always remember that its edge is never to be hit by the hammer. In cutting off a piece of hot iron or steel on the hardy, the hammer should stop before the iron or steel is cut through.

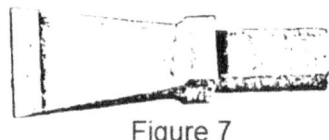

Figure 7

The shank of the hardy should be fitted to the hole in the anvil so that there will be no wobble or play to the tool when it is used. The shank should be long enough to extend through the tail of the anvil, so that in case it becomes stuck in the hole, the lower end may be tapped with the hammer to loosen it.

If a post drill can be afforded, one which will answer very well for the farm shop may be had for about $50. This price includes a chuck to hold drills of different sizes. See Figure 8.

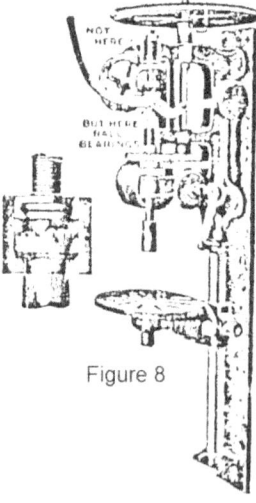

Figure 8

Two Useful Anvil Tools

The smith often has occasion to do small jobs requiring something smaller than the horn of the anvil for bending or shaping. In Figure 9 are shown two very convenient tools or pieces of equipment which the farm smith can easily make from a piece of shafting or other iron, or from mild steel which he may salvage from the scrap pile or "machinery graveyard" to be found on almost any farm. One is a straight, round mandrel which will be found handy for bending ferrules, small rings, etc. The other is a small horn to be used the same as an anvil horn in making small links or doing any kind of bending of small articles. Of course, both are to have shanks to fit the square hole in the anvil. In making either one of these tools, it is well to begin by first forming the shank and fitting it to its place in the anvil. It should be a tight fit; and in order that it may be easily loosened from the anvil after being used, it should have a shank long enough to extend a little below the tail of the anvil the same as in the case of the hardy above mentioned.

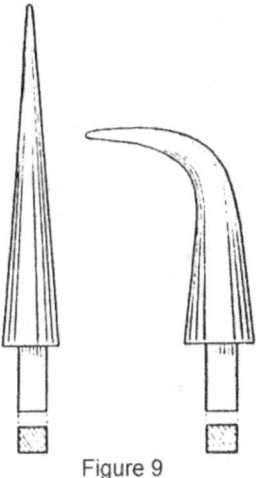

Figure 9

III. THE FORGE FIRE

Much of the success of forge work depends upon the care and management of the fire and the proper heating of iron and steel. Therefore, it is of great importance that the smith be thoroughly familiar with the different factors that go into making the right kind of fire in order that he may get the results that he wants.

SMITHING COAL

The most satisfactory coal for ordinary smithing work is what is known to the trade as Cumberland coal. It contains less sulphur and other impurities than any other mined coal and is easily packed about the forge fire. Coke, when broken up into small pieces, makes a good fire, particularly when a large fire is wanted, but it is not so easily managed as Cumberland coal.

Neither ordinary soft coal such as is used for making steam, nor hard (anthracite) coal is suitable for use in a forge. Both kinds contain impurities which make it impossible to use them in welding.

Charcoal makes a good fire if properly managed, and is very desirable for use in making fine steel tools, as it is wholly free from sulphur and other injurious chemicals; but in most parts of the country it costs more than mineral coal and has almost gone out of use as a smithing coal.

MANAGING THE FIRE

The first and most important thing for the amateur smith to learn is the proper management of his fire so as to get the heat where he wants it, and to do this without too much waste of fuel.

Let us suppose that the beginner has the equipment and the most necessary tools mentioned on the preceding pages, and that he is ready to start a fire in the new forge. The fire is started by using pine shavings or any fuel that would make good kindling for a fire in a kitchen stove. After a good blaze has started, a little coal is packed *around, not upon* the kindling, so that it will take fire slowly. After a forge has been in use, there will always be coke left over from the former fire to be used in starting a new fire; but for this first time there is only kindling and blacksmith's coal. It must be remembered that coal should never be put *on* the fire but *around* it. After being near the fire a short time, the coal is changed to coke because all its sulphur and other impurities are burned out of it. By continually packing the coal about the fire and crowding it toward the center, a supply of coke is kept burning in the middle of the fire, where the most heat is needed. The packing also prevents the fire from spreading out and becoming too flat. It is well to wet the coal about the fire in order to pack it harder and to keep the fire confined to the middle.

The fire will now present the appearance of a mound of coal, the interior of which is a mass of burning coke, with a somewhat loose center through which the blast is coming. The most common mistake of the beginner is to allow this mound to become too low and flat. The coal should be piled up quite high about the fire so there will be considerable depth to the mass of burning coke. Whatever is to be heated in the fire should be held midway between top and bottom, so as to have burning coke both below and above it. If held too low, it will be struck by the blast of air from the blower, and if too high it will be cooled by the air from above.

Experience will soon show how much blast should be given. The stronger the blast, the greater will be the heat, up to the point where the coke in the middle of the fire begins to be lifted out of place.

It is sometimes desirable to have a long fire instead of a round one in order to heat an iron for some length instead of in one spot; for example, the edge of a plow share. In such a case, it is easy to lengthen the fire by packing coal on two sides instead of all around the middle.

Too much blast will cool the fire. Just enough blast should be given to keep the coke at a white heat but not enough to lift it out of place. Long experience and practice are needed to enable one to manage a forge fire so as to get the best results; although to the onlooker it may appear to be a very simple matter.

A forge fire left to itself will soon die out. The experienced smith, when he leaves his fire for a short period of time, will place a small piece of hard wood in the fire knowing that it will hold the fire until he returns. Thrifty smiths save old wagon spokes and similar pieces of wood for this purpose. Often a forge fire which has apparently died out may be revived by a sprinkling of sawdust. If the old embers are still hot enough to cause sawdust to smoke, a handful of sawdust and a gentle blast will revive the fire and save the time that it would take to build a new fire in the ordinary way.

IV. FORGING IRON AND STEEL

Forging of iron and steel may be summed up in the following list of operations: *drawing*, *upsetting*, *bending*, *scarfing*, *welding*, *punching*, and *riveting*.

DRAWING

By drawing, the smith usually means making a piece of iron or steel smaller and longer. This is done by heating, then pounding it over the rounded edge of the anvil, trying at the same time to keep it as nearly square as possible. In the case of a large piece of iron or steel, a pair of fullers would be used (shown in Figure 6), and the helper would be called upon to use the sledge. The beginner will probably have a little trouble with his first trial at drawing because the iron will seem to insist on becoming diamond shaped instead of square. This is because the novice almost always turns the iron, between blows, a little further than through a quarter circle. But he will soon learn to turn it just enough to keep the square shape. No matter what is to be the final shape of the piece, it should be drawn square at first because it can be reduced in size much faster that way than in any other. After it is drawn down to about the desired size, it may be made octagonal by pounding down the four corners, or round by flattening out the remaining corners. Finishing is done with light blows of the hammer. All the finishing, after reducing to the proper size in the square shape, is done on the flat face of the anvil, and with a smooth faced hammer.

The heating for drawing should be done slowly enough so that the iron or steel has a chance to become as hot in the middle of the piece as it is on the surface. It is possible, especially with large pieces, to heat the surface to the desired temperature before the middle becomes hot enough to work well. The result will be that the surface will be drawn out faster than the rest of the piece. In the case of tool steel, this produces strains in the metal which hare troublesome when it comes to tempering the tool so made.

Not only should the metal to be drawn have an even heat throughout, but the hammer used and the blows struck should be heavy enough to affect the whole mass. Light blows would have the same effect as uneven heating; for the surface only would be drawn.

UPSETTING

This means enlarging a piece of iron or steel by heating it at the part to be made larger, and driving it together so as to swell the heated part. In case the end of a short piece of iron is to be upset, it should be heated to a white heat, the heated end placed on the anvil and the other end struck with the hammer. In the case of a longer piece of iron which is heavier than the hammer, it may be danced on the face of the anvil, letting its own weight do the work of pounding. The ends of long rods, like truss rods, may be upset by heating and butting the ends against the side of the anvil after the manner of a battering ram.

Wagon and carriage tires are shortened or made smaller by being upset by a special machine made for the purpose. A short section of the tire is heated to white heat and placed in the machine which grips the tire at both sides of the heated portion and pushes it together.

BENDING

There are several points in connection with bending iron that should be mentioned. The beginner should be warned against spoiling the shape of the iron he is bending by too much or too hard hammering. If the iron to be bent is made hot enough, it may be bent into almost any desired shape with very little pounding, and if it is a piece with sharp corners that would be marred by hammering, it is a good plan to use a wooden mallet or even a stick of stove wood or any hardwood club if a mallet is not at hand.

SCARFING

The term scarfing is used for the shaping of parts to prepare them for welding.

In the case of round irons, the ends are first upset enough to allow for the expected loss in heating and welding, and then are shaped as shown in Figure 10. Steps in the shaping of round irons for welding are shown in Figure 21. This shaping is done by first holding the hot upset iron on the anvil at an angle of about 30 degrees, and striking with the hammer held at a corresponding angle.

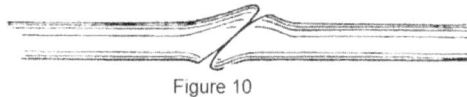
Figure 10

When the end of the iron assumes the shape shown at A in Figure 21, it is turned a quarter turn, laid flat on the anvil, as at B, and shaped as shown at C. Both the irons to be welded together are, of course, shaped alike. Notice that the faces which are to fit together are slightly convex so that when placed together the middles touch, and space is thus left for any scale to be pushed out when the weld is made.

Flat irons to be welded are upset and scarfed as shown in Figure 11. Notice that these faces also are convex instead of flat.

Figure 11

In preparing chain links for welding, it is not necessary to upset the ends for the reason that the ends are crossed in such a way as to provide plenty of iron at the welding point to take care of any loss in heating and welding. After the iron for a link has been bent in the form of a letter U, the ends are scarfed as shown in Figure 16, by flattening the inside corners of the ends, but leaving the outside of the ends as thick as they were originally.

WELDING

By the term welding, the smith means the joining of iron or steel parts by heating to the melting point. the metal is not actually melted so as to be in a liquid state, but the surface is hot enough to begin to flow, and when at this temperature is sticky, like a warm piece of molasses candy, and may be pressed or pounded together so as to make perfect joints.

Iron or steel at welding heat is perfectly white, and the surface is beginning to flow. It has the appearance of wet, white ice. If heated beyond this point, it will begin to burn and is in danger of being spoiled.

Wrought iron and mild steel may be welded without the use of any welding compound or flux of any kind; but the difference between welding heat and burning heat is so slight, especially in the case of mild steel, that it is often of advantage to use a flux to avoid burning. Clean sand is about as good as anything in this case. One should not get the idea that the flux is going to act in any magic way to help the iron to weld. It is used simply as a protection to the iron. Sand or borax will melt at a lower temperature than iron, but after melting it will stand a higher heat without burning than will the iron, and is used because it keeps the air away from the iron, and iron cannot burn without air.

The welding of chain links, rings, and of round and flat separate irons is explained in the following chapter.

PUNCHING

Punching is a quick, easy way of making holes in wrought iron. The amateur smith will often find himself debating the question whether to drill or punch holes in a certain job of work. As a help in deciding this question, the following story may be worth telling.

In making a certain machine, two pieces of iron one inch wide and a quarter-inch thick, were to have quarter-inch holes in them an inch apart for nearly their whole length. Two young apprentices decided to have a race. Each took one of the irons; one was to drill the holes in his piece, the other said he could do the job in less time by heating and punching. Which one came out ahead in point of time is a forgotten item. The lesson in the story lies in the fact that the iron that was punched was several inches longer than the other when the job was done. The boy who did the punching did not realize that the hot iron would spread both ways when the holes were punched.

In a job where a little spreading of the iron will make no difference, punching the holes may be a saving of time. To do a neat job of punching, the hot iron should be placed on the anvil, not over a hole, but on the solid face, and the punch should be driven till it feels as though it were solid against the anvil. Then the piece should be turned over, and the place where the punch nearly came through will show as a round dot. The punch should now be placed on this dot, over the round hole in the anvil, and driven through. In this way, a very neat hole may be made.

In punching thick iron with a small punch, the beginner should be warned of the danger of upsetting the end of the punch in the hot iron if he works too slowly.

RIVETING

Riveting may be thought of by the smith as such a simple operation as to need no explanation in a book of this kind. There are, however, a few points in connection with this form of forging that should be mentioned. The best material for rivets which are to be used for cold riveting is Norway iron; the next best is mild steel. If the latter is used to forge rivets for cold riveting, the rivets should be allowed to cool slowly after being formed, and not quenched in water. The reason for this is that most mild steel contains enough carbon to cause it to harden a little upon being suddenly cooled. Any degree of hardening would make the metal too brittle for riveting.

Norway iron rivets of all sizes and lengths are to be found in the hardware stores, and it is a good plan for the farm smith to keep on hand a few sizes which are most often used: for example, those that are used for replacing worn or broken mower sections. But special rivets will often have to be made to be used in repair jobs, and the smith should know how to make them. In many cases, simply cutting a section of rod the proper length and using it for a rivet will solve the problem. If a large head is needed, sometimes a bolt of the right size may be found which may be cut the right length. If neither a piece of rod nor a bolt of the right size is at hand, it will be necessary to forge a rivet. To do this in the right way, the smith should choose a piece of rod the next size larger than the desired rivet, heat it to a yellow heat and draw out the end by holding it against the near edge of the anvil so as to leave a shoulder between the part being drawn out and the part of the original rod which will form the head of the rivet. Just where this shoulder will be calls for the exercise of good judgment. It should be remembered that reducing the diameter of a piece of iron one-half will lengthen it four times. Most beginners start with too long a "bite" and are surprised at the way it stretches out in length before it is drawn down to the right diameter. As described under the head of "Drawing," the iron should be kept square until reduced to about the right size, then rounded. It should be cut from the rod while hot by holding it on the hardy at the proper place to leave the right sized head. The cutting should be done with light blows so as not to mar the head too much, and the rod should be turned round and round so as to make a smooth, even cut.

The two most common mistakes which beginners make in cold riveting are in having the rivet too long and in hitting it too hard. If, for example, in the case of fastening fish plates to the sides of a cracked wooden pump rod, the rivets used should be too long, they would be likely to buckled or bend in the middle and split the wood. In ordinary practice, it is usually a good plan to countersink the holes for rivets, and the rivets should extend through only far enough to allow for the making of a small head. This is usually a little less than one diameter of the rivet. Very light blows should be used in doing the riveting. Heavy blows would be likely to bend the rivet in the middle, especially in the case of a long rivet. Light blows will upset the extreme end and draw the rivet tight.

V. SIMPLE EXERCISES IN BLACKSMITHING

Assuming that the beginner has the necessary tools and equipment described in Chapter II, and that he has a fire properly built in the forge, he is ready to begin actual work. The best plan is to start with simple things and to lead by gradual steps to the more difficult jobs that require more practice and experience.

A FIRE POKER

As a first exercise, the poker, which has been mentioned as one of the necessary tools, furnishes a good example. It bring into use the three processes of heating, bending, and flattening. About 2 feet of round half-inch iron should be used. About 4 inches of one end should be heated to a light yellow heat and bent into the shape of a round eye. At his first trial, the beginner will have trouble in trying to make the eye round instead of oval unless he has been told that in starting the bend he should make a right angle bend between the shank of the poker and the part that is to be the eye; then bend the extreme end before closing up the circle. If the middle of the hot part is bent first, as a beginner is likely to do, there is left no handy way to make the bends in the end and next the shank, and an oval instead of a round eye results. After the eye end has been finished and cooled, the opposite end of the rod is heated and flattened out until it is about ¾ of an inch wide, then curved slightly as shown at A in Figure 12.

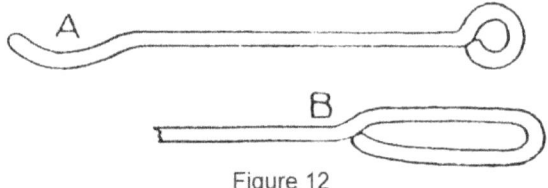

Figure 12

If a longer handle to the poker is preferred, it is an easy matter to form an oblong eye instead of a round one, as shown at B in the cut, but in this case it will be necessary to start with a rod about 6 inches longer than the one first described.

A STAPLE PULLER

In these days of wire fences, one of the handiest tools on the farm is a staple puller, such as is pictured in Figure 13. When the writer was a young farm boy he thought he had the champion staple puller. It was simply a long punch with a tapering end drawn to a fine point. This point he would drive under a staple and then pry it out. Sometimes in doing the driving he hit his knuckles with the hammer. When a neighbor showed him one like the tool here pictured, he immediately made one from a piece of old horse-rake tooth, tempered it blue, and liked it better than his old one. The best size stock for making one of these pullers is ½-inch tool steel. The point is made rather short and bent at a right angle, and tempered the same as a cold chisel as explained on page __. The handle end should be about 8 inches long.

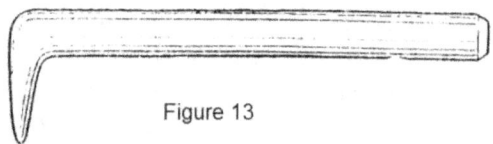

Figure 13

HOOK AND STAPLE

Another simple exercise in blacksmithing is the forging of a hook for a gate or a barn door, and the staple with which to fasten it in place. This exercise involves drawing, squaring, rounding, pointing, turning a round eye, and twisting.

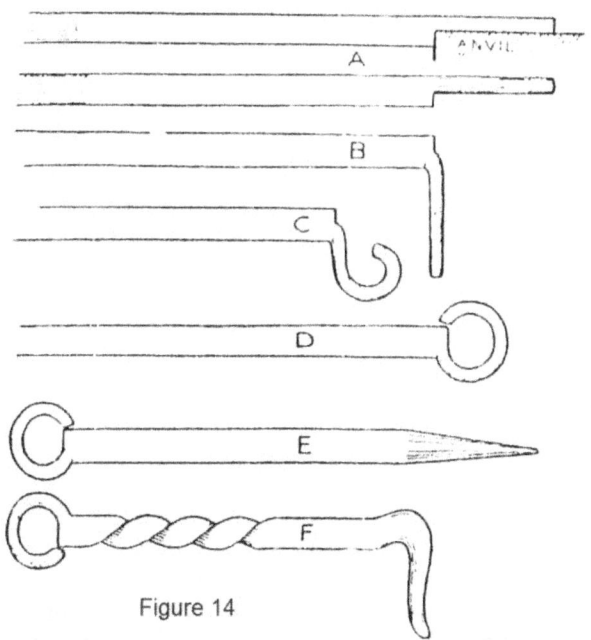

Figure 14

For an ordinary barn door hook, a piece of $3/8$-inch round iron is a convenient size to use. One end should be heated to a light yellow and drawn out square so that the corners come out sharp. (See what is said about drawing on page 10.) The end of this square part should next be heated and about $5/8$ inch of it drawn down to half the size of the square p art, then made round by hammering down the corners. In starting to draw out this last part, the iron should be held over the edge of the anvil as shown at A in Figure 14, so that when struck a flat blow by the hammer, the edge of the anvil will form a decided shoulder between the large square part and the part that is being drawn smaller. The small end is next to be made round and turned to form a round eye. To do this, it is best to start by bending at a right angle from the main parts, as shown at B, then bending the extreme end as much as it needs to be bent in the finished eye (C). It is then a simple matter to close the ring so as to form a perfect circle as shown at D. The hook is now to be cut from the original bar at a point that will make it the right length when the point is drawn out to form the hook end. This end should first be drawn out square, then rounded as shown at E, and the hook formed in the end as shown at F.

The twist shown at F is put in the middle of the hook by first heating to a yellow heat, then grasping with two pairs of tongs and turning through one complete revolution, so that the eye and the hook end are in the same relative position as before.

To make a staple for a hook of the size mentioned above requires a piece of ¼-inch iron. One end should be drawn out and rounded, then bent as shown at A and B in Figure 15. It should then be cut off at a point which will make the second leg the right length after it is drawn to a point. A pair of chain tongs should be used to hold the piece while the second leg is being drawn out as shown at C. The bend is completed by grasping the middle of the bent part with the chain tongs, as at D, and holding it over the horn or the rounded corner of the anvil, regulating the bend with light blows of the hammer.

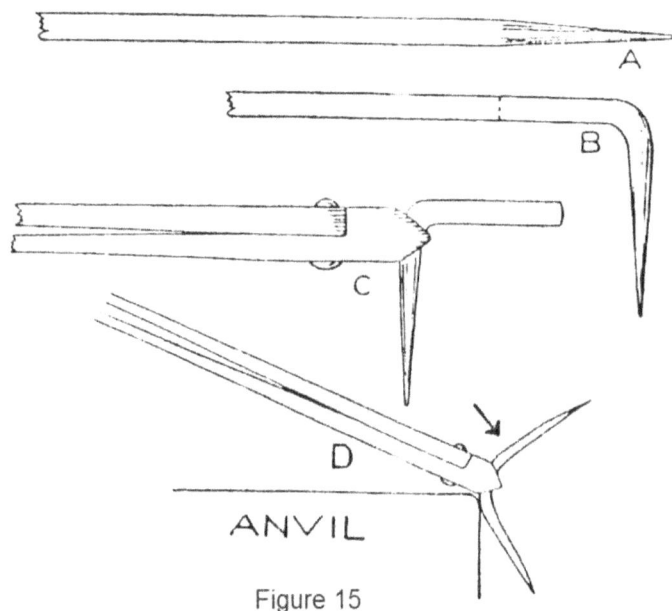

Figure 15

CHAIN LINKS

One of the jobs which the farm smith will often be called upon to do is to mend broken chains. The right way to do the job of mending, if time will permit, is to make a new link with which to join the broken parts. For temporary repairs there should be a supply of what are called cold-shut links which may be substituted for broken links without any loss of time.

To make a new link, take a piece of round rod of the same size as that used in making the chain, and bend it into the form of a capital letter U as shown at A in Figure 16; then, holding the bent pat with a pair of chain tongs, heat the two ends to a yellow heat and scarf the inside corner of each end by holding it at an angle on the edge of the anvil. Notice in B and C that only the corners are flattened, not the whole end. The ends are then bent so that the scarfed surfaces fit together as at D, and the joint is ready for welding. The heating for welding should be done in a clean fire and the link should be closely watched to see that one side does not heat faster than the other. It is a good plan to turn it over often, for the lower side is likely to become hot sooner than the upper.

When the end to be welded is perfectly white, and the surface is in a fluid condition, it should be quickly placed on the anvil and struck two quick, light blows: one on each side of the weld. The part at the weld should now be worked as nearly round as possible over the horn of the anvil. This will probably widen the link too much at one end, so that it will look more or less like E in the illustration. To shape it properly so it will resemble the link shown at F, it should be held as shown at E and struck where the small arrow is pointing. This will put the bend where it should be, in the end of the link. If it had been held with its side on the anvil and had been struck on the other side, as almost all beginners do in their first attempt, it would resemble the crooked link shown at G.

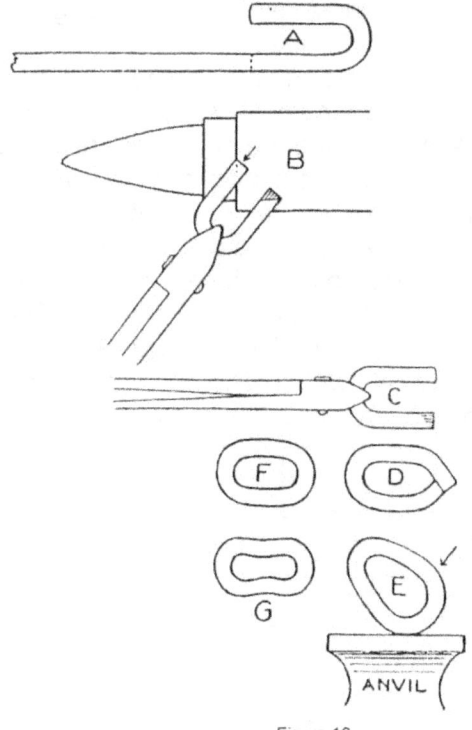

Figure 16

COLD SHUT LINKS

There are two good ways of making cold shut links to use as temporary repairs in log chains. In the one shown at A in Figure 17, a piece of rod the size of the iron in the chain is slightly upset at one end and a hole punched in it large enough to fit the other end of the rod which is bent around as shown. In use, this link takes the place of the broken link and is closed together and the end riveted.

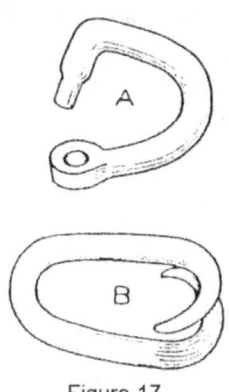

Figure 17

Another temporary link which is not quite as strong as the one just described, but which can be made in a little less time, is made by drawing out the two ends of a letter U and bending them around as shown at B in Figure 17. When this is hooked into the place of a broken link, a blow of the hammer will close it so it will answer very well as a temporary substitute for a link.

CHAIN HOOK

Hooks for log chains are of two kinds: round hooks large enough for the chain to slide through easily, and grab hooks made narrow with just enough room between the two sides to admit a link edgewise.

There are two common ways of making a chain hook. Where good, tough iron or mild steel of the proper size is at hand, the easiest way to make a hook is to upset the bar where the middle of the hook is to be and the end where the hole is to be punched, as shown at A and B in Figure 18. The hole is then punched, and the iron around the hole is worked as nearly round as possible over the horn of the anvil. The bar is then cut off at the point indicated by the dotted lines, and the end is drawn out and rounded as in B. The hook is next to be bent and beveled so as to have a cross-section through the largest part like that shown at C. It should be bent only about halfway at first as the beveling of the back causes it to bend more. The reason for beveling a hook is that it makes it stronger in the line of pull than it would be if left round. The most common weakness in a log chain is the hook which is not strong enough to stand a heavy pull without straightening.

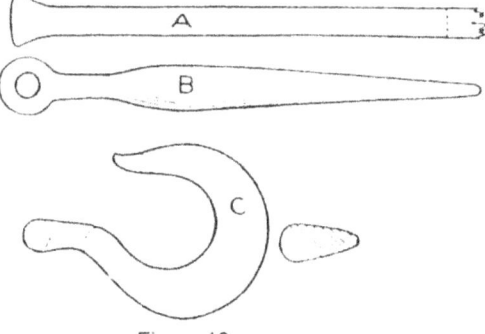

Figure 18

Another way to make a chain hook is shown in Figure 19. By this method, iron of smaller size may be used than in the hook just described, for the reason that the iron is doubled at the place where the strongest part of the hook is to be. In forging a hook by this method, a part of the rod, marked A, is drawn down to the proper size to form the eye of the hook; then the end of the rod is doubled back and welded as shown at B. The rod is then cut off and the hook shaped as in the case above described; or, if it is to be a grab hook, it should be bent on the corner as shown at C. The novice may have trouble in making the iron bend on the corner; but if he will start the bend by putting the end in the square hole of the anvil, then cool the end while the balance of the piece is left hot, then put the cool end in the vise, he will have no trouble in finishing the bend.

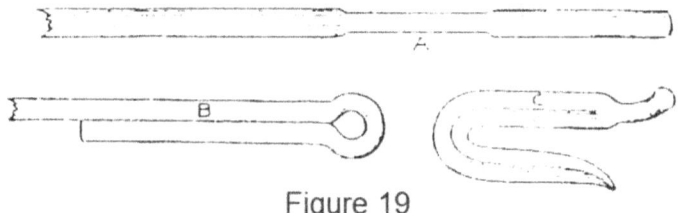

Figure 19

SWIVEL

Log chains are often broken because of becoming twisted. This is especially true in logging work. To avoid twisting, every log chain should have a swivel at about its middle point. Making a swivel is a good exercise in forging. To make a swivel, it is necessary first to have a mandrel over which to form the middle part of the swivel. For the mandrel it is best to use a piece of ⁷⁄₈-inch round, mild steel. One end of this should be heated and a very short piece of the end, about ½ inch, should be drawn out to about ½ inch in size as shown at A in Figure 20.

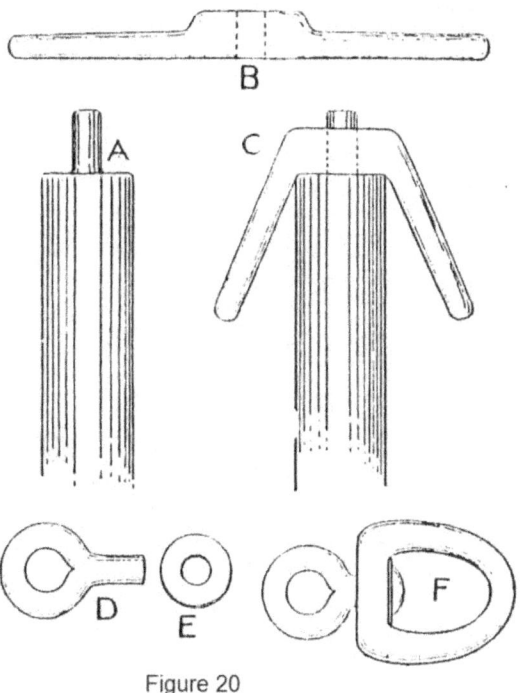

Figure 20

The material for the main part of the swivel should be a piece of mild steel 1 inch wide and ½ inch thick. One end of the bar should be drawn out to ³⁄₈ inch in size and 3 inches long; the middle section about 1 inch long should be left the original size; and the other end also drawn out to ³⁄₈ inch the same as the first part, as shown at B. A ½-inch hole is to be punched through the middle section, and the piece heated to a white heat and placed on the mandrel to be worked into the shape shown at C.

The eye is made by welding the end of a 7/16-inch road back on itself to form the opening, then working the shank down to ½ inch as shown at D. The shank should be just long enough to go through the main part of the swivel, through a washer, E, with enough space to make a good head when riveted. The riveting should be done while the end of the shank is red hot. The two arms of the swivel should then be bent together and welded in the same manner as the chain link described on page 16. The completed swivel is shown at F.

Riveting the shank in place will probably make it so tight that it will not turn easily. The cure for this condition is to heat the whole swivel to a light red heat and turn the shank around a few times while hot.

RING

The proper way to start a ring that will be of even thickness throughout, is to upset both ends of the rod from which the ring is to be made, enough so that there will be no thin spots at the sides of the weld when the job is finished. After the ends are upset, each one is to be heated in turn and scarfed for welding. This process consists in first shaping the end as at A in Figure 21, then holding the rod level on the anvil, as at B, and pounding the end back and rounding it slightly as shown at C. The scarfing of the second end should be made on the side opposite the first, as in D, so that when the iron is bent to form the ring, the two scarfs will fit together and their ends be, not one inside and outside the ring, but both out where the hammer can get at them, as shown at E.

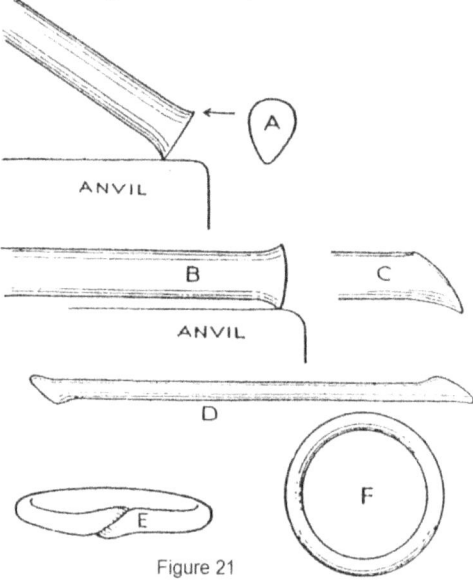

Figure 21

In heating the ring for welding, the same directions apply as for the chain link, described on page 16. After welding, the iron in the welded place and for a little space on each side will probably be a trifle larger than in other parts of the ring. This can be easily worked down to the proper size by heating to a low red heat, and going over it with light blows of the hammer. The finished ring is shown at F.

Where appearances make little difference, rings are sometimes made like chain links and rounded up afterward.

When a ring is made to go on the end of a chain, it should not be bent into the chain before welding, but should be finished as a separate ring, then joined to the chain by another link.

CLEVIS

To make an ordinary coupling clevis requires about 13 inches of ⅝-inch round, mild steel as shown at A in Figure 22. This bar should be upset in the middle, where the greatest wear will come, and at the ends where the holes are to be punched, as shown at B. The ends should be flattened out and rounded and holes punched in them as shown at C. The holes should be large enough to admit a ½-inch bolt easily. The clevis is then to be bent into shape so as to leave a space of 2¼ inches between the ends, as shown at D in the illustration.

21

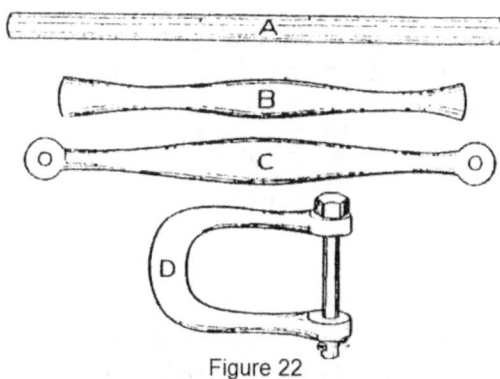

Figure 22

Another, and a quicker way, of upsetting the ends where the holes are to be punched, is shown in Figure 23. A short piece of the end of the iron is turned up at a right angle, as at A, then heated to a welding heat and pounded straight down so as to form a lump as shown at B. If carefully done, this makes a neat, round end with less labor than is necessary to round out and finish the kind of end shown in Figure 22.

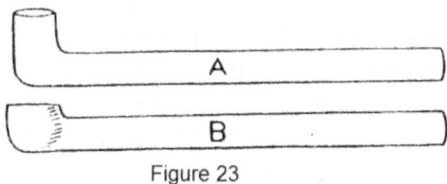

Figure 23

What might be called an emergency clevis may be made in a few minutes by using about 20 inches of $7/16$-inch round, mild steel, welding it in the form of a long link, then closing the sides together as shown in Figure 24, and bending to form the clevis.

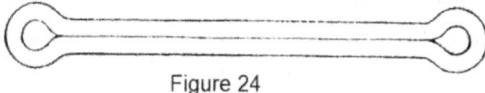

Figure 24

PIN OR BOLT FOR CLEVIS

The pin or bolt for the clevis should be made of ½-inch mild steel. The easiest way to make the head of the bolt is to upset the end a little, then drive the bolt into a heading iron. If the farm smith does not have a set of heading irons, perhaps he can find what he needs in the scrap pile or "machinery graveyard." Almost any heavy piece of cast iron with a ½-inch hole in it will answer for a heading tool for the clevis bolt. The upset end should be at welding heat when the bolt is driven into the heading tool, and the smith should be careful to drive it straight down over the hole so that the head may not be one-sided.

HEADING TOOL FOR BOLTS

Heading tools for bolts of the most commonly used sizes should be found in every shop. They are among those tools which the farm smith can make on rainy days. To make a heading tool, it is only necessary to upset one end of a large piece of mild steel, flatten and round it, as shown in Figure 25, then punch a hole of the proper size. Heading tools for small bolts and rivets are sometimes made with several holes of different sizes in one tool. In this case the head end of the tool is, of course, made long instead of round, and the holes are generally drilled instead of being punched.

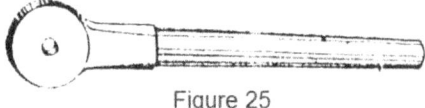

Figure 25

BOLTS AND NUTS

Small bolt heads are generally made by the upsetting method described in the making of the clevis bolt. This is the method used in making ordinary carriage bolts, although, of course, they are made by machinery.

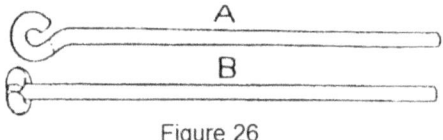

Figure 26

Heads on large bolts are generally welded on instead of being upset. In making a welded head, it is customary to use for the head a piece of rod one size smaller than the bolt itself. An eye is turned in the end of the rod as in Figure 26, A, which is fitted to the bolt. This eye is then cut nearly off on the hardy, but is cut so short that it will reach only about three-fourths of the way around the bolt, as shown at B. The end of the bolt is then heated and upset a trifle in the eye, then the eye is broken from the rod and struck with the hammer in such a way as to pinch it tight to the bolt. The whole is then heated to welding heat and welded. While welding, the piece should be held so that the open place in the smaller iron is at one side where it will be closed when struck by the hammer. The reason for making it so as to reach only part way around the bolt will now be seen. If it had been so made as to reach all the way around, it would have been too long and would have caused trouble by buckling up and spoiling the weld.

When it is necessary to put a head on a long rod, like a truss rod for a bridge, a short piece of rod the same size as the truss rod is headed, then welded to the long rod.

Nuts for bolts are easily made by simply punching holes of the needed size in iron or mild steel of the proper thickness and width, and then threading them to fit the bolts. On most farms, it will seldom be necessary for the farm smith to make any nuts for the reason that nuts of almost all sizes and kinds may be salvaged from the scrapped farm machinery.

Cutting threads on bolts and in nuts is such a simple proceeding that little instruction in this line is necessary. It will be very seldom that the farm smith will be called upon to cut threads on anything larger than ¾-inch in size. Dies that will take care of all threading on iron from ¼ inch up to ¾ inch may be had for about $50.

One or two precautions regarding the use of dies may be in order. Dies should never be used on hot metal, as this would spoil the die by removing the temper. Dies should not be expected to cut tool steel. Mild steel sometimes contains enough carbon to cause it to harden when suddenly chilled from a high temperature. It is, therefore, always wise to anneal (soften) a piece of mild steel by heating to a red heat, then allowing it to cool slowly in the air before attempting to cut threads on it with a die.

An assortment of carriage bolts of the most commonly used sizes and lengths should be found in every farm shop. Such an assortment properly kept where a bolt of any size or length may be found at a moment's notice, will prove a great timesaver on any farm.

A fairly complete list for such an assortment would be one package each of the following sizes and lengths:

¼ IN. DIAMETER	
Length	Price Per Pkg. of 25
1¼	$1.10
1½	1.10
1¾	1.30
2	1.40
2½	1.80
3	2.00
3½	2.10
4	2.50
4 ½	2.70
5	3.10
6	3.40

⁵/₁₆ IN. DIAMETER	
Length	Price Per Pkg. of 25
1½	$1.80
2	2.10
2½	2.80
3	3.10
3½	3.40
4	3.60
4½	4.00
5	4.30
5½	4.60
6	5.20

3/8 IN. DIAMETER	
Length	Price Per Pkg. of 25
1¼	$2.30
1½	2.40
2	2.80
2½	3.40
3	3.90
3½	4.30
4	4.50
4½	4.60
5	5.30
6	6.30

½ IN. DIAMETER	
Length	Price Per Pkg. of 25
2	$ 5.70
2½	6.80
3	7.60
3½	8.30
4	8.80
5	9.50
4½	9.00
5½	10.00
6	11.00

The farm smith should know of the saving which may be made by buying bolts in wholesale lots. A full package of 25 bolts may be had for about the same price as half that number bought at retail.

WELDING SEPARATE IRONS

In welding the link and the ring already described, the ends of iron to be welded were naturally held together. Welding separate irons introduces the new problem of placing them together while at welding heat, and getting them to stick together before the heat is lost. Figure 27 shows the proper way to place the two irons on the anvil when ready to weld.

Round irons to be welded together should first be upset and scarfed the same as the two ends of the iron for making a ring. They should be placed in the fire with the scarfed faces down, for the reason that the under part of anything in the forge fire heats faster than the upper side. Particular pains should be taken to get the two irons to heat evenly. If one should appear to be heating faster than the other, it should be pulled back a little until the other iron has had a chance to gain the same heat.

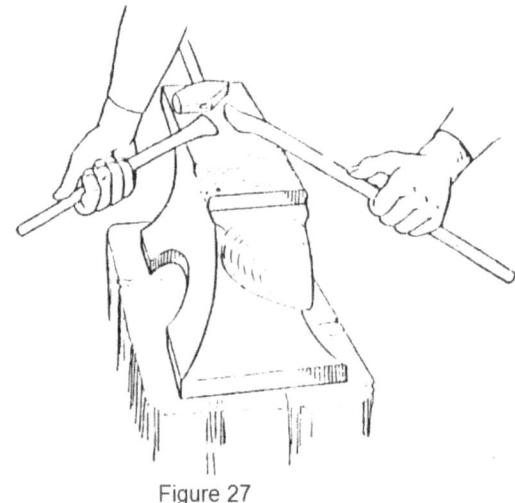

Figure 27

    Before heating the irons for welding, the beginner should practice getting them from the fire and on the anvil so that when they are ready to weld, he may get them together in the best way and in the shortest possible time. To do this he should grasp the right hand iron with the back of the hand uppermost and the little finger toward the fire. This will naturally bring the iron face side up on the anvil.
    Note in the illustration that the hands are holding both irons, not on the face of the anvil, but resting over the edge, so that they can be held steady while the left hand iron is being placed on the other one. If the end of the first iron were to be placed flat on the anvil before coming in contact with the second iron, the anvil, a very good conductor, would absorb enough heat to bring it below the proper welding heat. The result would be a poor weld, if, indeed, the irons chanced to stick at all.
    When both irons are at welding heat, that is, when they are perfectly white and the surface is in a melting condition so that it looks as though it were wet, they should be taken quickly from the fire, given a sharp rap against the anvil to shake off any scale or slag that might be sticking to the faces of the scarfed ends, then placed against the edges of the anvil as shown in the cut and the scarfs brought steadily together with the left hand iron on top of and holding the other. The right hand is now free to let go of its iron and pick up the hammer, which should be lying on the end of the anvil. The first blow struck should be light to help stick the irons together, then heavy blows should follow to perfect the weld. In welding large irons, it is often possible to make a complete weld and finish it down to the original size of the iron at one heat; but with small irons, which lose their heat quickly, it is usually necessary to heat several times in order to complete the weld. In welding, the smith should never strike a blow after the iron cools below welding heat, as that would only thin the iron and do the weld no good.
    In welding one long and one short piece of iron together, the short piece should be managed with the right hand, using a pair of tongs. This will put the short iron on the underside on the anvil where it may be held by the longer piece while the smith lets the tongs fall to the floor and picks up his hammer.
    In the case of irons so small that they would lose their heat while being carried from the fire to the anvil, it is well to protect them with a flux of sand or borax. With larger irons (½ inch or over), no such protection is necessary.

In welding together pieces of flat iron, they should be upset and scarfed as shown in Figure 11, page 12. The faces of the scarfs are a trifle convex as in the case of the round irons, and the process of welding is the same; but it is a little more difficult to make a finished, smooth job of welding with flat irons, because the corners and edges lose their heat sooner than the rest of the iron.

When flat irons are to be welded at right angles, they should be slightly upset and scarfed as shown at A, and put together as shown at B in Figure 28. After welding irons together in this form, it is unwise to try to forge a sharp inside angle as this is likely to start a crack. It is considered better practice to leave the inside corner a little rounding, or, if a sharp corner is required, to finish by filing after the iron is cold.

Figure 28

It is often required that flat irons be welded together in the form of a T. In such a case, the iron forming the head of the T should be slightly upset, then scarfed, as shown at A in Figure 29. The part which is to form the shank or upright of the T is upset and shaped as shown in the two views B and C in the cut. Before putting the two parts together for welding, the smith should be very sure that no scale is left in the hollowed scarf at A.

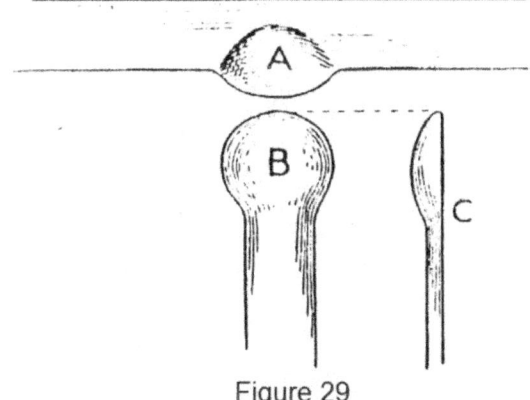

Figure 29

WELDING IRON AND STEEL

In the days of our great-grandfathers, when tool steel was very costly in comparison with the price of iron, many tools were made partly of iron and partly of steel. For example, hand hammers were made of iron with a face of steel welded on. Iron plow shares had a strip of steel welded, or "laid," as the old smiths expressed it, along the edge. This is what gives the commonly used name of "lay" to that part of a plow.

In these days of comparatively cheap steel, it is cheaper to make a whole tool of steel than to do the welding that formerly was done. There are, however, occasions when it is desirable and practical to weld steel and iron, and the farm smith should be able to do the trick and make a good job of it.

A very good crowbar may be made of a piece of mild steel shafting by welding a piece of tool steel in one end and drawing it down to the proper shape.

A good churning drill for work in rock may be made in the same way.

In making a heavy screwdriver, where it would seem a waste of tool steel to make it entirely of that material, mild steel may be used for all but a little wedge of tool steel welded in the end.

The method generally used in welding tool steel to iron or mild steel for the tools just mentioned is illustrated in Figure 30. The bar of iron or mild steel is first upset at the end as shown at A. It is then split with a thin chisel as at B, spread open as at C, and the two halves flattened out into the form of rather thin, wide lips as at D. A piece of tool steel of the proper size is then drawn out in the form of a wedge, and the two lips of the bar are wrapped around it as shown at E. The whole end is then covered with borax and welded.

Steel, enclosed in a coating of borax, will weld at a yellow heat. Beginners often make the mistake of getting the steel too hot.

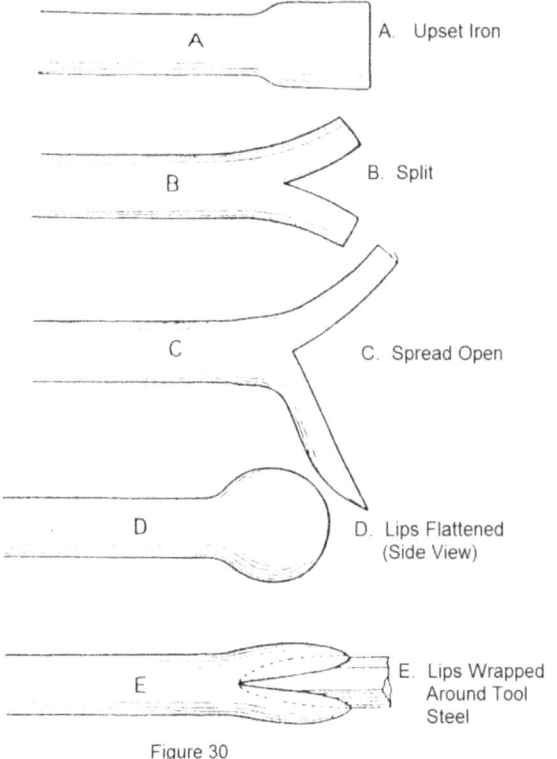

Figure 30

As a first attempt at this kind of welding, the amateur smith might well try to make a screwdriver by taking a piece of 7/16-inch mild steel about 16 inches long, and welding a wedge of 3/8-inch tool steel in one end. Then, if he will draw the other end to a short point and bend it around weld it as shown in A in Figure 31, then give it a twist as shown, he will have a good-looking screwdriver, the handle of which will never come off. The steel in the end may be refined by hammering, as in the case of the cold chisel (see page 27, and should be tempered a trifle softer than the cold chisel.

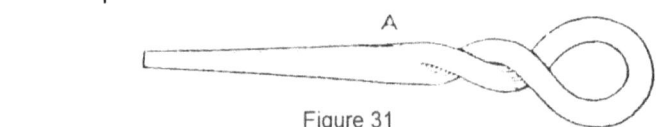

Figure 31

VI. FORGING AND TEMPERING STEEL TOOLS

Makers of tool steel make many different grades of steel according to the purposes for which they are to be used. This should be understood by the amateur smith, and he should always tell the dealer what he expects to make of the steel that he buys so that he may be sure to get the grade that will be most suitable. The main difference between the different grades of tool steel lies in the amount of carbon contained in each. A piece of steel that would make a good punch or cold chisel would not make the best kind of a rock drill because it would be lacking in the amount of carbon and could not be made to hold the edge that would be possible with a steel of higher carbon content. A spring cannot be made from an old file because the file contains altogether too much carbon, and would be too brittle to stand much bending. Many people harbor the delusion that the best kind of a knife blade can be made from an old file. The idea probably grew from the thought that the file is able to cut iron and steel, and, therefore, a knife made of the same material ought to cut almost anything. The truth of the matter is that steel suitable for making files contains such a high percentage of carbon that it is too brittle for making the best kind of knives.

A smith who is used to working with tool steel is able to make a good guess at the amount of carbon in a tool such as a chisel or punch, which has been used for some time, by the way the head or top end reacts to the blows of the hammer. If the end has spread out and turned down like the petals of a sunflower, it is steel of low carbon content. If, on the other hand, particles of steel have broken off instead of turning down, steel of high carbon content is indicated.

The beginner in blacksmithing, who has had some experience in forging iron, finds that he has some new points to consider when he begins to work with tool steel. In the first place, unless he has been warned and is on his guard, he will almost certainly burn the first piece of steel he attempts to heat in the forge fire. On account of the carbon which it contains, steel is much more easily heated than iron, and the margin between the proper heat for forging and the burning point is very much narrower than in the case of iron. Iron may be heated to the point of melting without any particular damage being done; but tool steel, heated to the same degree, would be totally ruined. It is also true that steel is more easily damaged than iron by being exposed to injurious chemicals. It is, therefore, very important that the fire in which steel is to be heated should be kept clean and free from ashes and cinders; and the coal used should be well coked before coming in contact with the steel.

In heating steel for forging, it is very necessary that it be heated slowly so that the center of the piece shall be of the same temperature as the outside; and if the steel is to be drawn out, as in the case of a cold chisel or punch, it is important that the hammer blows be heavy enough to affect the steel to the middle of the bar. If light blows should be used, the outside of the bar would be drawn out faster and farther than the middle, and strains would be set up in the metal which would be likely to show up as cracks when the tool so made came to be tempered.

A COLD CHISEL

After having had enough experience in the forging of steel so that he can heat his metal without burning it, the farm smith will be able to make better cold chisels than he can buy. But to do this he must use great care in heating, in forging, and in tempering. For forging, the steel should not be heated above a light yellow. For tempering, a cherry red is hot enough.

In forging a cold chisel, the steel should be drawn out in a wedge shape and not allowed to spread out, as it will be inclined to do, in the form of a dove's tail. After being drawn out in the form of a long, straight wedge, a little of the edge should be cut off; for, no matter how much care may have been used in the forging, the outside has been drawn out a little faster than the inside, and cutting off the extreme end—perhaps ½ inch or even less—will insure an edge of sound metal. The chisel is now ready to be cut from the bar. This should be done by heating at the right point to a light red, and cutting it round and round on the hardy so as to make an even, smooth job. If the hammer is held at the proper angle while this cutting is being done, it will help to make the slight bevel on the head of the chisel which is shown in the cut of the finished tool. The wedge-shaped part of the tool should next be refined by proper hammering. The right way to do this is to heat to a dull red and pound it well on both flat sides with a heavy hammer, beginning with heavy blows which should become lighter and lighter as the metal cools, and stopping when the red color has disappeared. If this pounding has spread the edge out too wide, it would be a mistake to try to remedy it by any pounding on the edges, for this would undo what has been done by the hammering on the flat sides. Any necessary trimming of the sides should be done by grinding or filing after the tool is cold.

The above-described refining process is what constitutes the main difference between a first class tool and an ordinary one. A tool so made and properly tempered will stand more hard usage, and even abuse, than one that has simply been shaped and tempered without the refining process.

After the chisel has been filed or ground to the proper shape, as shown in Figure 32, it will be ready for tempering.

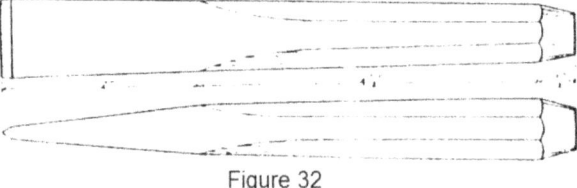

Figure 32

What is usually spoken of as tempering is in reality a double process; for the steel is first hardened, then softened to the desired degree to suit a particular need.

In the case of a cold chisel which needs to be hardened only at the edge, the easiest way to do the tempering is to chill the end and then let the heat from the balance of the tool bring it back to the proper temperature. The whole of the tool is first heated to a dull red color. Great care is necessary in heating to avoid getting the thin end too hot. Plenty of time should be taken to get an even heat throughout the whole piece. It is advisable to push the thin end through, beyond the middle of the fire, to allow the body of the tool to heat first. When the whole tool is of an even, dull red color, it should be taken from the fire and held in a vertical position over the water and an inch or two of the edge dipped beneath the surface. It should not be held still, but should be danced up and down until, when raised above the surface of the water, it remains wet for a few seconds. The reason for the dipping is that if the tool were to be held still in the water, the great difference in temperature between the two parts would be very likely to cause a crack to form at the water-line.

After the dipping, the chisel should be polished quickly on one flat side by rubbing with a piece of whetstone or brick. There will then appear on the polished surface a band of colors which will be seen to be passing from the hot tool toward the cool end. These colors indicate the degree of hardness of the steel. The first color to be seen is a very pale straw color, then follow in order—pale yellow, yellow, dark yellow, brownish yellow, brown, light purple, dark purple, darker blue, greenish blue. A cold chisel for ordinary work should be quite soft in comparison with other tools, and the proper temper is indicated by the *blue* color in the color band. When this color reaches the edge, the tool should be quickly dipped into the water again to prevent any further softening. If by this time the body of the tool has so far cooled off that no red color is to be seen, it will be safe to cool the whole chisel in the water.

A chisel made and refined and tempered as above described will easily cut a chip from the bar from which it was made. At the same time, the edge will not be too hard to be sharpened with a file. A chisel made from the same bar but without the refining process, in order to be able to cut steel would have to be tempered harder, and consequently would be more brittle and more likely to break than the one first described.

FORGING AND TEMPERING DRILLS

Flat drills for ordinary work may be made of the same kind of steel which is used for cold chisels, and the same rules for heating, drawing, and refining the steel apply as in the case of the chisel. In Figure 33 are shown two kinds of drills; one an ordinary flat drill, the other a drill with a twisted end. The latter will cut faster and easier than a flat drill, and is not so hard to make as one who had never learned the trick of making the twist might suppose.

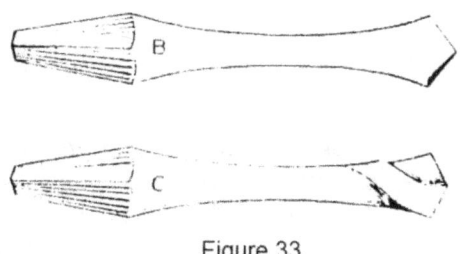

Figure 33

In making a flat drill, the steel is drawn out square to the size wanted for the neck of the drill, then it is rounded and the end flattened, as shown at A in Figure 33, and refined b pounding. The corners are then cut off on the hardy by being held in such a way as to give the proper angle and bevel to the two sides. The proper shape is shown at B. This will save some filing. The drill is allowed to cool slowly; then filed to the proper size and bevel.

In the case of large drills, the tempering may be done in the same way as in the case of the cold chisel. With small drills, it is better to chill the whole tool, then, after polishing, heat for the tempering by pinching between the jaws of a pair of hot tongs. For ordinary work, drills should be tempered to a purple color.

The drill with the twisted end, shown at C in Figure 33, is started in the same way as the flat drill, then the twist in the end is started by pulling the middle of the flat end in the corner of the vise, or holding it with a small pair of tongs and giving it a slight turn to the left. The rest of the twisting is done with a light hammer and by using very light blows. The steel is held in such a way that the blows of the hammer and to give it more twist; but the blows are so light that the edges of the steel only are upset—leaving the middle thin as in the case of a machine-made twist drill. It is well for the beginner to practice first with a piece of mild steel.

STONE DRILLS

Drills for working in stone should be made of steel having a higher percentage of carbon than that used for cold chisels, punches, etc. Because of the higher carbon content, this steel is more easily spoiled by overheating, and greater care must be used by the smith.

A drill intended for working in limestone, slatestone, or other comparatively soft rock may be finished with a thinner edge than one intended for use in granite. In Figure 34, an attempt has been made to show about the right angle to be given the edge for the different kinds of stone: A for soft stone, B for granite. The edge should be curved about as shown in the side view at C.

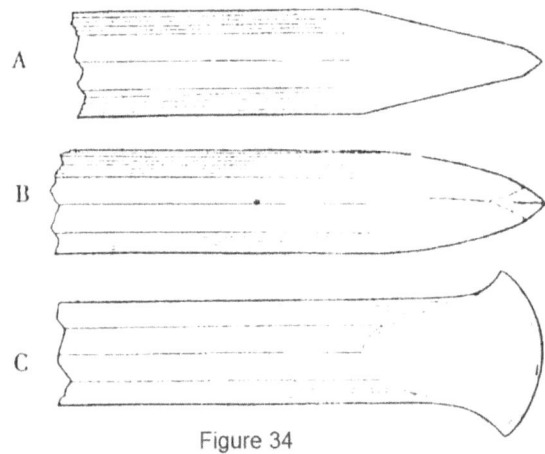

Figure 34

The steel in a stone drill may be refined by hard hammering on the sides, just as in the case of the cold chisel. In tempering, it should be brought to a dull red and chilled in salt water, following the same directions as for the cold chisel, except that the stone drill must be harder, and should be dipped again when the yellow color reaches the edge. Because of the curved edge, the corners become too soft before the middle is of the right temper if the smith does not do something to retard the heat. The usual custom is to touch the corners with a wet rag or sponge as soon as the right color reaches them, then to dip the whole end when the yellow color reaches the end.

KNIFE BLADES

Knives are made from steel having a rather low carbon content; about the same as that used for making springs. In forging a blade, it is necessary first to bend the steel in a decided curve in the direction of what is to be the edge. See Figure 35. Forging the edge thin will stretch that side of the steel enough to take out the curve and make it straight. If the attempt were made to forge it without doing this bending, the result would be a blade with a backward curve which would be difficult to straighten.

The proper way to harden a knife blade is to heat it to a dull red, then dip it in water, back edge first. After polishing, the color should be drawn by pinching the back edge with a pair of red hot tongs, moving them back and forth so as to secure an even heat the whole length of the blade. The right color for the edge is dark purple. Heating from the back, as just described, leaves the body of the blade softer than the edge and it is thus able to stand bending without danger of breaking.

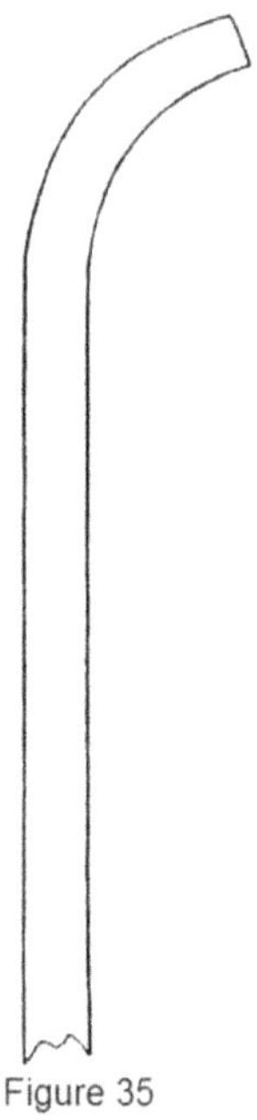

Figure 35

TEMPERING A HAMMER

The farm smith will probably never take the time to make a hammer, for he knows that he can buy one cheaper than he could buy the steel to make one. He will, however, probably have occasion to dress up hammers that have been pounded out of shape; and it will be necessary for him to do the tempering afterwards. If he should attempt to temper a hammer by dipping it into water while hot, in the same way as he would temper a cold chisel, the result would be exactly opposite from what he would like it to be. Dipping in water would chill the outside and leave the middle too soft. When used, the edges of the face would be likely to chip off, and the middle would be dented or sunken.

The right way to chill a hammer for tempering is to heat it to a full red heat, then hold it under a faucet where a stream of cold water will strike the middle of the face. It should be held there until entirely cold. If the work must be done where there is no running water, a large sprinkling can from which the sprinkling head has been removed, may be used to pour a stream of water on the face. To draw the temper, a large punch or any large piece of iron that will about fit the handle hole may be heated and driven in the hole. The face should be tempered to a dark purple.

BLACKSMITH'S TONGS

For making a pair of ordinary size tongs, the smith uses mild steel, ¾ inch for the jaws, $7/_{16}$ inch for the handles. To shape the jaw, the steel is heated to a white heat, and placed on the anvil as shown at A in Figure 36. It is struck with the hammer at the place shown by the arrow, causing the edge of the anvil to cut up into the steel and form a sharp angle, a front view of which is shown at B. The pounding at this point is continued until the end on the anvil is about half its original thickness. At the same time, the top line of A is kept straight. The piece is next given a quarter turn, so that what was the underside is now toward the right, and, after being heated again, it is placed across the anvil at an angle of 45 degrees, so that the inside angle made by the first process is exactly over the further edge of the anvil, as at C. The part C is now to be hammered down until it is half its original thickness. This will cause the edge of the anvil to cut a slanting shoulder from the underside. If given another quarter turn to the left, the end will look like D in the figure. E shows a side view at the same stage. This part is next to be cut off at the dotted line, and the end is to be scarfed for welding on the handle, as shown at F and G. This jaw is now to be laid astride, and another exactly like it is to be made.

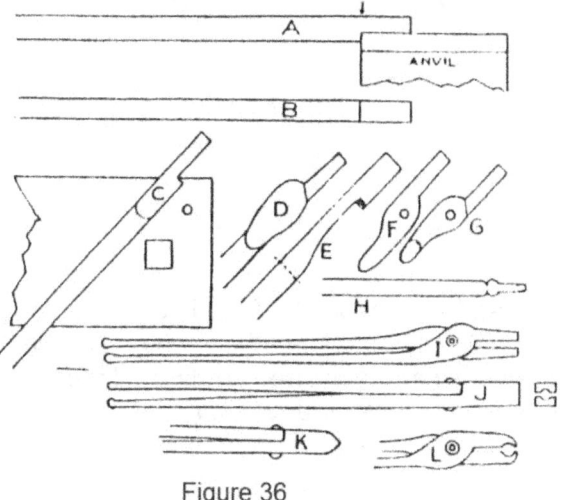

Figure 36

The best way to make handles is to use 2 feet of 7/16-inch rod, upsetting and scarfing each end, and welding a jaw to each end. The two handles are now to be cut apart at the middle point and drawn out a little and the ends finished off. The rivet holes, which should be about 5/16 inch in size, should then be punched and a rivet made to fit them. The handy way to get the rivet in place is to form it on the end of a ½-inch rod, and, after getting it the right size and length, to cut it nearly off on the hardy, as shown at H; then, after heating, put it in place, break it off, and rivet. While doing the riveting, the hammer should be held at a slant so as to give a beveled edge appearance to the rivet head. Riveting the two parts of the tongs together with a hot rivet (I) will probably tighten them so they will be hard to work. This condition may be cured by heating them to a red heat and working them open and shut a few times while hot.

If the tongs are to be used for ordinary work about the shop, they may be improved somewhat by making a groove in the jaws as shown in the front view at J. This grooving is done by heating the jaws of the tongs to a light yellow heat, closing them on a short piece of 3/8-inch iron, and hammering with a heavy hammer. If they are to be used for welding links of chain, the corners should be cut off as shown at K and the ends of the jaws formed as shown at L by closing them while hot over a piece of 3/8-inch iron.

Figure 37 illustrates the process of making a pair of bolt tongs. A 7/8-inch mild steel is used. A lump about 1 inch long is left at the end, as shown at A, while a short, round neck is drawn down to about 7/16 inch in size. The part marked B is then flattened down as shown, while the iron is laid across the anvil at a 45 degree angle, the same as in the case of the plain tongs already described. The lump at the end is flattened out as shown in C and shaped like a spout by holding in the angle between the horn and the face of the anvil, striking with the cross pein of the hammer as shown at D. The curve is next formed in the neck as at E, and the completed jaw is cut off at the dotted line and scarfed for the handle. The balance of the process is exactly the same as for the plain tongs.

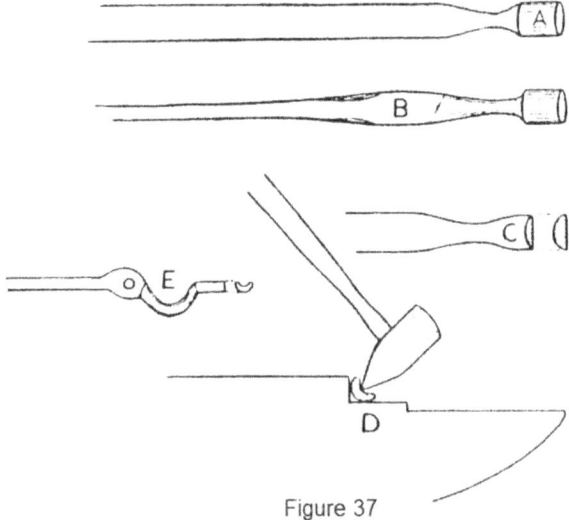

Figure 37

Tongs of various sizes and shapes will be found convenient for handling the many different kinds of work that will fall to the lot of the farm smith. The two kinds of tongs just described are those that will be used most frequently, and the smith who has learned to make them will have no trouble in making any others that he will need in his work.

Figure 38 pictures four kinds of tongs that are used for different kinds of work. The first, A, is used in dressing hand hammers and all kinds of flogging tools that have eyes for handles. B is shaped for handling ball pein hammers and short bolts. The tongs shown at C, with the jaws set off at a right angle, are used in making hoops, hub bands, and whiffletree clips. Horseshoer's tongs, shown at D, are short and light in weight and have jaws that are wide and round and generally cupped so as to give a better grip on the shoe.

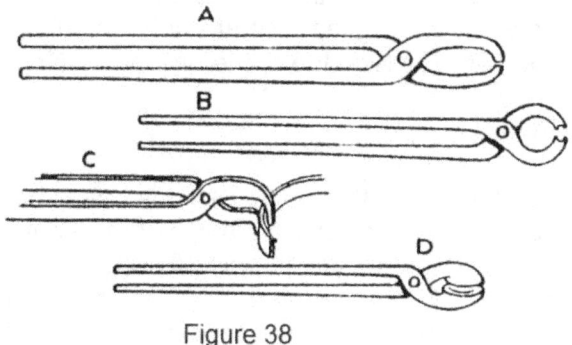

Figure 38

FILES

The files in a farm shop are so often misused that it may be well to give space here to a brief discussion of their proper use and care.

A file is a series of very sharp, very hard cold chisels. They have to be tempered very hard to do the work expected of them, and are, therefore, very brittle and easily broken. No mechanic would be guilty of keeping his sharp wood chisels and plane irons where they would come in contact with other metal tools that might dull them. If the smith can be taught that each tooth in his files is a sharp chisel, it may be possible to induce him to have a proper place for the files where they may never be injured by other tools. Each file should have its place on a shelf or on wooden pins, and the smith should train himself always to keep it in that place when it is not in use.

A good file should never be used on hot metal or hardened steel or on hard cast iron. Cast iron nearly always has an outside coating which is very hard, because when the casting was made, the surface, coming in contact with the cold, damp molding sand, was chilled enough to harden it. This coating is usually very thin, and if it is removed by grinding or by the use of an old, worn file, the iron below the surface may be safely filed with a sharp file.

The teeth of a file are so made that the file cuts in but one direction. It should be lifted from the work on the back stroke. In filing wrought iron or steel, the spaces between the teeth often become clogged with particles of the metal and should be brushed with a wire brush or card. Sometimes soft iron filings become so tightly lodged between the teeth that the wire brush will not remove them. In such a case, the smith may make what is called a scorer by flattening out the end of a soft iron rod and making a sort of comb of it by drawing it across the file lengthwise of the teeth. With this tool it is easy to poke out anything that is lodged between the teeth.

The writer once heard an old blacksmith tell his apprentice that the whole of the file he was working with was paid for. The young man took the hint and changed from short, jerky motions to long sweeping strokes which used the whole length of the file.

In order that it may be used properly, every file should have a handle, and the handle should be so attached that it will be in line with the body of the file. It is a good plan to bore a hole in the center of the handle a little smaller than the tang of the file, then heat the tang of an old file of the same size and burn the hole large enough to make a tight fit. The handle should have a tight-fitting, strong ferrule so that it will not split when the tang is driven in tight.

VII. PLOW WORK

Wherever steel plows are used, the smith will be called upon to sharpen dull plowshares and to apply new points. While these are not particularly difficult tasks, they require painstaking care and some knowledge of the proper working of steel.

SHARPENING PLOWSHARES

To sharpen plowshares without aid, the tool to use is a heavy hand hammer with a rounding face. With such a tool, it is possible to draw the share out to a thin edge by pounding on the upper side, at the same time keeping the bottom straight by holding it level on the face of the anvil. Drawing the edge out thin has a tendency to crowd the point around too much "to land." This tendency should be corrected from time to time as the drawing out process progresses, by holding the edge against a hardwood block and driving the point back to its proper position. Of course, it would dull the edge to hold it against the anvil while doing this straightening.

During the whole process of sharpening, the utmost care should be used to avoid burning the share. When the edge is drawn out much thinner than the rest of the share, it becomes hot so much more quickly than the thicker part that it is almost sure to be overheated unless the smith is very watchful. A light red heat is what is wanted. It is a good plan to have the fire rather long in shape and to hold the edge of the share out beyond the hottest part of the fire, especially after it is drawn out thin, so that it will not be in danger of burning before the thicker part back from the edge becomes hot enough to work.

Some plowshares are made from steel containing enough carbon to allow it being hardened like tool steel. Such shares, after being sharpened, should be heated to a dull red, care being used to see that all parts of the share are of an even heat, then plunged into cold water. The thick edge should go into the water first.

Shares made from mild plow steel containing too little carbon for self-hardening may be hardened on the surface—case hardened—by bringing to an even light red heat and sprinkling with prussiate of potash. The potash will melt and flow over the entire surface of the share which should then be plunged into water or brine.

Prussiate of potash is a dangerous poison. The smith, when using it for case hardening, should carefully avoid breathing any of the fumes which rises from it when heated. It goes without saying that it should be kept out of the reach of children.

NEW POINTS

After a plowshare has been sharpened a number of times, it will usually be found that the point has become so short that it no longer serves its purpose and a new point must be welded on. The new point should be made of plow steel and not from any high carbon steel such as an old rasp or file, as the latter will cause too much trouble in welding, and may discourage the amateur smith. A suitable piece for a new point may usually be cut from the back or upper part of an old share which has not been worn too thin.

Plow steel, or any mild steel, may be easily sheared into any form by heating to just the right heat and shearing it over the edge of the anvil by the use of the set hammer as the upper blade, so to speak, of the shear. The particular heat at which it may be most easily cut is between black and red; that is, when it is just cooling from red heat to black. No one seems to be able to explain why this is true, but such is the fact.

The new piece to be welded to the point should be shaped as shown at A in Figure 39. It is, of course, to be welded to the bottom of the share. In making the weld, it will be necessary to use great care to have the parts reach the welding heat at the same time. To do this, it is well to heat slowly so as to give the larger part time to get to the welding heat before the small point becomes too hot. Borax and iron filings should be used as a flux, and the first part of the welding should be done in the fire.

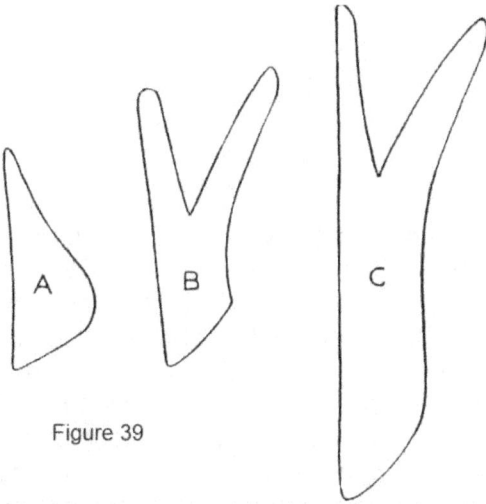

Figure 39

By this method, it is easier and more certain to get the parts welded in the right position than by trying to place them together on the anvil after taking from the fire. When the two parts are at welding heat and still in the fire, the point should be placed in the proper position and a few taps given with a light hammer. This will cause the point to stick fast where it belongs, and the whole may then be taken out on the anvil and the weld finished with a heavier hammer.

If the throat of the old share is worn away, a piece of plow steel shaped as shown at B should be welded on the bottom of the throat. Figure 40 illustrates the position of plowshare and point.

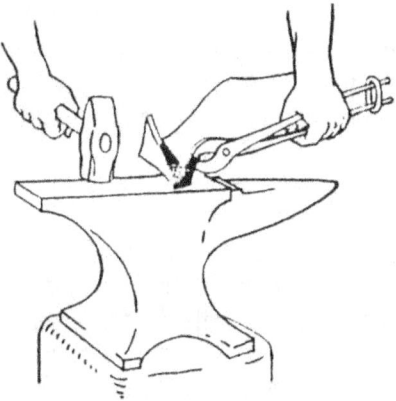

Figure 40

If the old point is worn very short, a piece shaped as shown at C in Figure 39 may be made. It should be long enough to bend over and weld to the top side of the share. The part to be welded to the top of the share should be thinned down to a feather edge before bending. The manner of welding on this type of point is shown in Figure 41.

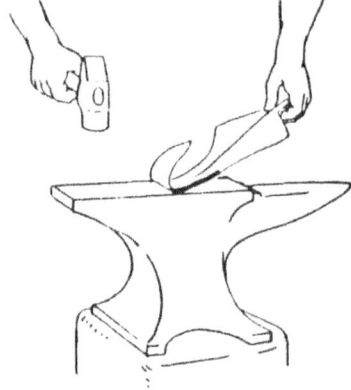

Figure 41

To make a new share for the style of plow using what is known as a slip share, plow steel $9/16$ by 3 inches in size should be used. A piece of this steel 9 inches in length will make two landsides if it is cut as shown in Figure 42. The long edge of the short landside should be bent to fit the curve of the share, then it should be fitted to the plow so that the bottom edge will extend below the main landside about $3/16$ of an inch, to allow for welding, which will narrow it up somewhat. The bolt hole should then be drilled and the short landside bolted to the plow, and the blank share put in place and marked. It should extend about $1/8$ inch beyond the edge of the landside. The short landside and blank share should be clamped together by using a clamp and wedge as shown in Figure 43.

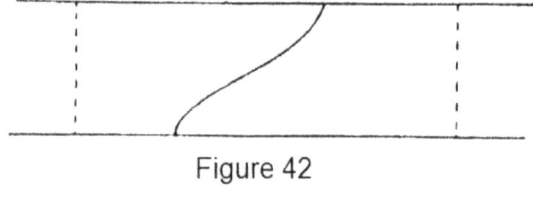

Figure 42

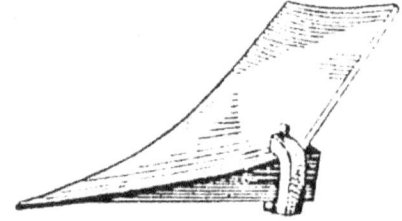

Figure 43

The whole is then to be unbolted from the plow, and a light weld taken at the point to hold it fast. The clamp is then to be moved down to the middle and a weld taken at the upper corner. This plan will avoid the creeping up out of shape which is sure to take place if the welding is followed up from the point, as is sometimes done. The whole should then be welded solidly and the point turned down under and welded and trimmed to shape.

HANDY TOOLS

In a shop without power, a very effective tool for shaping plow points after welding may be made from an old horse rasp, fitted with a rather long iron handle. This is to be used while the steel is hot, and is to be followed with the file after the metal cools.

To make a tool which is somewhat handier than ordinary tongs for handling slip shares while sharpening them, the writer once took a piece of $5/8$-inch round iron 2½ feet long, welded the ends together and shaped it like a long link, with just enough space between the two sides to hold a plow bolt. Another road of the same length was bent as shown in Figure 44, and the ends welded to the ends of the link. With the share bolted to the link, it was easy to handle, and the stiff link had a tendency also to keep the share from warping while it was heated and sharpened.

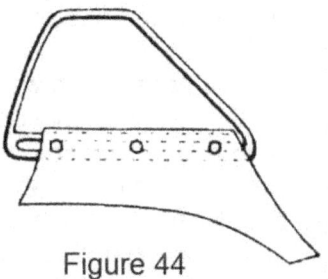

Figure 44

Trouble is often encountered in removing shares from plows because of rusted bolts which have a provoking way of turning when an attempt is made to screw off the nuts. Many tools have been invented to hold such bolts in place. One of the best simple tools of this kind is shown in Figure 45. It consists of two pieces of $7/16$-inch round, mild steel united by a hinge joint. One piece has a bit of tool steel welded in its end. The other has an end bent like a hook. The steel end is sharpened and tempered like a small cold chisel. In use the bent end is hooked over the edge of the moldboard or share, and the chisel end placed against the head of the bolt. This gives a purchase that holds the bolt from turning. The writer once saw such a tool made from the braces of an old buggy top which was found in a scrap heap. The two braces were joined by their original hinge joint, and all that was necessary to complete the tool was to finish the two ends as described above.

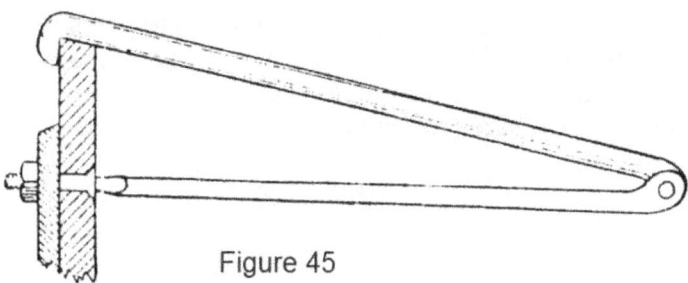

Figure 45

VIII. WAGON WORK

Wagons are becoming so scarce in these days of trucks and automobiles that the old-fashioned wagonmaker has almost passed from the scene. Similarly, there is no danger that the village blacksmith will also disappear for lack of work to do. In this case, the farmer who still uses wagons will be obliged to do his own repairing. He should at least know how to do the most important jobs in wagon repairs.

SETTING TIRES

The setting of wagon tires is a job which the average farmer would turn over to the village blacksmith, if one could be found, rather than tackle the job himself. However, it is not such a difficult piece of work as might be supposed. Any farmer with natural mechanical ability should be able to master the details of the work without much trouble.

When the tires of a wagon become loose, and are allowed to go for some time without attention, several bad symptoms are almost certain to develop. The spokes will become loose in the felloes, and, if further neglected, will become loose in the hub. The wood of the hub and the spokes may have shrunken so much that the wheel has become "felloe bound"; that is, the felloe has become too long and needs to be shortened as well as the tire. If a wheel is allowed to be used in this condition for any length of time, both spokes and felloes will be badly damaged. This is a case which well illustrates the old adage of the stitch in time. Loose wheels may be tightened up by soaking in the river or horse pond; but this is a temporary makeshift, and is only postponing the day of reckoning.

Let us suppose we have a wagon with wheels in the above-mentioned condition. The first thing to do is to mark the wheels and the tires in such a way that after setting the tires we may be sure to get each wheel back in its proper place and wearing its own tire. An old smith whom the writer once worked with always marked the wheels and tires in regular order by beginning with the near, (left), fore wheel, going to the left rear wheel, and so on around the wagon. (He said it meant bad luck to cross over the tongue of the wagon!) To do the marking, he used a center punch, and on the inside (wagon side) of the first wheel he made a single dot on the tire and a corresponding dot on the felloe. The second tire and felloe were marked with two dots, the third with three, and the last with four. He thus did a double job of marking, for his marks enabled him to know on which wheel each tire belonged and also where each wheel belonged on the wagon.

To get the tires off the wheels, the bolts should be removed and the felloes driven from the inside (wagon side) of the wheels. If light taps with the hammer do not start the tire loose, a block of wood held against the felloe will allow harder blows without injuring the felloe.

Trouble is often encountered in removing tire bolts. The nuts are found to be rusted fast to the bolts, and the bolts turn around when the attempt is made to unscrew the nuts. This calls for something to hold the bolts in place. One of the best tools for holding bolts is shown in Figure 46. It is a bar of ¾-inch mild steel with a bend in one end of the proper size to grasp the felloe, and a steel projection shaped like a cold chisel to hold the bolt.

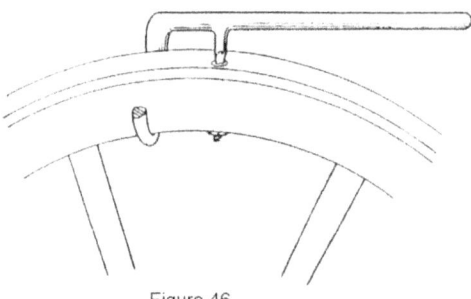

Figure 46

Each wheel should be taken in turn and placed on a table or bench where it may be easily turned about so that all the spokes and the felloes may be examined to find out what they need. If the spokes have been used a long time with a loose tire, and have become badly worn, it may be necessary to replace them with new ones. If the felloes have shrunken so much that some of the tenons of the spokes reach through and rest against the tire, giving us what is called a spoke-bound wheel, the ends of the long spokes should be cut off. If the felloes are too long to fit down to a snug fit on the spokes, a little should be sawed out at the ends of the felloes. In doing this, it is necessary to be very careful not to saw out too much. If the wheel is only slightly felloe-bound, the thickness of the handsaw blade will be enough to take out. The spokes should be wedged in the felloe so as to make the whole wheel tight, and a tracing wheel used to get the exact size of the wheel to compare with the size of the tire in order that we may know just how much shrinking will have to be done.

A picture of a tracing wheel is shown in Figure 4y7. A substitute for a tracing wheel may be made from a sheet of tin or sheet iron cut in the form of a circle, with a small hole drilled in the center and a handle made by sawing a keep kerf in the end of a pine stick about 1 inch square.

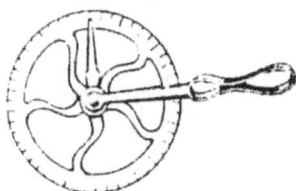

Figure 47

In use, the wheel to be measured is placed where it may be easily turned around and a mark is made on the face of the rim. A mark is then made on the tracing wheel (a slate pencil is a good marker to use) and the mark on the tracing wheel is placed against the mark on the wagon wheel. The tracing wheel is then pressed against the rim of the wagon wheel and the latter is turned around till the mark again comes to the starting place. Another mark is then made on the tracing wheel where it will match with the mark on the rim of the wagon wheel.

The tire is now to be measured with the same tracing wheel. To do this, the smith places the tire where it is supported at at least three points, and with himself on the inside of the tire he proceeds to measure by first making a mark with his pencil on the inside of the tire; then placing the first mark of the tracing wheel on the tire mark, he runs the tracer around in the same direction that it ran while measuring the wheel. When the complete circle of the tire has been made, a third mark is made on the tracer where it meets the mark on the tire. The space between the second and third marks on the tracing wheel will indicate the difference in size between the wheel and the tire.

We have now to shrink the tire to the proper size to fit the wheel. A regular tire shrinker such as is used in wagon shops, is a somewhat costly piece of machinery which a farmer who has but little tire setting to do can hardly afford. A homemade shrinker is something that the farm smith can make for himself. Figure 48, A, shows such a shrinker. It is a bar of iron 1 by 2 inches in size and about 1 foot long. A square piece of iron to fit the hardy hole is welded to the middle of the bottom. Two clamps provided with heavy set screws are fastened to the bottom iron base with plow bolts or rivets. The cut shows the shrinker in use. The tire is heated to a white heat and a bend or hump made in it as shown; then it is clamped so that it is held solidly while the hump in the tire is hammered down to the proper curve of the tire. This process will shrink an ordinary tire something like $3/8$ of an inch at a time. Another homemade tire shrinker is shown at B. It is made in the same way as that shown at A, except that wedges are used instead of set screws to hold the tire.

To save time, we can avoid using the tracer wheel after the first measurement of the wheel and tire, by employing what is known as the compass or divider method. After tracing the wheel and the tire and determining how much the tire is to be shortened, a dot is made with a center punch on each side of the place which is to be shrunken. The dividers are then set so that they measure the distance between these points. The amount of shrinkage is then carefully marked by another punch mark away from the part to be shrunken. The shrinking is then done and the distance between punch marks measured with the dividers. If the dividers just span the distance between the outside punch marks, the amount of shrinkage is just right. If the marks are still too far apart, a little more shrinking will have to be done. If the marks are too near together, the shrunken part can be very easily stretched the proper amount by light hammering on the anvil. Sometimes, in the case of a very loose tire which has to be shortened a good deal, two places instead of one are shrunken. These two places are chosen on opposite sides of the tire. This method is less likely to cause trouble in matching bolt holes in tire and felloe than where all the shrinking is done in one place.

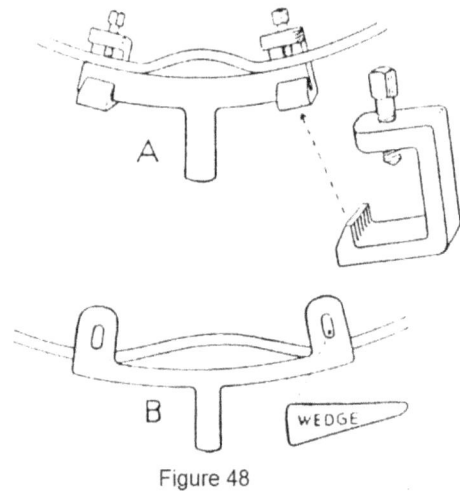

Figure 48

As to the amount that any tire should be shrunk, only this advice can be given: It is safer to shrink too little than too much. Too much shrinking will dish and spoil the wheel. For a light buggy wheel, shortening the tire $1/8$ of an inch is enough if the wheel is in fairly good condition. A heavy wagon wheel will stand about ½ inch.

In replacing the tire after shrinking, the wheel should be supported, inside (wagon side) uppermost, on four blocks high enough to lift the hub from the floor. If the tire is not too large and heavy, it may be heated in the forge by having a rather long fire and keeping the tire moving around till it is almost red hot. When it is in this condition, it ought to drop into position easily and without any trouble. The smith should know where the punch mark is on the felloe, and should put a slender punch in the bolt hole which is next to the punch mark on the tire. Holding the tire by this punch and a pair of tongs, he should be able to get the tire in its proper place without any loss of time. He should begin to cool the tire as soon as it is in place by pouring water on it so that the felloe will not be burned. As soon as the tire shrinks enough to be fairly tight, the wheel should be picked up and turned so as to run the tire through the water in the slack tub, which should be level full. Make sure, before the tire is cold, that the felloe and tire are in line all around; correcting it here and there with the hammer if necessary, by holding it level on the anvil.

MAKING NEW TIRES

To make a new tire for a wheel is not a hard job for the farm smith if he has mastered the art of welding. The proper way to measure the stock for a new tire is to roll the wheel over the bar from which the tire is to be made, and mark the exact circumference of the wheel. To this add three times the thickness of the tire and cut off at that point. The ends are then to be scarfed the same as for welding flat irons, as has been explained on page 12. The corners of the end which comes on top, when the tire is bent around into shape, should be flared out enough so that they may be bent down a little around the sides of the lower end. This will prevent the ends from sliding sidewise while being heated.

Most of the failures in welding tires are due to faulty placing of the tire on the anvil when the welding is being done. Beginners should be warned against allowing the lower end of the weld to touch the anvil before the smith is ready to strike the first blow. An anvil is a very good conductor of heat, and if the parts to be welded are placed flat upon the face of the anvil when taken from the fire, the chances are that the lower end will have lost heat enough to spoil the weld before the smith is ready to strike. The correct way is to rest that part of the tire which is just beyond the joint against the far edge of the anvil, so that when the tire is rolled toward the anvil, the joint will be at the middle of the face. This rolling should be done after the hammer is raised and ready to come down upon the joint the instant that it touches the anvil. It is well to use sand for a flux in making this kind of weld.

WIFFLETREE IRONS

A good way of iron wiffletrees is shown in Figure 49. The main advantage claimed for this method over the old-fashioned way is that the ends do not so easily catch fast to things. For example, in cultivating in the orchard, if the team is driven a little too close to a tree, the old-fashioned singletree end with its ferrule is too likely to rip off a piece of bark; whereas the newer kind will simply slip past. The newer style also has the advantage of being easily made and put on by the amateur smith.

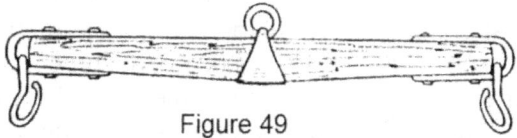

Figure 49

The hooks and the irons which hold them to the singletree are made of $7/16$-inch round, mild steel, which is flattened somewhat where the rivets hold them to the wood. The manner of making the hooks is shown in Figure 50. A piece of $7/16$-inch mild steel is heated and the end bent over upon itself, as shown in A, and welded; then cut off at the dotted line and the end drawn out to a point as shown at B. In bending the hooks, the points are bent back to within a trifle more than $7/16$ of an inch from the back of the eye, as drawn at C. This brings the points so close to the irons which hold them to the singletree that it is impossible for the tugs to become unhooked of themselves. To fasten or unfasten a tug, it is necessary to turn the hook up in the position shown at D.

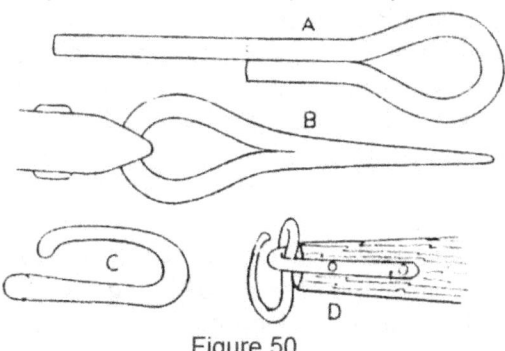

Figure 50

For heavy work, the kind of singletree shown at A in Figure 51 is recommended. The wooden part is of hickory or white oak, 1½ inches thick and 2¼ inches wide at the middle, tapering to 1½ inches at the ends. A band of mild steel $3/16$ inches thick and 1 inch wide is fastened to the back of the singletree with short screws. The ends of this band are rolled back to form eyes to hold the hooks. The hooks shown here have bars across their ends to prevent accidental unhooking. To make the cross bar, a lump of steel is left when the hook is drawn out which is flattened first one way in the vise, then the other way on the anvil, as shown at B; then the sides are drawn out round over the edge of the anvil, as shown at C.

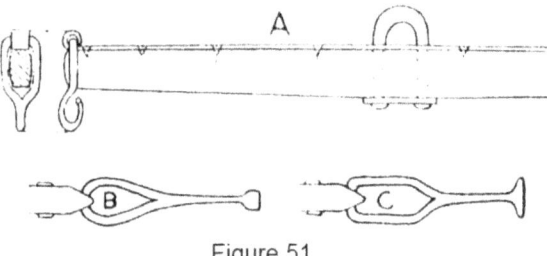

Figure 51

IX. HORSESHOEING

It is not to be supposed that all farmers, or even all of those who do most of their own blacksmithing and repair work, will care to shoe their own horses. It is true, however, that many farmers with a natural bent for that kind of work have found that they can do a workmanlike job of shoeing their own teams, and get some satisfaction from doing it.

Every horse owner should have a good knowledge of how the shoeing should be done in order to be able to judge a good job when he sees it, and to give sound advice to the man who does the shoeing. There are still some blacksmiths of the old school who might possibly be benefited by a little such advice.

Almost all farm horses, unless they are to be used for road work, would be better off without shoes for the greater part, and possibly all, of the year. Since gasoline motors and trucks now do most of the road work, it is probable that many farm horses will live a life of usefulness without having to submit to the wearing of shoes. This does not mean that the feet of such horses are to be neglected. They should be watched carefully and trimmed whenever there is need for such trimming. This care should begin with the young colt. Colts that get plenty of exercise in rocky pastures will probably wear away their hoofs fast enough to keep them in shape which nature intended them to have. But colts reared in stables and on soft ground will be found almost invariably to have overgrown hoofs that will bring about actual deformity of feet and legs if not properly cared for. Such colts should be carefully watched and their hoofs trimmed to the proper size and shape. Most of the trimming may be done with a chisel and mallet by placing the foot on a hardwood plank and having a helper hold up the opposite foot, so as to compel the animal to hold the first foot still. After being trimmed to the proper form with the chisel, the rough edges of the foot should be smoothed off with a rasp.

Time spent in handling young colts and having them get used to having their feet handled will pay good dividends. This kind of training should begin when the colt is but a few days old. Almost all colts will respond to kind treatment, and when very young may be taught many lessons that will be much easier for them to learn then than later in life. Colts so trained will give little trouble when it is necessary to trim their feet or to shoe them, or when they are harnessed and put to work.

The writer has known farmers who allowed their colts to grow up to the age when they were wanted for farm work with absolutely no training, excepting to wear a halter. These colts, wild as hawks, were taken to the shop, and the blacksmith was expected to shoe them for the same price per shoe that he charged for shoeing Old Dobbin. This is not fair to the smith.

Machine made horseshoes are now so cheap that no farm smith can afford to make his own. They may be had in all sizes and weights, and there has come upon the market a shoe that has the toe and heel calks forged in place, so that the smith has only to do a little shaping to fit the shoe to the foot.

When farm horses must be used for work on hard gravel roads or on icy roads in winter, it becomes necessary for them to wear shoes. For summer wear, when the only purpose of the shoe is to keep the hoof from wearing away too fast, a thin, flat shoe, or even a tip such as is shown in Figure 52, will serve the purpose. For use on icy roads in winter, some form of sharp calks will be required. Such calks should be made as short as possible to avoid the straining of tendons which is caused by high calks. To keep the calks sharp, especially when the horses are used on frozen gravel roads, is something of a problem. An improvement on the ordinary calk may be made by splitting the calk and inserting a steel center. This steel center will wear away much more slowly than the iron of the calk, and a constant sharp edge is the result. Pieces of old mower sections are good materials for the centers. The calk, when hot, is split with a thin chisel and the piece of section is inserted and welded. Cooling the calk suddenly in water hardens the center.

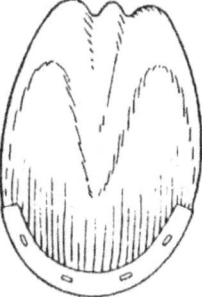

Figure 52

Another way of adding to the length of life of the calks is to give them a coating of cast iron. This is done by heating the calk to a welding heat, and at the same time heating the end of a piece of cast iron to the melting point and smearing the hot calk with the melting cast iron. The cast iron will form a coat over the calk, and on being plunged into water, becomes very hard. Calks treated in this way will outlast ordinary calks many days.

There are several kinds of patented calks which may be removed from the shoe without removing the shoe from the foot. These calks serve a good purpose if carefully watched and removed before they become too much worn. If allowed to wear down to the level of the shoe, it is impossible to remove them without taking off the shoe.

Whenever it becomes necessary to have horses shod, several points should be borne in mind. In the first place, shoeing is at best a necessary evil. A shoe cannot be nailed to a horse's hoof without doing at least some damage to the hoof. It becomes our business to do as little damage as possible when we fit the shoe and fasten it to the hoof.

Many old-fashioned smiths, and perhaps not all of them are dead yet, had the habit of cutting away the frog of the hoof as the first act in fitting the foot for the shoe. Just why they did this is one of those things that have never been satisfactorily explained. The hoof so treated became dry and contracted, and the horse became more or less lame; but the same old foolish practice went on for years, and, no doubt, still prevails in some places.

The frog is the natural cushion placed by nature where it relieves the foot from jar at every step and gives a springiness of gait which is entirely different from the gait of a horse whose feet have been deprived of this natural buffer.

In fitting the foot to receive the shoe, let us leave the frog in its natural condition. If the outline of the hoof is not what it should be, that is, if it has been allowed to grow out of shape instead of being trimmed as it should have been, this fault may be remedied by the use of hoof nippers. But most of the fitting should be done by rasping the bottom of the foot perfectly level and at the correct angle with the slant of the front of the hoof. See Figure 53. If the bottom of the foot is made perfectly level, and the shoe is made perfectly level, there will be no trouble about making a fit without touching the sole with the hot shoe, as is so often done. It should be unnecessary to say that the shoe should be shaped to fit the form of the foot, instead of trimming the foot to conform to the shape of the shoe.

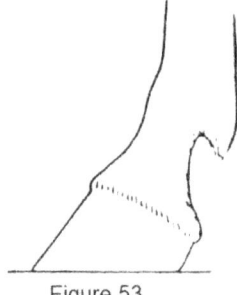

Figure 53

The shoe should be fastened to the hoof with as few and as small nails as will serve to hold it securely in place. The usual practice is to use four nails on each side of the shoe. Horseshoe nails may be had in such a variety of sizes that the proper size and length for any size or weight of shoe may be easily found.

When the bottom of the hoof is rasped level, a so-called white line is to be seen following the curve of the hoof just inside the horny wall. When the shoe is properly fitted, the nail holes will all be in such a position that the nails may be driven into this white line. In driving the nails they should be held with the bevel of the point toward the middle of the hoof so that they will tend to go outward through the wall of the hoof. It is a good plan to hold the nail tightly between finger and thumb while the first few blows are given so as to help guide it in the proper direction. It should come to the surface of the hoof between 1 and 1½ inches above the shoe. Driving the nails so that they will come out higher than this endangers the tender part of the hoof; while driving them lower may cause the hoof to break out when the clinching is done. It is a good plan for the novice to practice driving nails into a dead hoof held in the vise until he can be reasonably certain of having the points come out where he expects them.

The beginner should be warned against the too common mistake of nailing the shoe on too far back from the toe. The first nails driven have a tendency to draw the shoe back, and unless the smith is careful to watch this point, he is likely to find, after the nails are in, that the toe of the hoof overhangs the shoe a little at the front.

As fast as the nails are driven, the points should be bent over toward the shoe so that in case the horse should try to jerk his foot away, the point of the nail could not damage the wrist or hand or trousers of the smith.

After all the nails are driven and turned, they should be tightened by holding the clinch block, or any square-edged weight, at the bends and tapping on the heads with rather light blows of the shoeing hammer. The nails should then be cut off with the clippers and the stubs slightly thinned by filing. then the final clinching should be done with clinching iron and hammer, first by tapping the heads of the nails with the hammer while the clinch block is held under the clinches, then reversing the position of these tools, and the horse's foot, and smoothing down the clinches with the hammer while the clinch block is held under the heads of the nails. For this last operation, a foot rest, such as that shown in Figure 54, is a great help. A good workman should be able to do such a good job with his shoeing hammer that no roughness of the clinches can be felt with the hand. There will then be no excuse for using the rasp on the outside surface of the hoof. No rasping of the outside of the hoof should ever be necessary except possibly to smooth the extreme edge of the hoof where slivers may have been raised when the sole was rasped to make it level. The outside of the hoof is covered with a natural varnish which acts as a protection and a conserver of the moisture of the hoof. It cannot be disturbed without damage to the hoof.

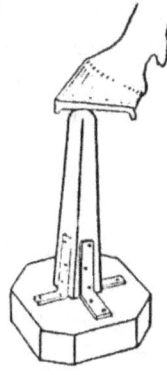

Figure 54

There are two problems that often trouble the horseshoer. They are found in connection with the proper shoeing of horses that "interfere," and those that "forge," or strike the front shoe with the hind toe.

Some horses will interfere when very tired and at no other time. This is especially true in the case of colts or young horses that are being worked too long at a time, or driven too far. Horses thin in flesh are more likely to interfere than when in good condition. Horses that "toe out" are very apt to interfere. Those that "toe in" seldom or never interfere. This is a point to remember when selecting a horse.

Many cases of simple interfering may be cured by trimming the inside edges of the hoofs to a line which is only a little straighter than the natural curve, and fitting the shoe to this straighter line. It is also a help in most cases to use a shoe with the outside web heavier than the inside, a so-called sideweight shoe.

The writer once knew a blacksmith who thought he had hit upon a brilliant idea in the line of curing a horse of interfering. He claimed that by having the feet trimmed lower on the *outside*, the ankles would be bent outward when the weight was on them so that the opposite foot would miss instead of striking as it went by. He shod a four-year-old colt after this fashion, not because the colt was interfering, but because he came so near striking at each step that it was thought wise to guard against it. The result was that immediately after being shod, the colt began to interfere. The owner brought the colt to the writer, who simply pulled the shoes off and rasped the hoofs to a perfect level and replaced the shoes. The owner afterward said that the colt did not interfere again. If the blacksmith in this case had done exactly the opposite of what he did—that is, if he had rasped the hoofs so that the outside edges would be a trifle higher than the inside, he would have been nearer right. Why is this so? The following experiment will explain the point. If a horse is allowed to stand at ease on a level floor, and the distance between his fore feet accurately measured, then if the inside walls of his feet are rasped so as to be a little lower, or shorter, than the outside walls, he will be found to stand with his feet a little further apart than the distance first measured. This is because he finds it to be more comfortable to stand on level feet; and to get each foot in a level position after the inside walls are trimmed shorter than the outside, he naturally spreads his feet apart. He will usually be found to travel with his feet further apart also, and thus this method is often found to cure interfering.

The bad habit known as "forging" or "clicking," which horses often have, is caused by the front foot being a little too slow in getting out of the way of the hind foot when the horse trots. This may be cured in some cases by shoeing in front with what are known as "roller motion shoes," and the hind feet with shoes with rather long toes.

By "roller motion shoes" is meant shoes with the toe so shaped as to cause the foot to "break over" sooner than would be the case with a shoe of ordinary shape. In a shoe without calks, the toe is shaped somewhat like the front of a sled runner. When calks are used, the same effect is produced by setting the toe calk back about an inch from the front rim of the toe on the front shoes, and well out to the front on the hind shoes.

X. SOLDERING AND BRAZING

Although soldering and brazing are not, strictly speaking, parts of the blacksmithing trade, they are operations which the farm smith will often be called upon to perform and he should have a knowledge of them in order to make repairs as the need arises. Few tools are required, and the work is easy to do if a few simple rules are followed.

SOLDERING

A one-pound soldering copper is about the right size. If much work is to be done, it is best to have a pair of coppers, so that one may be heating while its mate is being used. A pair of the size mentioned may be had for $7.50. Solder (half tin and half lead is most commonly used) costs about $4.50 a pound. Besides the coppers and the solder there will be needed some resin, some zinc chloride flux, a lump of sal-ammoniac and proper tools for cleaning the parts to be soldered.

The soldering coppers may be heated in the forge, or by a blow torch. A clean fire in the forge is an excellent place for heating. No attempt should ever be made to solder any metal of any kind until the parts to be soldered are cleaned of all rust, paint, grease, and foreign matter. Soldering is like welding; and the only way to make a strong job is to have the parts absolutely clean.

The soldering copper should be first heated to a red heat, then filed with a rather coarse file on all four of the flat sides. Care should be used to hold the file flat to keep the original bevel. It is then to be heated only just hot enough to melt solder or to cause a little smoke when touched to the sal-ammoniac. The tip of the copper is then to be "tinned" by rubbing it against the sal-ammoniac and solder till about a half-inch of the end is nicely covered with a coat of solder. After this is done, the copper should not be heated much beyond this heat or the "tinning" will be turned off.

The chloride of zinc flux is prepared by pouring 3 or 4 ounces of common muriatic acid into an old tumbler or any open glass dish, and putting into it scraps of zinc. This will cause it to boil. Zinc should be added till the boiling stops. Add about ¼ in volume of water to the solution in the tumbler, then procure, if possible, a bottle with a glass stopper in which to keep the flux. The tip end of a small feather makes a good swab for applying the flux, but should not be kept in the fluid when not in use. The flux just described is the most satisfactory soldering fluid for most kinds of work, but should not be used where it cannot be thoroughly washed off after the soldering is done, for fear of causing rust. For tin roofing jobs, resin makes a safe flux and is generally used.

By watching a tinsmith at work, a person might get the idea that all there is to doing a soldering job is to melt some solder on the place to be mended, and rub it around with the hot soldering copper. The main point that would be likely to be missed by the observer is the fact that there can be no real union of the metal to be mended and the solder, unless both are at the same degree of heat. It is necessary to go slowly enough so that the copper will heat the tin or whatever is being worked upon so that it will be as hot as the melted solder.

The beginner is apt to think that a good job of soldering depends upon getting a large quantity of solder to stick to the joint, whereas the right way is to use as little solder as possible. The right way to apply the solder is to touch the bar of solder with the tinned tip of the copper. If the copper is at the right heat, a small drop of solder will stick to the tip. This is to be applied to the seam or whatever is to be soldered, and the tip of the copper is to be held against the metal till it is hot enough to make a good union with the solder. If there is any tendency for the metals being soldered to spring apart, it will be necessary to hold them together till the joint has cooled below the melting point of solder.

To sum up, the points to be considered in doing a good job of soldering are:
1. All parts to be soldered must be absolutely clean.
2. Soldering copper must be well trimmed and heated to the right heat in a clean fire.
3. A good flux must be used.
4. As little solder as possible should be used.
5. Metals to be soldered must be heated to the melting point of solder, and held together till somewhat cooled.

BRAZING

Brazing bears a close relationship to soldering, the chief difference being that brass is used instead of solder. In certain kinds of jobs, thin iron parts may be more conveniently brazed together than welded. Take for example the case of ferrules for tools. After one becomes accustomed to brazing, he can make them easier and faster by this process than by welding.

For brazing it is necessary to use what is known as soft brass. Cast brass is not suitable for brazing. Old lamp tops, old clock wheels, or any form of sheet brass may be used. Suppose we try to braze a ferrule. The first thing to do is to bevel the ends of the piece of iron on opposite sides, so that when bent into the form of a ring the two beveled parts will fit together. Make sure that these two bevels are clean. If you do not have any pulverized borax, prepare some by heating some lump borax on a fire shovel till it swells up and becomes frothy, then cool it and rub it into the form of powder. Heat the ferrule in a clean fire until it is hot enough to melt borax. Put on a little of the powdered borax, then lay a little strip of the sheet brass on the joint and heat the iron until the brass melts, when it will run into and fill up the joint. Do not heat any more, but take it from the fire and allow to cool.

APPENDIX

TABLE 1

DECIMAL EQUIVALENTS

Equaling Parts of an Inch

Fraction	Decimal	Fraction	Decimal
1/64	.0156	33/64	.5156
1/32	.0313	17/32	.5313
3/64	.0469	35/64	.5469
1-16	.0625	9-16	.5625
5/64	.0781	37/64	.5781
3/32	.0938	19/32	.5938
7/64	.1094	39/64	.6094
1-8	.1250	5-8	.6250
9/64	.1406	41/64	.6406
5/32	.1563	21/32	.6563
11/64	.1719	43/64	.6719
3-16	.1875	11-16	.6875
13/64	.2031	45/64	.7031
7/32	.2188	23/32	.7188
15/64	.2344	47/64	.7344
1-4	.2500	3-4	.7500
17/64	.2656	49/64	.7656
9/32	.2813	25/32	.7813
19/64	.2969	51/64	.7969
5-16	.3125	13-16	.8125
21/64	.3281	53/64	.8281
11/32	.3438	27/32	.8438
23/64	.3594	55/64	.8594
3-8	.3750	7-8	.8750
25/64	.3906	57/64	.8906
13/32	.4063	29/32	.9063
27/64	.4219	59/64	.9219
7-16	.4375	15-16	.9375
29/64	.4531	61/64	.9531
15/32	.4688	31/32	.9688
31/64	.4844	63/64	.9844
1-2	.5000	1	1.

TABLE II

RULES RELATIVE TO THE CIRCLE

To Find Circumference:
    Multiply diameter by   3.1416
    or divide diameter by   0.3183

To Find Diameter:
    Multiply circumference by   0.3813
    or divide circumference by   3.14156

To Find Radius:
    Multiply circumference by   0.15915
    or divide circumference by   6.28318

To Find Side of an Inscribed Square:
    Multiply diameter by   0.7071
    or multiply circumference by   0.2251
    or divide circumference by   4.44218

To Find Side of an Equal Square:
    Multiply diameter by   0.8862
    or divide diameter by   1.284
    or multiply circumference by   0.2821
    or divide circumference by   3.545

To Find the Area of a Circle:
    Multiply circumference by one-quarter of the diameter,
    or multiply the square of diameter by   0.7854
    or multiply the square of circumference by   0.07958
    or multiply the square of ½ diameter   3.1416

To Find the Surface of a Sphere or Globe:
    Multiply the diameter by the circumference,
    or multiply the square of diameter by   3.1416
    or multiply four times the square of radius by   3.1416

To Find the Weight of Brass and Copper Sheets, Rods and Bars:
    Ascertain the number of cubic inches in piece and
    multiply same by weight per cubic inch—
        Copper   0.3212
        Brass   0.2972
    Or multiply the length by the breadth (in feet) and
    product by weight in pounds per square foot

TABLE II
CIRCUMFERENCES OF CIRCLES
In Inches

Diameter	Circumference	Diameter	Circumference
¼	.7854	18	56.54
½	1.570	18½	58.11
¾	2.356	19	59.69
1	3.141	19½	61.26
1½	4.712	20	62.83
2	6.283	20½	64.40
2½	7.854	21	65.97
3	9.424	21½	67.54
3½	10.99	22	69.11
4	12.56	22½	70.68
4½	11.13	23	72.25
5	15.70	23½	73.82
5½	17.27	24	75.39
6	18.81	24½	76.96
6½	20.42	25	78.54
7	21.99	25½	80.10
7½	23.56	26	81.68
8	25.13	26½	83.25
8½	26.70	27	84.82
9	28.27	27½	86.39
9½	29.84	28	87.96
10	31.41	28½	89.53
10½	32.98	29	91.10
11	34.55	29½	92.67
11½	36.12	30	94.24
12	37.69	30½	95.81
12½	39.27	31	97.38
13	40.84	31½	98.96
13½	42.41	32	100.5
14	43.98	32½	102.1
14½	45.55	33	103.6
15	47.12	33½	105.2
15½	48.69	34	106.8
16	50.26	34½	108.3
16½	51.83	35	109.9
17	53.40	35½	111.5
17½	54.97	36	113.0

TABLE IV
WEIGHT OF ROUND AND SQUARE MILD STEEL
Per Lineal Foot

Size	Pounds per Lineal Foot	
	Round	Square
3/16	0.094	0.120
1/4	0.167	0.213
5/16	0.261	0.332
3/8	0.375	0.478
7/16	0.511	0.651
1/2	0.668	0.850
9/16	0.845	1.08
5/8	1.040	1.330
3/4	1.500	1.910
7/8	2.040	2.600
1	2.670	3.400
1 1/8	3.380	4.300
1 1/4	4.170	5.310
1 3/8	5.050	6.39
1 1/2	6.010	7.650
1 5/8	7.050	8.93
1 3/4	8.180	10.410
1 7/8	9.390	11.88
2	10.680	13.600

TABLE V
WEIGHT OF FLAT MILD STEEL
Per Lineal Foot

Width in Inches	1/4	5/16	3/8	7/16	1/2	5/8	3/4	7/8	1
	Weight								
1/2	.425	.53	.638	.742	.850	1.062	1.275	1.488	1.700
5/8	.531	.66	.797	.924	1.056	1.320	1.593	1.855	2.124
3/4	.638	.797	.956	1.113	1.280	1.600	1.914	2.233	2.560
7/8	.744	.929	1.120	1.302	1.490	1.862	2.232	2.601	2.980
1	.850	1.060	1.280	1.490	1.700	2.130	2.550	2.975	3.400
1 1/8	.956	1.195	1.430	1.670	1.910	2.380	2.860	3.330	3.820
1 1/4	1.060	1.330	1.590	1.860	2.130	2.660	3.190	3.570	4.250
1 3/8	1.170	1.460	1.750	2.040	2.340	2.925	3.510	3.910	4.680
1 1/2	1.280	1.590	1.910	2.230	2.550	3.190	3.830	4.480	5.100
1 3/4	1.490	1.860	2.230	2.600	2.980	3.720	4.460	5.215	5.950
2	1.700	2.130	2.550	2.980	3.400	4.250	5.100	5.950	6.800

TABLE VI
SIZES OF WIRE
In Fractions of an Inch

No.	Inch	No.	Inch
000 is equal to 3/8		6 is equal to 3/16	
00 is equal to 11/32		8 is equal to 5/32	
0 is equal to 5/16		11 is equal to 1/8	
1 is equal to 9/32		12 is equal to 1/7	
3 is equal to 1/4		14 is equal to 3/32	
4 1/2 is equal to 7/32		16 is equal to 1/16	

GLOSSARY OF METAL WORKING

CONTENTS

	Page
Abrasive ...... Base Metal	1
Bastard ...... Brass	2
Brass Bound ...... Cadmium	3
Calipers ...... Cobolt	4
Cold Chisel ...... Drift	5
Drill Bit ...... Fish Plate	6
Flaring ...... Gunmetal	7
Hacksaw ...... Hollowing Hammer	8
Iron ...... Malleable	9
Mallet ...... Ore	10
Oxidation or Oxidization ...... Post vise	11
Pumice ...... Rust	12
Safe Edge ...... Smooth cut	13
Snap head ...... Steel sheet	14
Stock ...... Tinner's or Tinman's Solder	15
Tinning ...... Wing nut	16
Wiped joint ...... Zinc Chloride	17
Properties of Metals	18
Properties of Alloys	18
Soldering Fluxes	19
Composition of Some Alloys	19

GLOSSARY OF METAL WORKING

A

ABRASIVE
A natural or artificial substance used for grinding, polishing, buffing, lapping or sandblasting. Commonly includes garnet, emery, corundum, diamond, aluminum oxide and silicon carbide.

ACID PICKLE
Diluted acid used for cleaning metal.

AGE HARDEN
The capacity of some metals to get harder as they get older.

ALLOY
A substance having metallic qualities, composed of one or more chemical elements, at least one of which is a metallic element.

ALUMINUM
Lightweight soft white-colored metal, usually alloyed with other metals to increase its hardness and other qualities.

ANGLE IRON
Mild steel. Bars with 90 degree cross-section.

ANNEALING
Treating metal to make it as soft as possible (usually by heating and cooling slowly). The necessary technique varies between metals and alloys.

ANODIZING
Chemical surface treatment for protection and decoration of aluminum and its alloys.

ANTIQUEING
Darkening copper or brass by chemical treatment.

ASBESTOS
Fibrous silicate mineral that is incombustible.

ASH
Springy hard wood used for hammer and mallet handles.

B

BALL PEIN
Hemispherical end of a hammer head.

BASE METAL
At one time, the name for common metals. They are contrast to the "noble" metals which are valuable.

BASTARD
A grade of fairly coarse file.

BEAK OR BICK
Round conical end of an anvil or stake. Also horn.

BELL MOUTH
Spread end of tube.

BICK IRON
Light anvil for sheet metalwork.

BIT
Jaws of tongs. A drill.

BLIND RIVETING
Using tubular rivets on a mandrel with a device for closing each rivet from one side of the metal.

BLOCKING HAMMER
A hammer with two large flat faces.

BLOWLAMP
A torch burning gas, kerosene or other fuel to produce a flame in the form of a jet.

BOLSTER
Block with hole to support work being punched.

BOLT
Screw fastening with a head to take a nut. Only threaded part of its length. If it is threaded fully to its head, it is a metal-threaded screw.

BORAX
Flux for hard soldering and brazing.

BOSS
Center part of a wheel. A locally raised part of sheet metal. The punch used to raise it.

BOSSING MALLET
Wooden mallet with an egg-shaped head for shaping sheet metal.

BOUGE
Knock out dents in raised work over a stake.

BRAKE
Mechanical device for folding sheet metal.

BRASS
An alloy consisting mainly of copper and zinc to which small amounts of other metals may be added. Common brass is yellow.

BRASS-BOUND
　Strengthened with brass straps. Particularly a wooden box or chest.

BRASS SCRIBER
　Pointed brass rod used to mark tinplate.

BRASS TONGS
　Tongs for dipping non-ferrous metals in acid pickles.

BRAZING
　Joining by melting spelter or hard solder.

BRAZING HEARTH
　Trough to hold coke or asbestos and support work while it is brazed.

BRONZE
　Copper alloy with tin and other metals.

BRONZE AGE
　Early period after the Stone Age when primitive man made tools and implements from an early form of copper alloy.

BUFF
　To polish the surface of metal with a powered buffing wheel.

BUFFING WHEEL
　Fabric disks held together, usually by sewing, forming a wheel to be rotated at high speed and used for polishing. Also called a polishing mop.

BURIN
　An engraving tool.

BURNISHER
　Hard steel rubbing tool. Shaping tool used in metal spinning.

BURR
　Turned over edge. Small rotary file.

BUTTERFLY NUT
　A nut to fit on a bolt with projections for hand tightening. Also a wing nut.

BUTT STRAP
　Riveted strip over meeting edges. Also a fish plate.

C

CADMIUM
　Metal used for plating steel to protect it from corrosion.

CALIPERS
Tool with hinged curved jaws for checking thickness and diameters.

CANISTER STAKE
Cylindrical stake with a flat end.

CARBIDE TIP
A very hard tip to make a cutting edge bonded to tool steel, using carbide, which is a compound of carbon with one or more metallic elements.

CARBON
Element added to iron to make steel.

CARRIAGE BOLT
Bolt with a shallow domed head and square neck to prevent it from turning in wood.

CARRIAGE SCREW
A large wood screw with a head to take to wrench.

CASTING
Melting metal and pouring it into molds.

CENTER PUNCH
Pointed punch to make a dot in metal.

CENTIGRADE or CELSIUS
Temperature scale with the freezing point of water 0 degrees and the boiling point 100 degrees.

CHALK LINE
Fine cord that is used with chalk to strike a line.

CHATTER MARKS
Ridges produced by vibration during filing or other work.

CHISEL
An end-cutting tool for wood or metal.

CHROMIUM
Metal that can be alloyed with steel or used for plating.

CHUCK
A holding device for a drill or a lathe. A former for metal spinning.

CIRCUMFERENCE
Distance around a circle or other rounded shape. A similar distance around an angular shape is a perimeter.

COBOLT
Rare metal which can be added to steel to increase its magnetic properties.

COLD CHISEL
   A tool that is hammered for cutting cold metal.

CORROSION
   Oxidization of the surface of metal such as rust on iron.

CORRUGATED IRON
   Sheet iron or steel ridged and grooved regularly across its width. It is usually protected by galvanizing.

COPPER
   Red colored non-ferrous metal.

COUNTERSINK
   Bevelled edge of hole. The tool for doing this.

CREASING HAMMER
   A hammer with two narrow cross peins.

CREASING IRON
   Stake with grooves across.

CROCUS
   Fine polishing powder.

CURVE ALLOWANCE
   Size correction at a bend due to measuring around the neutral axis.

D

DEVELOPMENT
   Outline of the shape while metal is flat that will give the desired shape after bending.

DIAMETER
   Distance across a circle.

DIE
   Tool for cutting a screw thread on a rod. A form into which metal is pressed for shaping.

DIVIDERS
   Hinged pair of points for scratching a circle or comparing distances

DRAW FILLING
   Using a file sideways along an edge to remove cross file marks.

DRAWING
   Pulling metal through holes to form wire.

DRIFT
   Punch used to draw holes into line.

DRILL BIT
Tool for making a hole by cutting (as distinct from punching).

DRILL PRESS
A machine which uses drill bits to make holes.

E

ELEMENT
Any of about 100 substances that cannot be revolved by chemical means into simpler substances.

EMBOSS
Raise sheet metal, with a hammer, punch or boss from the reverse side.

EMERY
Grit used as abrasive on metal.

ESCUTCHEON
Key hole or the plate around it.

ETCHING
Eating into metal with acid to produce a design, usually a name.

EXCRUDING
Forcing metal through a die to form rods of special section.

EYE BOLT
Bolt with flattened or shaped end with a hole through.

F

FAHRENHEIT
Common temperature scale.

FERROUS
Alloy containing iron.

FERRULE
A tube or cap on a wooden handle to prevent it from splitting.

FILE
Tool with teeth made with grooves cut across it.

FILE CARD
Wire brush for cleaning files.

FISH PLATE
Alternative name for butt strap.

FLARING
Spreading the end of a tube. Giving it a bell mouth.

FLANGE
Folded edge.

FLASH
The movement of solder as it melts around a joint. Excess solder to be removed.

FLUX
Liquid or powder used to help a metal or an alloy to flow in welding, brazing or soldering.

FOCUS
Plural is foci. Point about which a curved shape is generated, The center of a circle is its focus. An ellipse has two foci.

FOLDING BARS
Parallel bars used for bending sheet metal.

G

GALVANIZED IRON
Iron coated with zinc as a protection against rust.

GAUGE
Size, particularly the thickness of sheets or the diameter of wires, according to a recognized scale. The tool for measuring this.

GILDING
Coating with gold leaf.

GILDING METAL
Alloy of copper and zinc with a greater proportion of copper than in brass.

GOLD
One of the rare or noble metals.

GRAVER
Cutting tool with a diamond-shaped cutting point.

GROOVING STAKE
Alternative name for a creasing iron.

GUILLOTINE
Large mechanical shearing machine.

GUNMETAL
Alloy of copper and tin.

H

HACKSAW
Metal-cutting handsaw with its blade tensioned in a frame.

HALF-MOON STAKE
A hatchet stake with a curved edge.

HARD SOLDER
Copper/zinc alloy with other metals added to lower its melting point.

HATCHET SOLDERING IRON
An iron with a copper bit at an angle to the shaft and a straight thin edge.

HATCHET STAKE
Stake with straight sharp edge for bending sheet metal across its top.

HEARTH
Any container for coke or other solid fuel.

HEAT TREATMENT
Heating steel to alter its character. This includes annealing, hardening, tempering and normalizing. Annealing other metals by heating.

HEEL
Opposite end of anvil or bick iron to the beak.

HICKORY
Springy wood used for mallet and hammer handles.

HIDE MALLET
A mallet with a head formed from rolled leather.

HIGH CARBON STEEL
Steel with sufficient carbon to permit hardening and tempering.

HOLD UP
Support one rivet head while the other is formed.

HOLLOW GROUND
A concave bevel on a cutting edge.

HONING
Sharpening or smoothing with a fine abrasive stone.

HORN
Alternative name for beak of anvil or bick iron.

HOLLOWING HAMMER
A hammer with two ball peins.

I

IRON
Silver-white common metal which can be alloyed with carbon to make steel.

IRON AGE
A prehistoric age when man first learned how to make tools and weapons from iron.

J

JAWS
Gripping surfaces of tongs or vise.

JENNY
Hand-operated machine for flanging and wiring sheet metal edges.

K

KILLED SPIRITS
Zinc chloride used as flux when soldering.

L

LEAD
Heavy and soft grey metal. The amount a nut moves forward in one revolution on a threaded rod.

LEG VISE
A strong vise attached to a bench, but with a leg extending to the floor.

LOW CARBON STEEL
Steel that does not contain the proper amount of carbon to permit tempering. Also called mild steel.

M

MACHINIST'S VISE
Vise with a parallel action to mount on a bench.

MAGNESIUM
Very light and combustible metal.

MALACCA
Species of cane used for mallot handles.

MALL OR MAUL
Large two-handed mallet.

MALLEABLE
Capable of being shaped.

MALLET
Type of hammer with wood, rawhide or plastic head.

MANDREL OR MANDRIL
Iron block on which parts are shaped. Particularly a round cone for shaping rings.

MEAN
Average or center. A mean line is the center of the thickness of bent sheet metal.

MILD STEEL
Low-carbon steel which cannot be tempered.

METALLURGY
The science and technology of metals.

MICROMETER
Instrument for making fine measurements using the rotation of a screw.

MUSHROOM STAKE
A round-topped steel anvil.

N

NEUTRAL AXIS
The mean line in the thickness of metal that is neither stretched nor compressed when it is bent.

NIBBLER
Shearing tool that removes particles along a line.

NICKEL
Metal alloyed with steel and used for plating.

NOBLE METALS
At one time the name for valuable metals in contrast with the "base" metals.

NON-FERROUS
Alloy that does not contain iron.

NORMALIZE
Reduce internal stresses after working by heating and allowing to cool slowly in the same way as annealing steel.

O

OFFSET
Double bend to alter alignment of a bar or sheet.

ORE
Solid naturally occurring mineral aggregate from which metal is extracted.

OXIDATION OR OXIDIZATION
    The effect of air on the surface of metal.

P

PATINA
    Colored oxidation on metal surfaces due to long exposure to air particularly on bronze. It can be simulated by chemical action.

PEEN, PEIN or PANE
    The shaped end of a hammer head.

PEENING
    Hollowing with ball peen hammer.

PERIMETER
    Distance around an angular outline. A similar measurement around a curve is a circumference.

PICKLE
    Dilute acid for cleaning metals.

PIERCING
    Cutting internal fretted shapes in sheet metal with a fine saw in a frame.

PITCH
    Composition for supporting repousse work. Distance between holes or the tops of a screw thread.

PLANISHING
    Hammering all over to harden and decorate.

PLANISHING HAMMER
    A hammer with highly polished flat or domed faces.

PLATE
    Alternative name for sheet metal. Usually of the thickert types.

PLATINUM
    Rare and valuable metal used especially in jewelry.

PLIERS
    Small gripping tool with tongs action.

POP RIVETING
    Alternative name for blind riveting.

POST VISE
    Alternative name for a leg vise.

PUMICE
    Volcanic powder used as a fine abrasive.

PUNCH
    Tool intended to be hit with a hammer to make a dent or hole.

Q

QUENCH
    To cool hot metal quickly in a liquid.

R

RADIUS
    Distance from the center to the circumference of a circle.

RAISING
    Making a deep bowl shape by hammering over a stake.

RAISING HAMMER
    A hammer with two cross peins.

RASP
    A coarse file type of tool with teeth individually raised.

RAKE
    Cutting angle of a drill or other tool.

REPOUSSÉ
    Method of raising a pattern from the back of thin metal.

REPOUSSÉ HAMMER
    Light hammer with broad-faced pein.

ROLLING
    Squeezing metal between rollers to form sheets.

ROUGE
    Fine polishing powder.

ROUT
    Cut grooves or hollows.

RULE
    Measuring tool. Not "ruler."

RUST
    Corrosion on iron steel.

S

SAFE EDGE
One edge of a file without teeth. Turned-in edge of sheet metal,

SAND BAG
Leather bag containing sand on which hollowing is done.

SATE
Alternative name for a sett. Used to flatten metal.

SCALLOP
An evenly waved edge.

SCREW
A fastening to take a nut that threaded to the head. If it is only threaded part way, it is a bolt. A screw can cut its own thread in wood or sheet metal.

SCOTS SHEARS
Large snips.

SCRIBE OR SCRIBER
Hard sharp steel point for scratching metal.

SECOND CUT
The grade of file commonly used on edges of sheet metal.

SELF-TAPPING SCREW
Hardened steel screw that cuts its thread in sheet metal.

SET
A hammer-like head on a wooden handle that is hit with a hammer to shape metal.

SET SCREW
Screw used to draw parts together.

SHANK
The neck or part of a tool between the handle and the blade.

SHEAR
Large snips that are often bench mounted with a lever handle.

SILVER SOLDER
Copper/zinc alloy with a small amount of silver included to lower its melting point.

SLEDGE
A large two-handed hammer.

SMOOTH CUT
The finest grade file normally used.

SNAP HEAD
Raised round head on a rivet.

SNIPS
Scissor action shears for cutting sheet metal.

SOFT SOLDER
Low melting point solder. A lead/tin alloy.

SOLDER
Alloy used to fuse into joints. The action of soldering.

SOLDERING IRON
Tool with copper bit that is heated to melt solder.

SPATULA
Iron rod with flattened end that is used to place flux and spelter in brazing or for hard soldering.

SPELTER
Form of brass used in brazing.

SPINNING
Shaping sheet metal in a lathe.

SPRING STEEL
High carbon steel that is similar to tool steel.

SQUARE
As a setting out term, this means at right angles.

STAINLESS STEEL
Steel alloyed with other metals to resist corrosion.

STAKE
Shaped block used as an anvil in sheet metalwork.

STAKE VISE
Alternative name for leg vise.

STEEL
Alloy of iron and carbon.

STEEL PLATE
Steel rolled into sheets more than about three-sixteenths of an inch thick.

STEEL SHEET
Steel rolled thinner than steel plate.

STOCK
Supply of metal. The body of a tool. One head of a lathe.

STRIKE A LINE
Draw a line using a chalked cord.

STROP
Leather strap used in the final stages of tool sharpening.

SULFURIC ACID
Corrosive fluid used in cleaning metal.

SWAGE BLOCK
Large block with many hollows and holes.

SWARF
Filings and other waste removed from metal.

T

TAIL
Oppposite end of anvil or bick iron to the beak. Also heel.

TANG
Part of a tool that is driven into a handle.

TAP
Tool for cutting a screw thread in a hole.

TEMPER
Reduced full hardened steel to a lesser hardness and less brittle form for a particular use.

TEMPLATE or TEMPLET
Pattern used for marking around to transfer an outline.

THREE-SQUARE FILE
A file with a triangular cross section.

TIN
White metal used in alloys and for coating steel for protection against corrosion.

TINMAN'S or TINNER'S MALLET
Mallet with a cylindrical wood head.

TINNER
Worker in tinplate.

TINNER'S or TINMAN'S SOLDER
Lead/tin alloy. Also called soft solder.

TINNING
In soldering, coating the bit or the surfaces to be joined with soft solder,

TINPLATE
Thin sheet steel that is coated with tin.

TINSNIPS
Small shears for cutting sheet metal.

TINSMITH
Alternative name for tinner or tinman.

TORCH
Device for burning gas to produce a forced flame that can be adjusted to size.

TRACER
Narrow-ended punch used for decorative lines.

TRAMMEL HEADS
Sliding heads on a bar for use as large compasses or dividers.

TRIPOLI
A fine polishing compound.

TRUNCATED
Cut off. Usually applied to part of a cone.

V

VISE
Two-jawed device with a tightening screw. Attached to bench and used to hold metal being worked on.

VISE GRIP PLIERS
Pliers that can be locked on to the work.

VISE CLAMPS
Sheet metal covers that are placed over vise jaws.

W

WELD
Fuse two pieces of metal together with heat.

WHITING
Powder used for polishing tinplate.

WING NUT
Alternative name for butterfly nut.

WIPED JOINT
   Joint between pipes made with plumber's solder.

WIRE EDGE
   Burr on the edge of a sharpened tool.

WIRED EDGE
   Wire enclosed in a rolled sheet metal edge.

WORK HARDEN
   Hardening due to hammering or other work on non-ferrous metals.

WRENCH
   Any tool for levering or twisting. Particularly useful for turning nuts and bolts.

WROUGHT IRON
   Iron with little or no carbon. Produced by the puddling process

Z

ZINC
   Grey/white metal used mainly in alloys and for coating steel

ZINC CHLORIDE
   Chemical used as a flux for soldering.

Properties of Metals

Metal	Chemical symbol	Pounds per cubic in.	Melting Point Degrees F
Aluminum	Al	0.0924	1218
Cadmium	Cd	0.3105	610
Chromium	Cr	0.2347	2939
Cobolt	Co	0.3123	2696
Copper	Cu	0.3184	1981
Gold	Au	0.6975	1945
Iron (wrought)	Fe	0.2834	2750
Lead	Pb	0.4105	621
Magnesium	Mg	0.0628	1204
Nickel	Ni	0.3177	2646
Silver	Ag	0.3802	1761
Tin	Sn	0.2632	449
Zinc	Zn	0.2587	787

Properties of Alloys

Alloy	Composition	Pounds Per Cubic Inch	Melting Point Degrees F
Brass Or	80 copper, 20 zinc	0.3105	1846
Spelter	60 copper, 40 zinc	0.3018	1634
	50 copper, 50 zinc	0.2960	1616
Solder	20 tin, 80 lead	-	532
	40 tin, 60 lead	-	446
	40 tin, 60 lead	-	446
	50 tin, 50 lead	-	401
	60 tin, 40 lead	-	369
	70 tin, 30 lead	-	365
	90 tin, 10 lead	-	419
Steel	-	0.2816	2500

Soldering Fluxes

Prepared fluxes can be purchased, but the following are traditional fluxes for soft soldering. For hand soldering all suitable metals, use borax.

Metal Or Alloy	Flux
Aluminum	Stearin
Brass	Chloride of zinc or resin
Copper	Chloride of zinc or resin
Lead	
Tinned steel	Tallow or resin
	Chloride of zinc or resin
Galvanized steel	Hydrochloric acid
Zinc	Hydrochloric acid
Pewter	Gallipoli oil
Iron and steel	Chloride of zinc or chloride of ammonia

Composition of Some Alloys

Alloy	copper	lead	tin	zinc	Antimony
Brass	32	-	1.5	10	-
Gunmetal	80	-	10	-	-
Gilding metal	60	-	-	40	-
Bell metal	80	-	20	-	-
Spelter	50	-	-	50	-
Solder	-	60	40	-	-
Britannia metal	2	-	90	-	8
Pewter	2	2	89	-	7
Type metal		50	25	0	25

GLOSSARY OF METALLURGICAL TERMS

CONTENTS

	Page
Abrasion resistance .... Allotropy	1
Alloy .... Bar mill	2
Base .... Bloom (Slab, Billet, Sheet Bar)	3
Blooming mill .... Bung	4
Burning .... Cementite	5
Critical range .... Dezincification	6
Die .... Elektron	7
Elongation .... Fillet	8
Film test .... Froth flotation	9
Full annealing .... Green sand	10
Green sand mold .... Hydrometallurgy	11
Hypereutectoid steel .... Iron-carbon constitutional diagram	12
Isothermal quench .... Liquation	13
Liquidus .... Match	14
Matchplate .... Nitriding	15
Normalizing .... Pearlite	16
Peen .... Precipitation hardening (Age hardening, Aging)	17
Precision casting .... Riddle	18
Rimmed steel .... Secondary hardness	19
Segregation .... Sintering	20
Sintering (Powder metallurgy) .... Solution Heat Treatment	21
Space lattice .... Strip (Hot-Rolled)	22
Strip mill .... Three-high plate mill	23
Time-temperature transformation curves .... Weldability	24
Welding .... Zyglo	25
Appendix - Reference Tables	A1-11

GLOSSARY OF METALLURGICAL TERMS

ABRASION RESISTANCE resistance of a material to being worn away by friction.

ACID in metallurgical terminology, the oxide of a nonmetal.

ACID BOTTOM AND LINING the inner bottom and lining of a melting furnace composed of materials having an acid reaction in the melting process. The materials may be sand, siliceous rock, or silica bricks.

ACID PROCESS a steel-making process, either bessemer, open hearth, or electric, in which the furnace is lined with a siliceous refractory, and for which the raw materials to be used are low in phosphorus and sulfur, because those elements are not removed by this process.

ACID STEEL steel melted under a slag that has an acid reaction, and in a furnace with an acid bottom or lining.

AGE HARDENING hardening caused by a change in the physical properties of a low-carbon alloy steel at room or elevated temperatures. It is an attempt to overcome an unstable condition by restoring real equilibrium.

AGING change in properties (for example, increase in tensile strength and hardness) that occurs in certain metals at relatively low temperature after a final heat treatment (as in duralumin) or after a final cold working (as in mild steel). The method employed to bring about aging consists of exposure to a favorable temperature subsequent to (a) a relatively rapid cooling from some elevated temperature (quench aging) or (b) a limited degree of cold work (strain aging).

AIR FURNACE a form of reverberatory furnace for melting ferrous and nonferrous metals and alloys. Flame from fuel burning at one end of the hearth passes over the bath to the stack at the opposite end of the furnace.

AIR-HARDENING STEEL an alloy steel that does not require quenching from a high temperature to harden, but which is hardened by simply cooling in air from above its critical range.

ALLOTRIOMORPHIC CRYSTAL a crystal the regular growth of which has been obstructed and distorted, causing it to lack external symmetry.

ALLOTROPY occurrence of an element in two or more modifications. For example, carbon occurs in nature as the hard crystalline diamond, soft

Glossary

crystalline graphite, and amorphous coal.

ALLOY a metallic material formed by mixing (in the molten state) two or more chemical elements. It usually possesses properties different from those of the components.

ALLOY STEEL a carbon steel to which is added a definite amount of one or more elements other than carbon, in order to impart special properties to the steel so that it can be used for specific purposes.

ALPHA-BETA BRASS brass which has zinc content of between about 39 per cent and about 45.5 per cent and contains the alpha solid solution and another known as beta.

ALPHA BRASS brass that contains about 38 per cent or less of zinc and consists of a solid solution designated alpha.

ALPHA IRON a magnetic allotropic form of iron; it crystallizes in the body-centered cubic structure.

AMORPHOUS SUBSTANCES substances that exhibit no crystalline structure because the atoms of which they are composed are not arranged in the geometrical structure of a space lattice. They may be considered solid solutions which can be supercooled to any degree without occurrence of crystallization.

ANISOTROPIC SOLIDS solids that possess directional properties because their atoms are arranged in a definite geometric order.

ANNEALING a heating and cooling operation implying usually a relatively slow cooling. In annealing, the temperature of the operation and the rate of cooling depend upon the material being heat treated and the purpose of the treatment.

ARC FURNACE an electric furnace in which an electric arc between carbon or graphite electrodes and the furnace charge is used to produce the heat required to melt metals in a confined space.

ARREST POINTS the various temperatures at which pauses occur in the rise or fall of temperature when steel is heated from room temperature or cooled from the molten state.

ATOM the smallest particle of an element, and the fundamental unit from which the grain structure of a metal is formed.

ATOMIC PLANES The layers of atoms or planes along which the atoms are arranged within the crystal.

AUSTEMPERING an interrupted quenching process the purpose of which is to produce a bainitic structure.

AUSTENITE a solid solution of iron carbide in gamma iron. It is stable at temperatures above the Ac transformation and has a face-centered cubic lattice structure. In some special steels it exists at room temperature.

AUSTENITIC STEELS steels containing sufficient amounts of nickel, nickel and chromium, or manganese to retain austenite at atmospheric temperature; for example, austenitic stainless steel, and Hadfield's manganese steel.

BABBIT a term applied to white metals having a tin base.

BAINITE a structure intermediate between pearlite and martensite, which is formed when steel is cooled rapidly to about 800°F and is held at any temperature between 800°F and about 400°F for a sufficient length of time. The structure depends upon the temperature at which transformation occurs.

BANDED STRUCTURE a segregated structure of nearly parallel bands which run in the direction of working.

BAR MILL a mill consisting of one or more stands of grooved rolls for reducing blooms or billets to bars.

Glossary

BASE in metallurgical terminology, the oxide of a metal.

BARS rounds, squares, flats, hexagons, octagons, half ovals, half rounds, special sections, and small shapes. Angles, channels, tees, or zees are *bar* size when their greatest diameter is under 3 inches. Flats are classified as bars when they are 6 inches or less in width and 0.250 inch or more in thickness.

BASIC BOTTOM AND LINING the inner lining and bottom of a melting furnace composed of materials having a basic reaction in the melting process. The materials may be crushed burnt dolomite, magnesite, magnesite bricks, or basic slag.

BASIC STEEL a steel melted in a furnace with a basic bottom and lining, and under a slag that is mainly basic. The raw materials used contain appreciable amounts of phosphorus and sulfur.

BAUXITE a residual clay, consisting essentially of aluminum hydroxide. It is the most important ore of aluminum.

BAYER PURIFICATION PROCESS a process for purification of bauxite, as the first stage in production of aluminum.

BEARING METALS alloys used for that part of a bearing which is in contact with the journal; for example, bronze or white metal, used because of their low coefficient of friction when used with a steel shaft.

BED CHARGE the charge of iron placed on the coke bed in a cupola.

BED COKE coke placed in the cupola well to support the following iron and coke charges.

BENEFICIATION the washing out of free sand and free clay from an ore.

BENTONITE a widely distributed and peculiar type of clay which is considered to be the result of devitrification and chemical alteration of the glassy particles of volcanic ash or tuff. Used in the foundry to bond sand.

BESSEMER ORE an iron ore containing not more than 0.045 per cent of phosphorus.

BESSEMER PROCESS a process for making steel by blowing air through molten pig iron contained in a converter. The process depends upon rapid oxidation of silicon and carbon to secure the necessary rise in temperature.

BETA BRASS copper-zinc alloys containing 46 to 49 per cent of zinc, which consists (at room temperature) of the intermediate constituent known as beta.

BILLET an ingot or bloom that has been reduced through rolling or hammering to an approximate square ranging from $1\frac{1}{2}$ to 6 inches square, or to an approximate rectangular cross section of an equivalent area. Billets are classified as semifinished products for rerolling or forging.

BINDER material to hold the grains of sand together in molds or cores. May be cereal oil, clay, resin, pitch, and the like.

BLACK-HEART American type of malleable iron. The normal fracture shows a velvety black appearance having a mouse-gray rim.

BLAST FURNACE a brick-lined cylindrical shell supplied with air blast, usually preheated in stoves, for producing pig iron by reduction of iron ore.

BLIND RISER an internal riser that does not reach to the exterior of the mold.

BLISTER a defect in a metal produced by gas bubbles either on the surface or beneath the surface.

BLOOM (SLAB, BILLET, SHEET BAR) semifinished products of rectangular cross section with rounded corners, hot rolled from ingots. The chief differences are in cross-sectional area and in their intended use.

Glossary

BLOOMING MILL a mill that rolls ingots usually to blooms, billets, and slabs. Sometimes called a *cogging mill*, and when so called in United States, refers to a mill producing shaped blooms used as blanks for subsequent rolling of I-beams, channels, and the like.

BLOW the forcing of air through the molten pig iron contained in a converter.

BLOWHOLE a casting defect caused by trapping of gas in molten or partially molten metal.

BODY-CENTERED CUBIC SPACE LATTICE (B.C.C.) in crystals, an arrangement of atoms in which the atomic centers are disposed in space in such a way that they may be presumed to be situated at the corners and centers of a set of cubic cells.

BOND cohesive material in sand.

BOSH the combustion zone of a blast furnace. It is the tapered zone just above the hearth.

BOTT (BOD) a piece of clay or other material to stop the flow of metal from the taphole.

BOTT-STICK a stick or rod on which the bott is mounted so that it may be forced into the taphole.

BOTTOM BOARD board supporting the mold.

BOX ANNEALING softening steel by heating it, usually at a subcritical temperature, in a suitable closed metal box or pot to protect it from oxidation, employing a slow heating and cooling cycle; also called *closed annealing* or *pot annealing*.

BRASS primarily an alloy of copper and zinc, but sometimes containing also small amounts of other elements such as aluminum, iron, lead, manganese, and tin.

BRAZING a method of joining by use of an alloy of lower melting point than that of the metal to be joined. Brazing is similar to soldering except that a higher temperature is required.

BRIDGING (in a blast furnace) sticking or arching of fine ore against the walls.

BRIDGING (in a cupola furnace) material adhering to the wall that retards or prevents descent of the stock charges.

BRIDGING (in an electric furnace) formation by the upper layers of scrap of a bridge over the pool of steel.

BRINELL HARDNESS value of hardness of a metal or alloy, tested by measuring the diameter of an impression made by a ball of given diameter applied under a known load. Values are expressed in Brinell hardness numbers obtained from tables.

BRIQUETTES compact blocked formed of finely divided materials by incorporation of a binder, by pressure, or both.

BRIQUETTING the process of feeding a predetermined quantity of metal powders into hardened steel dies and pressing the powders into a *slug* or *green briquette* of the desired shape.

BRITTLENESS the tendency to fracture without appreciable deformation and under low stress.

BROACHING a machining operation in which a long cutting tool having a series of cutting teeth (broaches) of continuously changing dimensions, is forced through a roughly finished hole or over a surface to produce the desired shape or size of the article.

BRONZE primarily an alloy of copper and tin, but the name is now applied to alloys with aluminum, silicon, and some other metals.

BRUCITE a naturally occurring magnesium hydrate $Mg(OH)_2$.

BUNG a section of the removable roof of an air furnace or reverberatory furnace. Also used to indicate choking or plugging up.

Glossary

BURNING the heating of a metal to temperatures sufficiently close to the melting point to cause permanent injury. Such injury may be caused by the melting of the more fusible constituents, by the penetration of gases such as oxygen into the metal with consequent reactions, or by the segregation of elements already present in the metal.

BUSTLE PIPE in a blast furnace, the large pipe that encircles the bosh and receives the hot blast of air from the stoves in order to distribute it to the tuyeres.

BUTT the large flat round end of the rammer used in the foundry.

BUTT-RAMMING ramming the molding sand with the large round end of the molder's rammer.

BUTT WELD the welding of two abutting edges. Used in the manufacture of steel pipe, the pipe so made being called *butt-weld pipe*. Also applied to butt-welding of ends of two bars.

CALCINING the removal of chemically held water by the prolonged heating of a material at fairly high temperatures.

CAPPED STEEL a rimmed steel in which the rimming action is intentionally stopped shortly after the mold is filled.

CARBIDE a compound of carbon with a more positive element such as iron.

CARBIDE FORMER an alloying element that reacts chemically with the carbon present in a steel to form a carbide.

CARBOMETER TEST testing a steel for carbon (on a carbometer) by determining its magnetic properties. These properties bear a definite relationship to the carbon content.

CARBON STEEL a steel in which carbon is the only alloying element added to the iron to control its properties; also known as *ordinary steel*, or *straight carbon steel*, or *plain carbon steel*.

CARBURIZING adding carbon to the surface of iron-base alloys by heating the metal below its melting point in contact with carbonaceous solids, liquids, or gases.

CASE the surface layer of a steel that has been made substantially harder than the interior by a process of case hardening.

CASE HARDENING a heat treatment or combination of heat treatments by which the surface layer of steel is made harder than the interior. The processes of carburizing, nitriding, and cyaniding accomplish this result by changing the composition of the case.

CASTING the metal shape that is obtained as a result of pouring metal into a mold.

CASTING the act of pouring molten metal into a cavity and allowing it to harden so that it will assume and retain the size and shape of the cavity when cold.

CAST IRON alloys of iron containing so much carbon that, as cast, they usually are not appreciably malleable at any temperature. Usually from 1.7 to 4.5 per cent carbon is present and in most cases an important percentage of silicon.

CEMENTED or SINTERED CARBIDES powdered carbides of tungsten, tantalum, or titanium cemented into solid masses by mixing with powdered cobalt or nickel, then compressing and sintering. Used instead of high-speed steel to form cutting tips of cutting tools, and in parts subjected to heavy wear.

CEMENTITE a chemical compound of iron and carbon, also known as iron carbide (Fe_3C), which contains about 6.8 per cent carbon. It occurs as grain envelopes or as needles within a grain of hypereutectoid steel. It occurs as in a metal as it is heated from room temperature to its melting point or is cooled from the molten state to room temperature.

CRITICAL RANGE the range of temperature in which occurs the reversible change from austenite, which is stable at high temperature, to ferrite, pearlite, and cementite, which are stable at low temperature.

CRITICAL RANGE the range between the recalescence point and the decalescence point.

CRITICAL TEMPERATURE the temperature at which some change occurs in a metal or alloy during heating or cooling; for example, the temperature at which an arrest or critical point occurs on heating or cooling curves.

CROP the end or ends of a rolled or forged product containing the pipe or other defects that are cut off and discarded.

CRYOLITE (ICE STONE) sodium aluminum fluoride, a mineral found in Greenland or produced synthetically. It is used as the electrolyte and solvent in the electrolytic process of obtaining pure aluminum from alumina.

CRYSTAL a homogeneous solid of regular geometrical structure peculiar to the element, compound, or isomorphous mixture of which it is composed. Within each crystal the atoms are spaced in characteristic pattern.

CRYSTAL BOUNDARIES the surfaces of contact between adjacent crystals in a metal.

CRYSTAL NUCLEI the minute crystals the formation of which is the beginning of crystallization.

CUPOLA FURNACE a stack-type melting unit in which metal is melted in direct contact with the fuel.

CYANIDING surface hardening by carbon and nitrogen absorption of an iron-base alloy article or portion of it by heating at a suitable temperature in contact with a molten cyanide salt, followed by quenching.

DAMPING CAPACITY the ability to absorb vibration. More accurately defined as the mount of work dissipated into heat by a unit volume of material during a completely reversed cycle of unit stress.

DECALESCENCE POINT the first critical point, 1333°F, at which a change of structure occurs in steel. The steel absorbs a considerable amount of heat as the structure changes in part to the face-centered cubic form.

DECARBURIZATION removal of carbon from the surface of solid steel by the (normally oxidizing) action of media that react with carbon. The media may be gaseous, solid, or liquid.

DEFORMATION change of form under mechanical stress (see ELASTIC DEFORMATION, PERMANENT DEFORMATION).

DEGASIFIER a material employed for removing gases from metals and alloys.

DENDRITE a crystal formed during solidification of a metal, or in any other way, having many branches and a treelike pattern; also termed *pine tree* and *fir tree* crystals.

DEOXIDATION the process of elimination of oxygen from molten metal before casting by adding elements with a high oxygen affinity, which form oxides that tend to rise to the surface.

DEOXIDIZER a material used to remove oxygen or oxides from metals and alloys.

DEPRESSANT a chemical that causes a finely powdered sulfide mineral to sink through a froth, in froth flotation. The mineral so sunk is said to be depressed.

DEZINCIFICATION that corrosive action which acts on brass, removing the surface zinc, leaving the copper exposed.

Glossary

DIE a solid or split block of metal used for cold drawing.

DIE a set of metal blocks used for blanking, coining, or forging various shapes.

DIE CASTING a method of casting which makes use of external pressure to shape the molten metal.

DIFFUSION migration of atoms through a solid metallic lattice. It takes place between cores and encasements of solid-solution alloys and is the basis for heat treating many alloys.

DISSOLVED CARBON carbon in solution in either the liquid or solid state.

DOLOMITE a mixed carbonate of magnesium and calcium. Calcined dolomite is used as a basic refractory for withstanding high temperatures and attack by basic slag in metallurgical furnaces.

DOUBLE BELL AND HOPPER a contrivance located in the furnace top of a blast furnace to prevent the escape of gas during the charging of the furnace. It also permits even distribution of the charge into the stack.

DOWNCOMER the pipe attached to the top of the stack of the blast furnace which conducts the hot gases to the auxiliary units.

DRAFT taper allowed on the vertical faces of a pattern to permit removal from the sand mold without excessive rapping and tearing of the mold walls.

DRAG the lower or bottom section of a mold or pattern.

DRAWING TEMPER or **DRAWING BACK** the operation of tempering hardened steel by heating it to some specific temperature and quenching in order to obtain some definite degree of hardness.

DRIFT a level or tunnel pushed forward underground in a metal mine, for purposes of exploration or exploitation.

DROP FORGING the process of shaping metal parts by forging between two dies, one fixed to the hammer and the other to the anvil of a steam or mechanical hammer. It is used for mass production of such parts as connecting rods, crankshafts, and similar articles.

DROSS similar to slag but consisting of metallic oxides that rise to the surface in metallurgical oxidation processes.

DRY SAND MOLD a mold made of prepared molding sand dried thoroughly before being filled with molten metal.

DUCTILITY the property permitting permanent deformation by stress in tension without rupture.

DUPLEX STEEL a steel which is refined in two stages. In one method the steel is first refined partially in a bessemer converter before final refinement in an open-hearth furnace. In another method the steel is refined partially in either the bessemer converter or open-hearth furnace before final refinement in an arc furnace.

DUST CATCHER a cylindrical chamber, part of the auxiliary apparatus of the blast furnace, in which the direction of flow of the gases of combustion and of decomposition is reversed suddenly, causing some of the dust to settle on the bottom.

ELASTIC DEFORMATION deformation which is removed with removal of load, permitting the body to revert to its original form.

ELASTIC LIMIT the limit of an applied stress, which, if exceeded will cause permanent deformation. For commercial purposes elastic limit is considered as yield strength.

ELECTRIC FURNACE STEEL steel produced in electrically heated furnaces of arc, induction, or resistance type.

ELECTRON a negatively charged particle that revolves about the heavy positive nucleus of an atom.

ELEKTRON the trade name for magnesium alloys in Europe.

Glossary

ELONGATION the amount of permanent extension in the vicinity of the fracture in the tension test; usually expressed as a percentage of the original gage length, such as 25 per cent in 2 inches. It may also refer to the amount of extension at any stage in any process which continuously elongates a body, as in rolling.

ENDOTHERMIC REACTION a chemical reaction accompanied by the absorption of heat.

ENDURANCE LIMIT a limiting stress, below which metal will withstand without fracture an indefinitely large number of cycles of stress. Above this limit failure occurs by the generation and growth of cracks until fracture results in the remaining section.

ENERGIZER a chemical mixed with charcoal to increase the speed with which steel will absorb carbon in the carburizing process.

EQUILIBRIUM DIAGRAM (CONSTITUTIONAL DIAGRAM) a curve that shows all relationships between composition and temperature of the various constituents in an alloy when that alloy is in equilibrium, its most stable and permanent condition.

ETCHING the process of revealing the structure of metals and alloys by attacking a highly polished surface with a reagent that has a differential effect on different crystals or different constituents.

EUTECTIC ALLOY the composition in an alloy system at which two descending liquidus curves in a binary system intersect at a point. Such an alloy has thus a lower melting point than neighboring compositions.

EUTECTOID a solid solution of any series which cools without change to its temperature of final composition.

EUTECTOID STEEL a steel of the eutectoid composition. Composition S on the iron-carbon diagram. This composition in pure iron-carbon alloys is 0.83 per cent carbon, but variations from this composition are found in commercial (impure) steels, and particularly in alloy steels in which the eutectoid composition is usually lower.

EXOTHERMIC REACTION a chemical reaction accompanied by evolution of heat.

EXTRUSION a method of shaping solid metal by forcing it through a die.

FACE-CENTERED CUBIC STRUCTURE an arrangement of atoms in crystals in which the atomic centers are disposed in space in such a way that they may be supposed to be situated at the corners and the middle of the faces of a set of cubic cells.

FACING refractory material applied to the face of a mold.

FATIGUE the phenomenon of progressive fracture of metal by a crack that spreads under repeated cycles of stress.

FERRITE nearly pure iron which contains less than 0.05 per cent of carbon and minor amounts of other elements. In its exact meaning, a solid solution of any element in alpha iron.

FERROMANGANESE an alloy of iron and manganese consisting of 80 per cent manganese, 12 per cent iron, $6\frac{1}{2}$ per cent carbon, $1\frac{1}{2}$ per cent silicon, which is added to the ladle to deoxidize steel and to increase the content of manganese and carbon in the steel.

FIBER a characteristic of wrought metal manifested by a fibrous or woody appearance of fractures and indicating directional properties. Fiber is caused principally by extension in the direction of working of the constituents of the metal, both metallic and non-metallic.

FILLET an arc connecting two surfaces converging at less than 180 degrees.

Glossary

FILM TEST the time required for a spoonful of metal to skin over.

FIN a thin piece of metal projecting from a casting at the parting line or at the junction of cores, or of cores and mold, etc.

FINE GRAIN the grain obtained when simultaneous crystallization occurs on many nuclei during solidification.

FINE GRAIN STEELS steels which resist grain growth over a considerable temperature range, when held at temperature for a reasonable length of time as is customary in heat treatment of steel.

FINISH. See machine finish allowance.

FIRE REFINING subjecting a liquid melt to slow, limited oxidation so that the impurities are oxidized but only a minimum of the metal oxidizes.

FLAME HARDENING a surface hardening method in which a highly concentrated oxyacetylene flame is passed rapidly over the portions of the pieces of work which are to be hardened. The flame is followed immediately by a jet of water or an air blast to quench the heated surface layer.

FLASH a protrusion or overfill of excess metal in the form of a fin, usually occurring on forgings made in dies and sometimes on semifinished rolled products. It is the result of excess metal forcing out at the parting of dies and rolls.

FLASK a wooden or metal frame in which a mold is made.

FLOTATION an ore concentration process in which air is blown into a mixture of ore pulp, water, oil, and various chemicals. The oil forms a film on the mineral particles and air bubbles adhere to this. Thus the mineral particles are floated while other matter sinks.

FLUORESCENCE the unique property of emitting light during activation by ultraviolet light.

FLUORSPAR commercial grade of calcium fluoride.

FLUSH SLAG see runoff slag.

FLUX a material added to a charge to react with the gangue and to reduce its melting point to such a value that the entire charge melts and produces a slag sufficiently fluid to be handled readily.

FLUX a material which dissolves oxides that form on the surface of a metal being heated preparatory to soldering, brazing, galvanizing, etc., thus affording increased contact of the metals. The surfaces being joined must be wet by it.

FOLLOW BOARD board shaped to fit the pattern and form the joint.

FOREHEARTH a reservoir, connected to the cupola by a short spout, which holds a supply of the molten metal.

FORGING a mechanical method for hot working steel into specific shapes or parts. It may be accomplished by forcing plastic metal to flow in dies and conform to the shape of the impressions which have been sunk in the dies.

FORGING STEELS steels that contain between 0.3 per cent and 0.6 per cent carbon, and which may be heat treated to increase hardness and strength.

FRACTURE TEST a test for carbon in which a specimen of metal is drawn off, cooled rapidly in water, and broken with a sledge hammer. The appearance of the metal exposed in the fracture permits a fairly accurate estimate of carbon content or the presence of internal defects.

FRANKLINITE a zinc ore, practically free of sulfur, which is mined in Franklin, New Jersey.

FREE FERRITE ferrite in steel or cast iron other than that associated with cementite in pearlite.

FROTH FLOTATION separating of finely crushed minerals from one another

Glossary

by causing some to float and others to sink in a froth. Oils and various chemicals are used to activate, make floatable, or to depress the minerals.

FULL ANNEALING heating iron-base alloys above the critical temperature range, holding the alloy above that range for a proper period of time and then slowly cooling it to below the range either in the furnace or in some thermal insulating material.

GAGGER (JAGGER) an L-shaped rod used for reinforcing sand in the cope mold.

GALVANIZING a process used to coat iron or steel with zinc.

GAMMA IRON one of the allotropic forms of iron which crystallizes in the face-centered cubic lattice form. Its range of stability when pure is 2552 to 1670°F. It dissolves carbon up to 1.7 per cent. Its range of stability is lowered by carbon, nickel, and manganese, and it is the basis of the solid solution known as austenite.

GANGUE a claylike mixture of oxides of aluminum and silicon, found as an impurity in iron ore.

GAS CARBURIZING a method of carburizing carried out in an atmosphere of carburizing gases, including carbon monoxide and such hydrocarbons as butane, ethane, methane, and propane.

GATE specifically, the point where molten metal enters the casting cavity. Sometimes employed as a general term to indicate the entire assembly of connected columns and channels carrying the metal from the top of the mold to that forming the casting cavity proper. Term also applied to the pattern parts which form the passages, or to the metal that fills them.

GATE CUTTER a U-shaped piece of thin metal used to cut a shallow trough in a mold which will serve as a passage for the hot metal.

GATED PATTERNS one or more patterns with gating systems attached. They are so assembled that they can be molded at one time.

GRAINS crystals in metals.

GRAIN BOUNDARY a layer only a few atoms thick which constitutes the zone of contact between adjacent grains having differently oriented space lattices.

GRAIN GROWTH an increase in the average grain size resulting from some crystals absorbing adjacent ones when the metal is raised to a temperature above that necessary for recrystallization and kept at that temperature for a sufficient length of time.

GRAIN SIZE this is usually defined as the average diameter of the grains or by the number of grains per unit area in any cross section under examination. In steel, grain size affects the critical rate of cooling; in alloys, the ductility.

GRANULAR PEARLITE (GLOBULAR and DIVORCED PEARLITE) a structure formed from ordinary lamellar pearlite by long annealing of steel or at a temperature below but near to the lower critical point, causing the cementite to spheroidize in a ferrite matrix.

GRAPHITIZATION decomposition of carbide to give free carbon as graphite or as temper carbon.

GRAVITY CASTING a casting process in which the metal flows into the mold by gravity.

GRAY CAST IRON cast irons which as cast have combined or cemetitic carbon not in excess of a eutectoid percentage—the balance of the carbon occurring as graphite flakes. The term *gray iron* is derived from the characteristic gray fracture of this metal.

GREEN SAND prepared molding sand in the moist or *as-mixed* condition.

Glossary

It is sand in its natural condition that contains just enough clay and water to hold it together.

GREEN SAND MOLD a mold made from moist refractory sand that is not dried before use.

GUIDE the strip or other suitable device used to locate the cope in the proper place on the drag.

GYRATORY CRUSHER a device which has a fixed crushing surface in the form of a frustrum of an inverted cone, within which is a moving crushing surface in the form of a frustrum of an erect cone. The ore is crushed in the downward converging annular space between the two crushing surfaces.

H-STEELS steels made under specifications that include hardenability tolerances.

HALL-HÉROULT PROCESS an electrolytic process in which alumina is dissolved in cryolite and then reduced to metallic aluminum by means of electricity.

HARDENABILITY the depth to which steel can be hardened to martensite under stated conditions of cooling.

HARDNESS resistance to plastic deformation by penetration, scratching or bending.

HEARTH in the blast furnace, the zone or basin at the bottom of the furnace into which molten pig iron and slag trickle and are stored until tapped off.

In other furnaces, the basin which holds the charge during the refining period.

HEAT-RESISTANT STEEL steel that resists scaling (oxidation) and creep when heated to a high temperature.

HEAT TREATMENT an operation or combination of operations involving the heating and cooling of a metal or an alloy in the solid state for the purpose of obtaining desirable conditions or properties. Heating and cooling for the sole purpose of mechanical working are excluded from the meaning of this definition.

HEMATITE the iron ore mined in greatest quantity in the United States; it is essentially ferric oxide.

HETEROGENEOUS FIELD or STRUCTURE the field between the liquidus and solidus curves in an equilibrium diagram. In this field any alloy is partly liquid and partly solid and is said to be in the mushy state and not uniform in chemical composition.

HIGH-SPEED TOOL STEEL a hard steel used to make tools that can cut while red hot and running at high speeds. It permits fast working and deep cuts while hot.

HOMOGENIZING a heat treating process to make cast solid solution alloys uniform. It is carried out at a temperature below the melting point.

HOT COLLAR see SHRINKHEAD.

HOT JUNCTION the measuring junction or junction of the thermocouple placed at the point of measurement.

HOT ROLLING see HOT WORKING.

HOT SHORTNESS brittleness in metal when hot. Steels that are hot short have a tendency to crack and tear during rolling.

HOT TOP see SHRINKHEAD.

HOT WORKING (HOT ROLLING or HOT FORGING) work carried out at a temperature at or above the recrystallization temperature of the metal in question. During hot working the grains are constantly being deformed and broken up but new ones are constantly forming to take their place.

HYDROMETALLURGY extraction of metals by leaching with an aqueous solvent that dissolves the valuable metal without attacking the gangue and permits subsequent recovery of the dissolved metal from the solution. It is really a large-scale application

Glossary

of the process known as extraction in the chemical laboratory—the separation of a soluble substance from an insoluble one by means of a solvent.

HYPEREUTECTOID STEEL a steel containing more carbon than the eutectoid composition, which is about 0.83 per cent.

HYPOEUTECTOID STEEL a steel containing less carbon than the eutectoid composition, which is about 0.83 per cent.

IDIOMORPHIC CRYSTAL a crystal of definite external shape.

IMPACT TEST a test in which one or more blows are applied suddenly to a specimen. Results usually are expressed in terms of energy absorbed or number of blows (of a given intensity) required to break the specimen. Izod impact or charpy impact are the common methods of studying impact resistance.

INCLUSIONS nonmetallic matter in metals.

INDUCTION HARDENING a surface hardening process based upon the heating effect produced in a piece of steel by placing it in a high-frequency electric field generated in a suitably shaped water-cooled coil of copper wire or tubing.

INGOT IRON an open-hearth product low in carbon, manganese, and impurities.

INGOT MOLD a thick-walled cast-iron mold in which molten metal is cast and allowed to solidify to form an ingot.

INGOTISM a coarse dendritic structure that forms when metals solidify.

INGOTS metal castings of uniform sizes and shapes for subsequent rolling, forging, or processing.

INOCULATION a process of adding some material to molten gray cast iron in the ladle for the purpose of controlling the structure to an extent not possible by control of chemical analysis and other normal variables.

INTERGRANULAR (INTERCRYSTALLINE) FRACTURE metal fractures that follow the crystal boundaries instead of passing through the crystals, as in the usual transcrystalline fracture.

INTERMETALLIC COMPOUND a constituent of alloys that is formed when atoms of two metals combine in certain proportions to form crystals with a different structure from that of either of the metals. The proportions of the two kinds of atoms may be indicated by formulas, as for example (CuZn).

INTERNAL STRESS a residual stress that may exist between different parts of metal products as a result of the differential effects of heating, cooling, working operations, or of constitutional changes in the solid metal. It may be relieved by heating to a low temperature without affecting the mechanical properties.

INTERRUPTED QUENCH a quench that is not carried through to the temperature at which transformation of austenite into martensite commences, but is interrupted at some higher temperature, in order to suppress transformation of austenite into pearlite and at the same time avoid formation of martensite.

INTERSTITIAL SOLID SOLUTION a solid solution in which the solute (stranger) atoms occupy positions in the host lattice and by becoming part of the lattice distort it.

INVESTMENT the refractory material that completely clothes or invests the model in precision casting.

IRON-CARBON CONSTITUTIONAL DIAGRAM a constitutional diagram each point of which represents the composition of steel or cast iron that is in equilibrium and that contains only iron and carbon.

Glossary

ISOTHERMAL QUENCH an interrupted quench requiring three steps.

ISOTHERMAL TRANSFORMATION DIAGRAMS diagrams that illustrate graphically the changes that take place when steel is cooled at various rates.

ISOTROPIC a material lacking directional properties.

IZOD TEST a notched-bar or impact test in which a notched specimen held in a vise is struck on the end by a striker carried on a pendulum; the energy absorbed in fracture is obtained from the height to which the pendulum rises.

JOLTER (JOLT RAMMING or JAR RAMMING) machine for ramming sand in a flask by repeated jarring or jolting action.

JOMINY TEST a standardized procedure by which the hardenability of a steel is determined.

KILLED STEEL molten steel held in a ladle, furnace, or crucible (and usually treated with aluminum, silicon, or manganese) until no more gas is evolved and the metal is perfectly quiet. When a killed steel solidifies the top surface of the ingot freezes immediately and subsequent shrinkage produces a central pipe. The steel is sound, and free from blowholes and segregation.

KISH graphite thrown out by liquid cast iron in cooling.

LADLE a vessel lined with refractory material; used for conveying molten metal from the furnace to the mold or from one furnace to another.

LAMELLAR PEARLITE pearlite crystals covered by a thin layer of cementite.

LAMINATED STRUCTURE a structure containing alternate layers of different forms of iron, such as pearlite.

LANCE a long slender steel pipe connected to an oxygen line and pushed into the taphole to ignite the carbon and thus melt through the crust of iron which has solidified around the bottom of the hearth.

LAP WELD a term applied to a weld formed by lapping two pieces of metal and then pressing or hammering, particularly to the longitudinal joint produced by a welding process for tubes or pipe in which the edges of the skelp are beveled or scarfed so that when they are overlapped they can be welded together. The product is known as a lap-weld or lap-welded pipe.

LAW OF HORIZONTALS the law used to determine the composition of the liquid of any alloys, in the series of a constitutional diagram, at any stated temperature. It applies to any two-phase heterogeneous field.

LEACHING the extraction of a soluble metal compound from an ore by dissolving in a solvent that does not dissolve the gangue. The metal is subsequently precipitated from the solution.

LEDEBURITE the cementite-austenite eutectic forming at point C on the iron-carbon diagram. During cooling the austenite in ledeburite may transform to ferrite and cementite. It is found in cast iron and high-speed steels.

LEVER ARM PRINCIPLE a principle used to determine the amount of phase or constituent present at any stated temperature on a constitutional diagram.

LIME BOIL that period in the open-hearth process when carbon dioxide gas released from the limestone on the hearth bottom causes the bath to bubble violently.

LIMONITE hydrated ferric oxide ($2 Fe_2O_3 \cdot 3 H_2O$), an important iron ore mineral.

LIQUATION separation of a metal from dross by heating to the melting point

Glossary

of the metal. The metal is permitted to flow out while the dross is left behind.

LIQUIDUS the upper curve in a constitutional diagram which is the locus of temperatures at which each alloy starts to solidify.

LIXIVIATION identical with leaching.

LOAM a coarse, strongly bonded molding sand used for loam and dry sand molding.

LOAM MOLDING a system of molding, especially for large castings wherein the supporting structure is constructed of brick. Coatings of loam are applied to form the mold face.

LOCAL CELLS cells set up during corrosion by impurities in the metal, causing a difference in potential and therefore corrosion.

LOOSE PATTERNS patterns not attached to a frame or rigid body.

LOST WAX PROCESS a method of casting in which an expendable wax pattern is used for making the molds. See precision casting.

MACHINABILITY a property of metals that permits them to be cut, turned, broached, or otherwise formed by machine tools.

MACHINE FINISH ALLOWANCE the allowance made for machining the finished part.

MACHINING STEEL steel having a carbon content of only 0.1 or 0.2 per cent, which is used widely for carburizing purposes.

MACROETCHING OF IRON AND STEEL subjecting the metal to the action of a reagent in order to bring out the structure for visual inspection.

MACROSCOPIC visible either to the naked eye or under low magnifications (up to about 10 diameters).

MACROSTRUCTURE the structure and internal condition of metals as revealed on a ground or polished (and sometimes etched) specimen, by the naked eye or under low magnifications (up to about 10 diameters).

MAGNAFLUX TEST a magnetic test used to detect defects on or near the surface of metals.

MAGNESITE a natural magnesium carbonate used as a basic refractory in open-hearth and other high-temperature furnaces; it is resistant to attack by basic slag.

MAGNETIC PERMEABILITY the ratio of the magnetic induction of a substance to the magnetizing field to which it is subjected.

MAGNETITE an iron ore mineral which has the chemical composition Fe_3O_4.

MALLEABILITY the property of being permanently deformable mechanically by rolling, forging, extrusion, etc., without rupture and without pronounced increase in resistance to deformation (as in case of ductility). Malleability generally increases at elevated temperature.

MALLEABLE IRON a mixture of iron and carbon including smaller amounts of silicon, manganese, phosphorus, and sulfur, converted structurally by heat treatment into a matrix of ferrite containing nodules of temper carbon.

MALLEABLEIZING an annealing operation performed on white cast iron partially or wholly to transform the chemically combined carbon to temper carbon, and in some cases wholly to remove the carbon from the iron by decarburization. Temper carbon is free graphitic carbon in the form of rounded nodules composed of an aggregate of minute crystals.

MARTEMPERING an interrupted quenching process the purpose of which is to produce a fully martensitic structure.

MARTENSITE a supersaturated solid solution of carbon in ferrite.

MATCH a form of wood, plaster of Paris, sand, or other material on

Glossary

which an irregular pattern is laid while the drag is rammed.

MATCHPLATE a metal or other plate on which patterns split along the parting line are mounted back to back with the gating system to form an integral piece.

MATRIX the principal substance in which a constituent is embedded.

MATTE a solution of mixed sulfides produced in smelting sulfide ores.

MECHANICAL PROPERTIES properties of a metal determining its behavior under stress.

MECHANICAL WORKING subjecting metal to pressure exerted by rolls, presses, or hammers, to change its form, or to affect the structure and therefore the mechanical and physical properties.

METALLIZING a method used to spray zinc on large articles.

METALLOGRAPHY the branch of metallurgy which deals with the study of the structure and constitution of solid metals and alloys, and the relation of this to properties on the one hand and manufacture and treatment on the other.

METALLOID in metallurgical practice, elements such as carbon, silicon, phosphorus, sulfur, and manganese, which are commonly present in small amounts in iron and steel.

METALLURGIST a technically trained person who has specialized in that science which deals with the separation of metals from the earthy materials with which they are combined.

METALLURGY the art and science of extracting metals from their ores and other metal-bearing products and adapting these metals for human utilization.

MICROSCOPIC visible under a magnification of about 10 diameters or more.

MICROSTRUCTURE the structure and internal condition of metals as revealed in polished, and usually etched, samples when examined under a microscope magnifying 10 diameters or more.

MILL SCALE a pure oxide of iron which forms on the surface of steel as it cools and which is removed when the steel is rolled in the rolling mill.

MILLING reduction in the size of ore particles by crushing and grinding, and classification of these particles by size and specific gravity.

MINERAL an inorganic substance occurring in nature with a characteristic chemical composition, and usually possessing a definite internal atomic structure which may produce a typical external form called a crystal.

MIXER a large vessel used to store molten pig iron coming from the blast furnace until it is required in one of the steel furnaces in the same plant.

MOLD the form containing the cavity into which molten metal is poured to make a casting.

MOLD BOARD the board on which the pattern is placed when ramming the drag.

MOLD WASH usually an aqueous emulsion containing various organic or inorganic compounds or both, which is used to coat the face of a mold cavity. Materials include graphite, silica flour, etc.

MOTTLED white iron structure interspersed with spots or flecks of gray.

MOUNTED PATTERNS patterns mounted in a frame or on a plate.

NITRIDING a hardening operation during which nitrogen is added to iron-base alloys by heating the metal in contact with ammonia gas or other suitable nitrogenous material. Nitriding is conducted at a temperature usually in the range 935°F to 1000°F

Glossary

and produces surface hardening of the metal without quenching.

NORMALIZING   heating iron-base alloys to approximately 100°F above the critical temperature range, followed by cooling to below that range in still air at ordinary temperature.

NUCLEI   points at which crystals begin to grow during solidification. In general, they are minute crystal fragments formed spontaneously in the melt, but frequently nonmetallic inclusions act as nuclei.

OIL-HARDENING STEELS   alloy steels, the S-curves of which lie to the right, and which therefore can be cooled slowly either in oil or air instead of in water.

OPEN-HEARTH FURNACE   a refractory-lined, shallow-bath, rectangular furnace in which both hearth and charge are subjected to direct action of the fuel flame. The fuel may be producer gas, natural gas, coke oven gas, powdered coal or oil.

OPTICAL PYROMETER   a temperature-measuring device through which the observer sights the heated object and compares its incandescence with that of an electrically heated filament the brightness of which can be regulated.

ORE   a natural mineral deposit from which a useful, valuable metal can be extracted profitably.

ORE BOIL   that period in the open-hearth process when the iron ore and the iron oxides in the slag act on the carbon of the pig iron to form carbon monoxide gas, causing the bath to froth and rise.

ORE DRESSING   a process of mechanically eliminating a portion of the waste material present in the ore, thus increasing the metal content of the product to be sent to the smelter.

OXIDATION   in the restricted sense in which the term is used in a discussion of smelting processes, the combination of an element with oxygen to form an oxide, or the combination of an oxide with more oxygen to form a higher oxide.

PACK CARBURIZING   a method of carburizing in which the articles to be carburized are cleaned and packed loosely in a metal box with carbonaceous material or with a commercial carburizing compound.

PANCAKE TEST   a rapid method of testing the iron oxide and the basic qualities of a slag by using a small shallow spoon in which the slag forms a pancake.

PARTING LINE   the line along which a pattern is divided for molding, or along which the sections of a mold separate.

PARTING SAND   sharp or burned sand sprinkled on the joint of the mold to prevent the sand cope and drag from adhering.

PATENTING   heating iron-base alloys above the critical temperature range followed by cooling below that range in air, molten lead, or a molten mixture of nitrates and nitrites. It is really normalizing carried out at a high temperature.

PATTERN   model of wood, metal, plaster, or other material used in making a mold.

PATTERNMAKER'S SHRINKAGE   shrinkage allowance made on all patterns to compensate for the change in dimensions as the solidified casting cools in the mold from freezing temperature of the metal to room temperature. Pattern is made larger by the amount of shrinkage characteristic of the particular metal in the casting and the amount of hindered contraction to be encountered. Rules or scales are available for use.

PEARLITE   the lamellar aggregate of ferrite and carbide resulting from

Glossary

the direct transformation of austenite at A_{r_1}. It is recommended that this word be reserved for the microstructures consisting of thin plates or lamellae—that is, those that may have a pearly luster in white light. The lamellae can be very thin and resolvable only with the best microscopic equipment and technique.

PEEN small end of a molder's rammer.

PERITECTIC REACTION a reaction that occurs between a solid and liquid phase resulting in a second solid phase. A typical example is the decomposition of an intermetallic compound before it reaches its melting point.

PERMANENT DEFORMATION deformation which remains after an externally applied load is removed from a body.

PERMANENT MOLD a foundry mold, made of metal or refractory material, that is capable of producing a large number of castings identical in shape.

PERMEABILITY the property in sand molds which permits passage of gases.

PHASE a constituent that is completely homogeneous both physically and chemically, separated from the rest of the alloy by definite bounding surfaces; for example, austenite, ferrite, cementite. Not all constituents are phases, pearlite for example.

PHYSICAL PROPERTIES those properties familiarly discussed in physics, exclusive of those described under mechanical properties; for example, density, electric conductivity, coefficient of thermal expansion.

PICKLING removing oxide scale from metal objects by immersion in a diluted acid bath so as to obtain a chemically clean surface preparatory to cold rolling or wire drawing.

PIG IRON the product obtained by reduction smelting in the blast furnace.

PINHOLES very small gas cavities generally found in alloy castings which are probably caused by the evolution of occluded gases during the process of solidification. They show up during machining.

PIPE a shrinkage cavity formed in metal (especially ingots) during solidification of the last portion of liquid metal. Contraction of the metal causes this cavity or pipe.

PLAIN CARBON STEEL see CARBON STEEL.

PLASTIC DEFORMATION permanent change in the shape of a piece of metal, or in the constituent crystals, brought about by the application of mechanical force which causes the crystals to slide or glide along slip planes.

PLATES (COMMERCIAL DEFINITION) flat rolled steel.

POLING insertion of timber or green trunks of hardwood trees into the molten metal during fire refining.

POLYCRYSTALLINE an aggregate of crystal grains. Most metals are polycrystalline and therefore stronger than single crystals because of slip interference.

PORPHYRIES large bodies of low-grade ores in which the copper minerals are disseminated relatively uniformly.

POURING BASIN reservoir on top of the mold to receive molten metal.

POWDER METALLURGY the art of converting metals or alloys into powders, plus the compressing or otherwise forming of these powders into desired articles, and the heat treating of these articles to provide desired physical properties.

PRECIPITATION HARDENING (AGE HARDENING, AGING) the phenomenon which results in an increase in hardness with the passage of time at room or elevated temperature. The increase is produced by a change in structure associated with precipitation of a constituent from solid solution along the grain boundaries.

Glossary

PRECISION CASTING a casting process in which the wax pattern used is destroyed by melting and burning in order to remove it from the mold.

PRIMARY DEPOSITS the first step involved in the accumulation of iron in the earth's crust into iron formations known as *primary* deposits.

PROCESS ANNEALING same as subcritical annealing.

PROPORTIONAL LIMIT the load per unit area beyond which the increases in strain cease to be directly proportional to the increases in stress.

PULLOVER MILL a rolling mill using a single pair of rolls. The metal, after passing through the rolls, is pulled back over the top roll in order to be fed through the mill a second time.

PYROMETALLURGY a metallurgical process which uses fuel as the source of heat.

PYROMETER an instrument for determining elevated temperatures.

QUENCHING rapid cooling of steel from above the critical range by immersion in liquids or gases, or by contact with metal, in order to harden it.

RAISES short vertical shafts extended upward from different depth headings or haulways which are used as chutes for handling the mined material from the upper levels of an iron ore mine.

RAM to pack the sand in a mold.

RAMMER a hand tool for packing the sand of a mold evenly round the pattern. One edge of the rammer is wedge-shaped and is called the peen end; the other edge is flat and is called the butt end.

RECALESCENCE the phenomenon of steel becoming brighter in color, for a limited time, by the steel heating itself spontaneously as it is cooling through the critical range. This causes a retardation of the cooling, which is shown on cooling curves and can be seen by the eye in a darkened room.

RECARBURIZER any carbonaceous material, pig iron, or alloy added to molten steel to increase the carbon content.

RECRYSTALLIZATION formation of new crystals or grains from deformed metal, accomplished by suitable heat treatment.

RED SHORTNESS brittleness in steel when it is red hot.

REDUCING SLAG a slag which aids in the removal of oxygen.

REDUCTION partial or complete removal of oxygen from an oxide.

REFRACTORIES materials capable of resisting high temperatures, changes of temperature, the action of molten metals, and slags, and hot gases carrying solid particles. They are used to line furnaces.

REGENERATIVE SYSTEM a system in which the waste heat of the escaping gases is used to preheat the incoming air. The regenerator is a chamber containing hot firebrick loosely stacked and laid in a checkerboard pattern.

RETAINED AUSTENITE the austenite that remains in tool steels after quenching. It usually can be eliminated by suitable tempering.

REVERBERATORY FURNACE a furnace in which the charge is melted on a shallow hearth by flame passing over the charge and heating a low roof. Firing may be with coal, pulverized coal, oil, or gas. Much of the heating is done by radiation from the roof.

REVERSING MILL a two-high mill in which a bar is passed back and forth between the rolls by reversing the direction of rotation of the rolls.

RIDDLE hand- or power-operated device for removing large particles of sand or foreign material from foundry sand.

Glossary

RIMMED STEEL an incompletely deoxidized steel normally containing less than 0.25 per cent carbon. A rimmed steel possesses 3 fairly well defined zones in its cross section: (a) an outer wall of clean, solid metal which is lower in carbon than the inner zone; (b) an intermediate zone that contains gas pockets or blowholes that vary in size and extent and that are welded during rolling; and (c) a central zone that contains a considerable concentration of metalloids.

RISER
(a) an opening in the cope into which the metal rises when the mold is filled.
(b) that part of the casting formed in the opening.
(c) reservoir of molten metal attached to the casting to compensate for the internal contraction of the casting as it solidifies. (It also allows dirt to escape and indicates that the mold is full.)

ROASTING the operation of heating sulfide ores in air to convert to oxide.

ROCKWELL HARDNESS TEST a method of determining the hardness of metals by indenting them with a hard steel ball or a diamond cone under a specified load, measuring the depth of penetration, and subtracting the latter from an arbitrary constant. Rockwell hardness numbers are based on the difference between the depths of penetration at major and minor load; the greater this difference, the less the hardness number.

ROD MILL a mill for rolling rods from billets.

RODS wire rods are semifinished hot-rolled rounds of great length, usually coiled, and used principally for drawing to wire.

ROLLING MILLS mills in which a preheated steel ingot is passed between heavy chilled cast steel rolls.

RUNNER that portion of the gate assembly connecting the downgate or sprue with the casting.

S-CURVE same as isothermal transformation diagrams.

SAGGERS or RINGS metal pots in which castings that are to be malleableized are placed for annealing.

SALT BATH a molten bath of special chemical salts used for heating metal, for hardening or tempering. Salt baths give uniform heating and prevent oxidation.

SAND SLINGER molding machine that throws sand into a flask or core box by centrifugal action.

SCARFING (DESEAMING) removal of seams and other surface defects by cutting with the gas torch; also beveling skelp with a cutting tool.

SCLEROSCOPE an instrument for determining hardness which is measured by the drop and rebound of a diamond-tipped hammer.

SCREW-DOWN MECHANISM a device used to adjust the distance between rolls.

SEAM a crack on the surface of metal that has been closed but not welded; usually produced by blowholes which have become oxidized.

SEAMLESS TUBE a tube other than that made by bending over and welding the edges of flat strip.

SEASON CRACKING stress corrosion of brass which has been cold worked. Ammonia aids it. Low temperature annealing relieves the stresses without affecting the mechanical properties.

SECONDARY DEPOSITS iron ore deposits which passed through a process of natural concentration, thus raising their iron content in places.

SECONDARY HARDNESS a further increase in hardness developed by tempering high-alloy steel after quenching.

Glossary

SEGREGATION nonuniform distribution of impurities, inclusions, and alloying constituents in metals.

SELF-HARDENING STEEL a steel carrying sufficient carbon or alloy content to produce hardening on cooling in air, without the necessity for quenching in oil or water. The alloying elements lower and retard the normal transformation from austenite to pearlite.

SELF-LUBRICATING BEARINGS oil-soaked porous bearings in which the pores serve as reservoirs for the oil which, later, is brought to the surface by capilliary action.

SEMIDEOXIDIZED STEEL a steel which gives off but little gas during solidification in the ingot mold, thus producing steel free from surface blowholes and piping.

SEMIFINISHED STEEL blooms, billets, slabs, sheet bars, rods, and other products, for rerolling or forging.

SEMIKILLED STEEL a type of steel obtained when deoxidation is not complete.

SHEAR STRESSES (TANGENTIAL) stresses effective in a direction along the plane of application.

SHEARED PLATE MILL a mill having horizontal rolls used for rolling ingots and slabs to plates, all margins of which are irregularly formed and require shearing to produce the finished plate.

SHEET MILL a mill that ordinarily rolls sheet bar to sheets.

SHEETS
Cold-rolled: the flat products resulting from cold rolling, after pickling, of sheets previously produced by hot rolling.
Hot-rolled: the flat rolled products resulting from reducing sheet bars on a sheet mill.

SHERARDIZING the process of coating small finished parts of iron and steel, such as nuts, screws, and bolts, with a corrosion-resistant layer of zinc.

SHOCK RESISTANCE the manner in which a metal reacts when subjected to sudden shock.

SHOTTING pouring molten metal through a screen contained in a tall tower before dropping it into water or bins.

SHRINK HOLE a hole or cavity in a casting resulting from contraction and insufficient feed metal, and formed during the time the metal changed from the liquid to the solid state.

SHRINK RULE patternmaker's rule graduated to allow for metal contraction.

SHRINKAGE ALLOWANCE the compensation required in a pattern to take care of the natural shrinkage of a solidified casting as it cools in the mold.

SHRINKAGE CAVITY see SHRINK HOLE.

SHRINKHEAD or **HOT TOP** the heat-insulated reservoir for excess metal on top of an ingot mold which feeds the shrinkage of the ingot that occurs during solidification.

SHRINKHEAD CASING see HOT COLLAR.

SIEMENS-MARTIN PROCESS another name for the open-hearth process.

SILICA silicon dioxide used to manufacture refractory materials. When the latter contain more than 90 per cent silica they are known as acid refractories (for example, ganister) and are used in open-hearth and other metallurgical furnaces to resist high temperatures and attack by acid slags.

SINTERED CARBIDES see CEMENTED CARBIDES.

SINTERING the fritting together of small particles to form larger particles, cakes, or masses; in case of ores and concentrates it is accomplished by fusion of certain constituents.

Glossary

SINTERING (POWDER METALLURGY) a heating operation in which a briquette is heated until the particles bond together and until it hardens sufficiently to permit handling and, when necessary, shaping.

SKELP mill steel strip from which tubes are made by drawing through a bell at welding temperature, to produce lap-welded or butt-welded tubes.

SKIM GATE an arrangement which changes the direction of flow of molten metal in the gating system and thereby prevents passage of slag and other extraneous materials beyond that point.

SKIN the surface of a mold or casting.

SKIN-DRIED MOLD a green sand mold, the face of which is sprayed with an additional special bonding material and then dried by rapid application of localized heat to the depth of a fraction of an inch.

SKIPWAY (SKIP HOIST) a steel incline which runs to the top of the blast furnace.

SLAB an ingot reduced, generally by rolling, to a thickness better suited to the operation that follows. A slab, as distinguished from a bloom, has width at least twice its thickness and a minimum thickness of $1\frac{1}{2}$ inches. It is rerolled to plates and to sheet bar. Slabs are classified as semifinished products.

SLAG a nonmetallic covering on molten metal as the result of the combining of impurities contained in the original charge, some ash from the fuel, and any silica and clay eroded from the refactory lining. Except in bottom-pour ladles it is skimmed off prior to pouring the metal.

SLAG HOLE an opening in a furnace for the removal of slag.

SLIP a displacement of a portion of a grain with respect to another portion.

SLIP INTERFERENCE interference of crystals of a metal with each other during slip. Sometimes called work hardening.

SLIP LINES OR BANDS the fine dark lines or bands seen on a stressed metal under the microscope, that is, on crystals of metals which have been cold worked.

SLIP PLANES the particular set or sets of crystallographic planes along which slip or sliding takes place in metal and other crystals during the process of plastic deformation.

SMELTING any metallurgical operation in which the metal sought is separated in a state of fusion from the impurities with which it may be chemically combined or physically mixed.

SOAKING PIT an underground furnace in which a stripped ingot is heated or soaked in heat until it is uniformly heated throughout to its rolling temperature.

SOLDER usually an alloy of two or more metals used for joining other metals together by surface adhesion. Most common solder is an alloy of tin and lead; hard solder is composed of copper and zinc.

SOLDERING the lowest temperature method of joining metals without melting.

SOLID PATTERNS one-piece patterns, so constructed that they can be molded with a single joint.

SOLID SOLUTION an alloy in which metals remain dissolved in each other when solid.

SOLIDIFICATION RANGE the temperature range through which metal freezes or solidifies.

SOLIDUS the lower curve in a constitutional diagram which indicates the temperature at which each alloy has completed solidification.

SOLUTION HEAT TREATMENT the operation of heating suitable alloys (for

Glossary

example, duralumin) in order to take the hardening constituent into solution. This is followed by quenching to retain the solid solution, and the alloy is then age-hardened at atmospheric or elevated temperature.

SPACE LATTICE   the orderly geometric form into which atoms tend to arrange themselves during the process of crystallization.

SPALLING   cracking and flaking of small particles of metal from the surface.

SPARK ARRESTER   device over the top of a cupola to prevent emission of sparks.

SPARK TEST   classification of steels according to their chemical analysis by visual examination of the sparks thrown off when the steels are held against a high-speed grinding wheel.

SPHEROIDAL or SPHEROIDIZED CEMENTITE   a rounded or globular form of carbide resulting from a spheroidizing treatment. The initial structure may be either pearlitic or martensitic.

SPHEROIDIZING   any process of heating and cooling steel that produces a rounded or globular form of carbide.

SPIEGELEISEN   a pig iron containing 15 to 30 per cent manganese and 4.5 to 5.5 per cent carbon. It is added to steel as a deoxidizing agent and to raise the manganese content of the steel.

SPLIT PATTERN   a pattern divided at the parting line or lines to facilitate molding by eliminating coping down by the molder.

SPRUE   the channel that conveys the molten metal from the pouring basin to the runner. Also, the metal which solidifies in these channels and is found attached to the casting after the casting has solidified.

STEADITE   a hard phosphorus-rich component found in gray iron, containing 10.2 per cent phosphorus and 89.8 per cent iron.

STEEL   an alloy of iron and carbon. It contains up to 1.7 per cent carbon plus minor amounts of other elements such as manganese, silicon, phosphorus, sulfur, and oxygen.

STELLITE   a series of alloys containing cobalt, chromium, tungsten, and molybdenum in various compositions. Stellites are used for high-speed cutting tools and for protecting surfaces subjected to heavy wear.

STOPE   see CONTRACT.

STOVES   steel structures that contain firebrick laid loosely in a checkerwork pattern in order to absorb heat and at the same time permit ready flow of gas used to preheat the air entering the blast furnace.

STRAIN HARDENING   increase in hardness and yield strength produced by straining metals.

STRAINS (CASTING)   strains produced by internal stresses resulting from unequal contraction of the metal as the casting cools.

STRESS   internal forces produced by application of external load, tending to displace component parts of the stressed material.

STRESS RELIEF   a thermal treatment in which the locked-up stresses in a bar caused by cold working are removed by heating the bar close to but below the lower limit of the critical temperature range, or to approximately 100°F below the tempering temperature.

STRIKE OFF (STRIKE)   a straight edge to cut the sand level with the top of the drag or cope flask.

STRIP (COLD-ROLLED)   the flat products resulting from cold rolling, after pickling of strip previously produced by hot rolling.

STRIP (HOT-ROLLED)   the flat products resulting from reducing sheet bars by hot rolling on a sheet mill; or slabs, blooms, and billets on a continuous strip mill.

Glossary

STRIP MILL a mill for rolling slabs, blooms, and billets to strip thickness. Commonly a continuous mill with rolls revolving at high speed in order to finish the rolling at sufficiently high temperature.

SUBCRITICAL ANNEALING heating steel to a temperature below its critical temperature, and subsequently cooling at a rate dependent upon the carbon content; also called *process annealing*.

SUBLIMATION vaporization of a solid without intermediate formation of a liquid.

SURFACE TENSION force that causes the surface of a free liquid to assume a spherical shape.

SWAB a piece of hemp or other material to put water in the sand around the pattern before it is rapped and drawn from the mold or to put liquid facing on the surface of a mold or core.

SWABBING dampening the mold surface next to the pattern to strengthen the sand and cause it to be more plastic and consistent.

TAILINGS a waste product from a mill or concentrator.

TAPHOLE a furnace opening through which the refined molten metal flows.

TAPPING the process of removing molten steel from a melting furnace by opening the taphole and allowing the metal to run out into molds or into a ladle.

TEEMING the operation of filling ingot molds from a ladle of molten metal.

TEMPER CARBON carbon in nodular form, characteristic of malleable iron.

TEMPERATURE DIFFERENTIAL the difference in temperature between the center and surface of a metal during the quenching period.

TEMPERING (also termed DRAWING) re-heating hardened steel to some temperature below the lower critical temperature, followed by any desired rate of cooling, in order to decrease the hardness.

TEMPERING MOLDING SAND mixing and moistening molding sand until it sticks together when squeezed in the hand.

TENSILE STRENGTH the maximum normal load, per unit area, which a material is capable of withstanding before rupturing. It is lowest in the annealed state. Also known as *maximum strength* and *ultimate strength*.

TENSILE STRESSES (COMPRESSIVE STRESSES) stresses effective in a direction perpendicular to the direction of application.

TENSION TEST application of a pulling force to a specimen of material and measurement of the reactions that occur. In steel these reactions occur in two distinct phases: the elastic phase wherein the material is not permanently deformed by the pulling force, and the plastic or yield phase wherein the material becomes either permanently deformed or ruptured.

THERMOCOUPLE a combination of dissimilar metallic conductors so joined that they produce an electromotive force when the junctions are at different temperatures. The junction can be maintained at the temperature which it is desired to measure in terms of the thermoelectric current produced.

THREE-HIGH MILL a mill having three horizontal rolls, one above another. The piece being rolled goes in one direction through the bottom and middle rolls and returns through passes in the middle and top rolls. A three-high mill performs the same service as a two-high reversing mill.

THREE-HIGH PLATE MILL a three-high mill in which the upper and lower rolls are of the same diameter but the

Glossary

middle roll is smaller. The latter can be raised or lowered to work with either of the rolls above.

TIME-TEMPERATURE TRANSFORMATION CURVES same as isothermal transformation diagrams.

TIN PLATE thin sheet steel covered with an adherent layer of tin formed by passing the steel through a bath of molten tin. It resists atmospheric oxidation and attack by many organic acids.

TOOL STEEL a steel used for cutting tools. Tool steels are those which contain more than 0.6 per cent carbon and nominally 0.25 per cent silicon and 0.25 per cent manganese.

TOUGHNESS the ability to withstand load without breaking.

TRANSCRYSTALLINE FRACTURE (FAILURE) the normal type of failure observed in metals. The line of fracture passes through the crystals, and not around the boundaries as in intercrystalline fracture.

TRANSFORMATION a constitutional change in a solid metal; for example, the change from gamma to alpha iron or the formation of pearlite from austenite.

TRANSFORMATION RANGE the range of temperatures at which changes in phase of iron-carbon alloys occur.

TRANSFORMATION TEMPERATURES the temperatures at which changes in phase of iron-carbon alloys occur.

TRANSITION POINT the temperature at which one crystalline form of a substance is converted into another solid modification.

TRANSVERSE FISSURE a physical rupture through or practically through the horizontal section of an ingot.

TRANSVERSE WEAKNESS a weakness through the horizontal section of an ingot.

TREE the pattern formed when several wax patterns are joined together by means of wax in precision casting.

T.T.T. CURVE same as isothermal transformation diagram.

TUYERES openings through which the air blast enters any metallurgical furnace.

TWO-HIGH MILL a mill having two horizontal rolls generally used for rolling rails, structural shapes, bars, etc.

TWO-HIGH REVERSIBLE MILL a two-high mill in which it is possible to reverse the direction in which the rolls are rotating so that the cross section of the ingot is reduced each time the metal passes back and forth.

UNIVERSAL PLATE MILL a mill having horizontal and vertical rolls. The horizontal rolls control the thickness, and the vertical rolls control the width during the rolling of ingots and slabs into plates.

VENT (VENT HOLE) an opening in a mold or core to permit the escape of steam and gases.

VENT ROD (WIRE) a piece of wire or bar used to form the vents in sand.

VENT WAX wax in rod shape placed in the core during manufacture. In the oven the wax is melted out, leaving a vent or passage.

VIBRATOR a device that jars or vibrates the pattern or matchplate as it is withdrawn from the sand.

WASH ORES ores that require concentration by removal of the sand remaining after crushing by washing with water in agitators.

WATER-HARDENING STEELS low-carbon and low-alloy steels that must be quenched in water for hardening.

WELDABILITY the ease with which simple metal parts made of similar and dissimilar metals may be joined together in order to form complicated structures.

Glossary

WELDING the process of joining two metals by a similar metal at a temperature above the melting point of the metal; suitable only for low carbon steels.

WELDING ROD filler metal in the form of a wire or rod, used in electric welding when the electrode itself does not furnish the filler metal.

WELL or CRUCIBLE that section of the cupola furnace which lies below the tuyeres.

WHITE or HARD IRON iron of suitable composition in which the castings, later to be malleableized, are originally cast. Carbon is in the combined form; hence its white fracture and name.

WHITE METAL BEARING ALLOYS alloys in which lead, tin, and cadmium are the major elements.

WIDMÄNSTATEN STRUCTURE a pattern formed when one or more ferrite grains alternate with areas of pearlite of the same general shape when a low carbon steel composed of large austenite grains is cooled at a moderately fast rate.

WIND BOX chamber surrounding the cupola furnace at the tuyeres, to equalize the volume and pressure of the blast and deliver it to the tuyeres.

WORK HARDENING hardening that takes place in a metal when work of any sort, such as bending, rolling, hammering, drawing, punching, and the like, is done at a temperature below that at which recrystallization takes place. Lead, tin, and zinc are not appreciably hardened by cold working, because they can recrystallize at room temperature.

WORKING FACES sidewise extensions in an iron ore mine.

WORKING PERIOD (REFINING PERIOD) the interval between the end of the lime boil and the time of tapping in the open-hearth process or electric steel process. During this period the molten metal is refined or worked by the action of the slag, additions of ore, limestone, and the like in order to obtain the steel desired.

WROUGHT IRON (ASTM DEFINITION) a ferrous material, aggregated from a solidifying mass of pasty particles of highly refined metallic iron with which, without subsequent fusion, is incorporated a minutely and uniformly distributed quantity of slag.

YIELD POINT the load per unit area at which a marked increase in deformation of the specimen occurs without increase of load; the stress at which there occurs a marked increase in strain without an increase in stress.

YIELD STRENGTH the load per unit area at which a material exhibits a specified permanent deformation or a specified elongation under load.

ZYGLO a highly fluorescent nondestructive penetrant inspection test applied to nonmagnetic materials to detect flaws.

Tables

MELTING POINTS AND SPECIFIC GRAVITIES

	Chemical Symbol	Melting Point Centigrade	Fahrenheit	Specific Gravity
Aluminum	Al	660	1220	2.7
Antimony	Sb	630	1166	6.7
Arsenic	As	sublimes		5.7
Beryllium	Be	1350	2462	1.8
Bismuth	Bi	271	520	9.8
Boron	B	2300	4172	2.5
Cadmium	Cd	321	610	8.6
Carbon (graphite)	C	3500	6330	2.3
Chromium	Cr	1615	2939	7.1
Cobalt	Co	1480	2696	8.8
Copper	Cu	1083	1981	8.9
Gold	Au	1063	1943	19.3
Iridium	Ir	2350	4262	22.4
Iron	Fe	1535	2795	7.9
Lead	Pb	327	621	11.3
Magnesium	Mg	651	1204	1.7
Manganese	Mn	1260	2300	7.2
Molybdenum	Mo	2625	4757	10.2
Nickel	Ni	1452	2646	8.9
Niobium	Nb	1950	3542	8.4
Phosphorus (yellow)	P	44	111	1.8
Potassium	K	62	144	0.86
Selenium	Se	220	428	4.8
Silicon	Si	1420	2588	2.4
Silver	Ag	961	1762	10.5
Sodium	Na	98	208	0.97
Sulfur	S	113	235	2.1
Tantalum	Ta	2850	5162	16.6

Tables

MELTING POINTS AND SPECIFIC GRAVITIES—Continued

	Chemical Symbol	Melting Point Centigrade	Melting Point Fahrenheit	Specific Gravity
Tellurium	Te	452	846	6.2
Thallium	Tl	304	579	11.9
Thorium	Th	1845	3353	11.2
Tin	Sn	232	450	7.3
Titanium	Ti	1800	3272	4.5
Tungsten	W	3370	6098	19.3
Uranium	U	1850	3362	18.7
Zinc	Zn	419	786	7.1
Zirconium	Zr	1700	3092	6.4

HARDNESS CONVERSION TABLE

The following values are to be considered only as rough approximations due to variables of size, shape, and mass:

(1) Brinell values over 578.
(2) All Shore Scleroscope values.
(3) Rockwell C scale figures under 20.
(4) Rockwell B scale figures over 104.

Approximate Relations between Brinell, Rockwell, and Shore Hardnesses and the Tensile Strengths of AISI Carbon and Alloy Constructional Steels

Brinell		Rockwell			
Dia. in mm, 3000 kg load 10 mm ball	Hardness No.	C 150 kg load 120° Diamond Cone	B 100 kg load $\frac{1}{16}$ in. dia. ball	Shore Scleroscope No.	Tensile Strength psi
2.05	898	..	..	..	440,000
2.10	857	..	..	..	420,000
2.15	817	..	..	..	401,000
2.20	780	70	..	106	384,000
2.25	745	68	..	100	368,000
2.30	712	66	..	95	352,000
2.35	682	64	..	91	337,000
2.40	653	62	..	87	324,000
2.45	627	60	..	84	311,000
2.50	601	58	..	81	298,000
2.55	578	57	..	78	287,000
2.60	555	55	120	75	276,000
2.65	534	53	119	72	266,000

Tables

HARDNESS CONVERSION TABLE—Continued

Brinell		Rockwell			
Dia. in mm, 3000 kg load 10 mm ball	Hardness No.	C 150 kg load 120° Diamond Cone	B 100 kg load $\frac{1}{16}$ in. dia. ball	Shore Scleroscope No.	Tensile Strength psi
2.70	514	52	119	70	256,000
2.75	495	50	117	67	247,000
2.80	477	49	117	65	238,000
2.85	461	47	116	63	229,000
2.90	444	46	115	61	220,000
2.95	429	45	115	59	212,000
3.00	415	44	114	57	204,000
3.05	401	42	113	55	196,000
3.10	388	41	112	54	189,000
3.15	375	40	112	52	182,000
3.20	363	38	110	51	176,000
3.25	352	37	110	49	170,000
3.30	341	36	109	48	165,000
3.35	331	35	109	46	160,000
3.40	321	34	108	45	155,000
3.45	311	33	108	44	150,000
3.50	302	32	107	43	146,000
3.55	293	31	106	42	142,000
3.60	285	30	105	40	138,000
3.65	277	29	104	39	134,000
3.70	269	28	104	38	131,000
3.75	262	26	103	37	128,000
3.80	255	25	102	37	125,000
3.85	248	24	102	36	122,000
3.90	241	23	100	35	119,000
3.95	235	22	99	34	116,000
4.00	229	21	98	33	113,000
4.05	223	20	97	32	110,000
4.10	217	18	96	31	107,000
4.15	212	17	96	31	104,000
4.20	207	16	95	30	101,000
4.25	202	15	94	30	99,000
4.30	197	13	93	29	97,000
4.35	192	12	92	28	95,000
4.40	187	10	91	28	93,000
4.45	183	9	90	27	91,000
4.50	179	8	89	27	89,000

Tables

HARDNESS CONVERSION TABLE—Continued

Brinell		Rockwell			
		C	B		
Dia. in mm, 3000 kg load 10 mm ball	Hardness No.	150 kg load 120° Diamond Cone	100 kg load $\frac{1}{16}$ in. dia. ball	Shore Scleroscope No.	Tensile Strength psi
4.55	174	7	88	26	87,000
4.60	170	6	87	26	85,000
4.65	166	4	86	25	83,000
4.70	163	3	85	25	82,000
4.75	159	2	84	24	80,000
4.80	156	1	83	24	78,000
4.85	153	..	82	23	76,000
4.90	149	..	81	23	75,000
4.95	146	..	80	22	74,000
5.00	143	..	79	22	72,000
5.05	140	..	78	21	71,000
5.10	137	..	77	21	70,000
5.15	134	..	76	21	68,000
5.20	131	..	74	20	66,000
5.25	128	..	73	20	65,000
5.30	126	..	72	..	64,000
5.35	124	..	71	..	63,000
5.40	121	..	70	..	62,000
5.45	118	..	69	..	61,000
5.50	116	..	68	..	60,000
5.55	114	..	67	..	59,000
5.60	112	..	66	..	58,000
5.65	109	..	65	..	56,000
5.70	107	..	64	..	55,000
5.75	105	..	62	..	54,000
5.80	103	..	61	..	53,000
5.85	101	..	60	..	52,000
5.90	99	..	59	..	51,000
5.95	97	..	57	..	50,000
6.00	95	..	56	..	49,000

Tables

TEMPERATURE CONVERSION TABLE

Albert Sauveur type of table. Values revised.

−459.4 to 0			0 to 100						100 to 1000					
C	$\frac{C}{F}$	F	C	$\frac{C}{F}$	F	C	$\frac{C}{F}$	F	C	$\frac{C}{F}$	F	C	$\frac{C}{F}$	F
−273	−459.4		−17.8	0	32	10.0	50	122.0	38	100	212	260	500	932
−268	−450		−17.2	1	33.8	10.6	51	123.8	43	110	230	266	510	950
−262	−440		−16.7	2	35.6	11.1	52	125.6	49	120	248	271	520	968
−257	−430		−16.1	3	37.4	11.7	53	127.4	54	130	266	277	530	986
−251	−420		−15.6	4	39.2	12.2	54	129.2	60	140	284	282	540	1004
−246	−410		−15.0	5	41.0	12.8	55	131.0	66	150	302	288	550	1022
−240	−400		−14.4	6	42.8	13.3	56	132.8	71	160	320	293	560	1040
−234	−390		−13.9	7	44.6	13.9	57	134.6	77	170	338	299	570	1058
−229	−380		−13.3	8	46.4	14.4	58	136.4	82	180	356	304	580	1076
−223	−370		−12.8	9	48.2	15.0	59	138.2	88	190	374	310	590	1094
−218	−360		−12.2	10	50.0	15.6	60	140.0	93	200	392	316	600	1112
−212	−350		−11.7	11	51.8	16.1	61	141.8	99	210	410	321	610	1130
−207	−340		−11.1	12	53.6	16.7	62	143.6	100	212	413.6	327	620	1148
−201	−330		−10.6	13	55.4	17.2	63	145.4	104	220	428	332	630	1166
−196	−320		−10.0	14	57.2	17.8	64	147.2	110	230	446	338	640	1184
−190	−310		−9.4	15	59.0	18.3	65	149.0	116	240	464	343	650	1202
−184	−300		−8.9	16	60.8	18.9	66	150.8	121	250	482	349	660	1220
−179	−290		−8.3	17	62.6	19.4	67	152.6	127	260	500	354	670	1238
−173	−280		−7.8	18	64.4	20.0	68	154.4	132	270	518	360	680	1256
−169	−273	−459.4	−7.2	19	66.2	20.6	69	156.2	138	280	536	366	690	1274
−168	−270	−454	−6.7	20	68.0	21.1	70	158.0	143	290	554	371	700	1292
−162	−260	−436	−6.1	21	69.8	21.7	71	159.8	149	300	572	377	710	1310
−157	−250	−418	−5.6	22	71.6	22.2	72	161.6	154	310	590	382	720	1328
−151	−240	−440	−5.0	23	73.4	22.8	73	163.4	160	320	608	388	730	1346
−146	−230	−382	−4.4	24	75.2	23.3	74	165.2	166	330	626	393	740	1364
−140	−220	−364	−3.9	25	77.0	23.9	75	167.0	171	340	644	399	750	1382
−134	−210	−346	−3.3	26	78.8	24.4	76	168.8	177	350	662	404	760	1400
−129	−200	−328	−2.8	27	80.6	25.0	77	170.6	182	360	680	410	770	1418
−123	−190	−310	−2.2	28	82.4	25.6	78	172.4	188	370	698	416	780	1436
−118	−180	−292	−1.7	29	84.2	26.1	79	174.2	193	380	716	421	790	1454
−112	−170	−274	−1.1	30	86.0	26.7	80	176.0	199	390	734	427	800	1472
−107	−160	−256	−.6	31	87.8	27.2	81	177.8	204	400	752	432	810	1490
−101	−150	−238	0	32	89.6	27.8	82	179.6	210	410	770	438	820	1508
−96	−140	−220	.6	33	91.4	28.3	83	181.4	216	420	788	443	830	1526
−90	−130	−202	1.1	34	93.2	28.9	84	183.2	221	430	806	449	840	1544
−84	−120	−184	1.7	35	95.0	29.4	85	185.0	227	440	824	454	850	1562
−79	−110	−166	2.2	36	96.8	30.0	86	186.8	232	450	842	460	860	1580
−73	−100	−148	2.8	37	98.6	30.6	87	188.6	238	460	860	466	870	1598

Tables

TEMPERATURE CONVERSION TABLE—Continued

Albert Sauveur type of table. Values revised.

-459. to 0			0 to 100						100 to 1000					
C	$\frac{C}{F}$	F	C	$\frac{C}{F}$	F	C	$\frac{C}{F}$	F	C	$\frac{C}{F}$	F	C	$\frac{C}{F}$	F
− 68	− 90	− 130	3.3	38	100.4	31.1	88	190.4	243	470	878	471	880	1616
− 62	− 80	− 112	3.9	39	102.2	31.7	89	192.2	249	480	896	477	890	1634
− 57	− 70	− 94	4.4	40	104.0	32.2	90	194.0	254	490	914	482	900	1652
− 51	− 60	− 76	5.0	41	105.8	32.8	91	195.8				488	910	1670
− 46	− 50	− 58	5.6	42	107.6	33.3	92	197.6				493	920	1688
− 40	− 40	− 40	6.1	43	109.4	33.9	93	199.4				499	930	1706
− 34	− 30	− 22	6.7	44	111.2	34.4	94	201.2				504	940	1724
− 29	− 20	− 4	7.2	45	113.0	35.0	95	203.0				510	950	1742
− 23	− 10	14	7.8	46	114.8	35.6	96	204.8				516	960	1760
− 17.8	0	32	8.3	47	116.6	36.1	97	206.6				521	970	1778
			8.9	48	118.4	36.7	98	208.4				527	980	1796
			9.4	49	120.2	37.2	99	210.2				523	990	1814
						37.8	100	212.0				538	1000	1832

Look up reading in middle column. If in degrees Centigrade, read Fahrenheit equivalent in right-hand column; if in degrees Fahrenheit, read Centigrade equivalent in left-hand column.

1000 to 2000							2000 to 3000					
C	$\frac{C}{F}$	F	C	$\frac{C}{F}$	F	C	$\frac{C}{F}$	F	C	$\frac{C}{F}$	F
538	1000	1832	816	1500	2732	1093	2000	3632	1371	2500	4532
543	1010	1850	821	1510	2750	1099	2010	3650	1377	2510	4550
549	1020	1868	827	1520	2768	1104	2020	3668	1382	2520	4568
554	1030	1886	832	1530	2786	1110	2030	3686	1388	2530	4586
560	1040	1904	838	1540	2804	1116	2040	3704	1393	2540	4604
566	1050	1922	843	1550	2822	1121	2050	3722	1399	2550	4622
571	1060	1940	849	1560	2840	1127	2060	3740	1404	2560	4640
577	1070	1958	854	1570	2858	1132	2070	3758	1410	2570	4658
582	1080	1976	860	1580	2876	1138	2080	3776	1416	2580	4676
588	1090	1994	866	1590	2894	1143	2090	3794	1421	2590	4694
593	1100	2012	871	1600	2912	1149	2100	3812	1427	2600	4712
599	1110	2030	877	1610	2930	1154	2110	3830	1432	2610	4730
604	1120	2048	882	1620	2948	1160	2120	3848	1438	2620	4748
610	1130	2066	888	1630	2966	1166	2130	3866	1443	2630	4766
616	1140	2084	893	1640	2984	1171	2140	3884	1449	2640	4784

Tables

TEMPERATURE CONVERSION TABLE—Continued

Albert Sauveur type of table. Values revised.

1000 to 2000						2000 to 3000					
C	C/F	F	C	C/F	F	C	C/F	F	C	C/F	F
621	*1150*	2102	899	*1650*	3002	1177	*2150*	3902	1454	*2650*	4802
627	*1160*	2120	904	*1660*	3020	1182	*2160*	3920	1460	*2660*	4820
632	*1170*	2138	910	*1670*	3038	1188	*2170*	3938	1466	*2670*	4838
638	*1180*	2156	916	*1680*	3056	1193	*2180*	3956	1471	*2680*	4856
643	*1190*	2174	921	*1690*	3074	1199	*2190*	3974	1477	*2690*	4874
649	*1200*	2192	927	*1700*	3092	1204	*2200*	3992	1482	*2700*	4892
654	*1210*	2210	932	*1710*	3110	1210	*2210*	4010	1488	*2710*	4910
660	*1220*	2228	938	*1720*	3128	1216	*2220*	4028	1493	*2720*	4928
666	*1230*	2246	943	*1730*	3146	1221	*2230*	4046	1499	*2730*	4946
671	*1240*	2264	949	*1740*	3164	1227	*2240*	4064	1504	*2740*	4964
677	*1250*	2282	954	*1750*	3182	1232	*2250*	4082	1510	*2750*	4982
682	*1260*	2300	960	*1760*	3200	1238	*2260*	4100	1516	*2760*	5000
688	*1270*	2318	966	*1770*	3218	1243	*2270*	4118	1521	*2770*	5018
693	*1280*	2336	971	*1780*	3236	1249	*2280*	4136	1527	*2790*	5036
699	*1290*	2354	977	*1790*	3254	1254	*2290*	4154	1532	*2790*	5054
704	*1300*	2372	982	*1800*	3272	1260	*2300*	4172	1538	*2800*	5072
710	*1310*	2390	988	*1810*	3290	1266	*2310*	4190	1543	*2810*	5090
716	*1320*	2408	993	*1820*	3308	1271	*2320*	4208	1549	*2820*	5108
721	*1330*	2426	999	*1830*	3326	1277	*2330*	4226	1554	*2830*	5126
727	*1340*	2444	1004	*1840*	3344	1282	*2340*	4244	1560	*2840*	5144
732	*1350*	2462	1010	*1850*	3362	1288	*2350*	4262	1566	*2850*	5162
738	*1360*	2480	1016	*1860*	3380	1293	*2360*	4280	1571	*2860*	5180
743	*1370*	2498	1021	*1870*	3398	1299	*2370*	4298	1577	*2870*	5198
749	*1380*	2516	1027	*1880*	3416	1304	*2380*	4316	1582	*2880*	5216
754	*1390*	2534	1032	*1890*	3434	1310	*2390*	4334	1588	*2890*	5234
760	*1400*	2552	1038	*1900*	3452	1316	*2400*	4352	1593	*2900*	5252
766	*1410*	2570	1043	*1910*	3470	1321	*2410*	4370	1599	*2910*	5270
771	*1420*	2588	1049	*1920*	3488	1327	*2420*	4388	1604	*2920*	5288
777	*1430*	2606	1054	*1930*	3506	1332	*2430*	4406	1610	*2930*	5306
782	*1440*	2624	1060	*1940*	3524	1338	*2440*	4424	1616	*2940*	5324
788	*1450*	2642	1066	*1950*	3542	1343	*2450*	4442	1621	*2950*	5342
793	*1460*	2660	1071	*1960*	3560	1349	*2460*	4460	1627	*2960*	5360
799	*1470*	2678	1077	*1970*	3578	1354	*2470*	4478	1632	*2970*	5378
804	*1480*	2696	1082	*1980*	3596	1360	*2480*	4496	1638	*2980*	5396
810	*1490*	2714	1088	*1990*	3614	1366	*2490*	4514	1643	*2990*	5414
			1093	*2000*	3632				1649	*3000*	5432

Look up reading in middle column. If in degrees Centigrade, read Fahrenheit equivalent in right-hand column; if in degrees Fahrenheit, read Centigrade equivalent in left-hand column.

Tables

STANDARD CLASSIFICATION FOR COPPER AND COPPER ALLOYS
Wrought Products Only

COPPER NUMBER	PREVIOUS COMMONLY ACCEPTED TRADE NAME	Copper plus Silver(% min.)	Silver (oz./ton)	COMPOSITION, PER CENT MAXIMUM (Unless shown as a range or minimum)							
				Arsenic	Antimony	Phosphorus	Tellurium	Nickel	Bismuth	Lead	Other named elements
101	Oxygen Free Certified	99.96	–	–	–	.0003	–	–	–	–	.004 Sulfur .0003 Zinc .0001 Mercury
102	Oxygen Free	99.95	–	–	–	–	–	–	–	–	–
104	Oxygen Free with Silver	99.95	8(min)	–	–	–	–	–	–	–	–
105	Oxygen Free with Silver	99.95	10(min)	–	–	–	–	–	–	–	–
110	Electrolytic Tough Pitch	99.90	–	–	–	–	–	–	–	–	–
111	Electrolytic Tough Pitch Anneal Resistant	99.90	–	–	–	–	–	–	–	–	⊙
113	Tough Pitch with Silver	99.90	8(min)	–	–	–	–	–	–	–	–
114	Tough Pitch with Silver	99.90	10(min)	–	–	–	–	–	–	–	–
116	Tough Pitch with Silver	99.90	25(min)	–	–	–	–	–	–	–	–
120	Phosphorus Deoxidized Low Residual Phosphorus	99.90	–	–	–	.004-.012	–	–	–	–	–
121		99.90	4(min)	–	–	.005-.012	–	–	–	–	–
122	Phosphorus Deoxidized High Residual Phosphorus	99.90	–	–	–	.015-.040	–	–	–	–	–
123		99.90	4(min)	–	–	.015-.025	–	–	–	–	–
125	Fire Refined Tough Pitch	99.88	–	.012	.003	–	.025	.05	.003	.004	–
127	Fire Refined Tough Pitch with Silver	99.88	8(min)	.012	.003	–	.025	.05	.003	.004	–
128	Fire Refined Tough Pitch with Silver	99.88	10(min)	.012	.003	–	.025	.05	.003	.004	–
130	Fire Refined Tough Pitch with Silver	99.88	25(min)	.012	.003	–	.025	.05	.003	.004	–
141	Arsenical Tough Pitch	99.40	–	.15-.50	–	–	–	–	–	–	–
142	Phosphorus Deoxidized Arsenical	99.40	–	.15-.50	–	.015-.040	–	–	–	–	–
145	Phosphorus Deoxidized Tellurium Bearing	99.90	–	–	–	.004-.012	.40-.60	–	–	–	–
147	Sulfur Bearing	99.90	–	–	–	–	–	–	–	–	.2-.5 Sulfur
150	Zirconium Copper	99.80	–	–	–	–	–	–	–	–	.10-.15 Zirconium

COPPER ALLOY NUMBER	PREVIOUS COMMONLY ACCEPTED TRADE NAME	Copper+Silver +elements with specific limits(% min.)	COMPOSITION, PER CENT MAXIMUM (Unless shown as a range or minimum)								
			Iron	Tin	Nickel	Cobalt	Chromium	Silicon	Beryllium	Lead	Cadmium	Other named elements
162	Cadmium Copper	99.75	.02	–	–	–	–	–	–	–	.7-1.2	–
164		99.75	.02	.2-.4	–	–	–	–	–	–	.6-.9	–
165		99.75	.02	.5-.7	–	–	–	–	–	–	.6-1.0	–
172	Beryllium Copper	99.5	⊙	–	⊙	⊙	–	–	1.80-2.05	–	–	–
182	Chromium Copper	99.5	.10	–	–	–	.6-1.2	.10	–	.05	–	–
184	Chromium Copper	99.75	.15	–	–	–	.40-1.20	.10	–	–	–	.005 Arsenic .005 Calcium .05 Lithium .05 Phos. .70 Zinc
185	Chromium Copper	99.75	–	–	–	–	.40-1.00	–	–	.015	–	.04 Phos. .08-.12 Silver
190		99.5	.10	–	.9-1.3	–	–	–	–	.05	–	.75 Zinc .15-.35 Phos.
191		99.5	.2	–	.9-1.3	–	–	–	–	.1	–	.5 Zinc .15-.35 Phos. .35-.65 Tellurium

COPPER ALLOY NUMBER	PREVIOUS COMMONLY ACCEPTED TRADE NAME	COMPOSITION, PER CENT MAXIMUM (Unless shown as a range or minimum)									
		Copper	Iron	Tin	Nickel	Cobalt	Chromium	Zinc	Aluminum	Lead	Cadmium	Total other elements
193		92.0-94.0	2.05-2.60	.03	–	–	–	Rem.	.02	.03	–	.05

Tables

STANDARD CLASSIFICATION FOR COPPER AND COPPER ALLOYS—*Continued*

COPPER ALLOY NUMBER	PREVIOUS COMMONLY ACCEPTED TRADE NAME	Copper	Lead	Iron	Tin	Zinc	Nickel	Aluminum	Phosphorus	Arsenic	Antimony	Manganese	Silicon	Total other elements a
210	Gilding, 95%	94.0-96.0	.05	.05	–	Rem.	–	–	–	–	–	–	–	.10
220	Commercial Bronze, 90%	89.0-91.0	.05	.05	–	Rem.	–	–	–	–	–	–	–	.10
226	Jewelry Bronze 87½%	86.0-89.0	.05	.05	–	Rem.	–	–	–	–	–	–	–	.15
230	Red Brass, 85%	84.0-86.0	.05	.05	–	Rem.	–	–	–	–	–	–	–	.15
234		81.0-84.0	.05	.05	–	Rem.	–	–	–	–	–	–	–	.15
240	Low Brass, 80%	78.5-81.5	.05	.05	–	Rem.	–	–	–	–	–	–	–	.15
260	Cartridge Brass, 70%	68.5-71.5	.07	.05	–	Rem.	–	–	–	–	–	–	–	.15
261		68.5-71.5	.05	.05	–	Rem.	–	–	.02-.05	–	–	–	–	.15
262		67.0-70.0	.07	.05	–	Rem.	–	–	–	–	–	–	–	.15
268	Yellow Brass 66% (Sheet)	64.0-68.5	.15	.05	–	Rem.	–	–	–	–	–	–	–	.15
270	Yellow Brass 65% (Rod and Wire)	63.0-68.5	.10	.05	–	Rem.	–	–	–	–	–	–	–	.15
274	Yellow Brass 63%	61.0-64.0	.10	.05	–	Rem.	–	–	–	–	–	–	–	.20
280	Muntz Metal 60%	59.0-63.0	.30	.07	–	Rem.	–	–	–	–	–	–	–	.20
298	Brazing Alloy	49.0-52.0	.50	.10	–	Rem.	–	.10	–	–	–	–	–	–
310	Leaded Commercial Bronze (Low Lead)	89.0-91.0	.3-.7	.10	–	Rem.	–	–	–	–	–	–	–	.50
314	Leaded Commercial Bronze	87.5-90.5	1.3-2.5	.10	–	Rem.	–	–	–	–	–	–	–	.50
316	Leaded Commercial Bronze (Nickel Bearing)	87.5-90.5	1.3-2.5	.10	–	Rem.	.7-1.2	–	–	–	–	–	–	.50
320	Leaded Red Brass	83.5-86.5	1.5-2.2	.10	–	Rem.	–	–	–	–	–	–	–	.50
325		72.0-74.5	2.5-3.0	.10	–	Rem.	–	–	–	–	–	–	–	.50
330	Low Leaded Brass (Tube)	65.0-68.0	.2-.8	.07	–	Rem.	–	–	–	–	–	–	–	.50
331		65.0-68.0	.7-1.2	.06	–	Rem.	–	–	–	–	–	–	–	.50
332	High Leaded Brass (Tube)	65.0-68.0	1.3-2.0	.07	–	Rem.	–	–	–	–	–	–	–	.50
335	Low Leaded Brass	62.5-66.5	.3-.7	.10	–	Rem.	–	–	–	–	–	–	–	.50
340	Medium Leaded Brass 64½%	62.5-66.5	.8-1.4	.10	–	Rem.	–	–	–	–	–	–	–	.50
342	High Leaded Brass 64½%	62.5-66.5	1.5-2.5	.10	–	Rem.	–	–	–	–	–	–	–	.50
344		62.0-66.0	.5-1.0	.10	–	Rem.	–	–	–	–	–	–	–	.50
347		62.5-64.5	1.0-1.8	.10	–	Rem.	–	–	–	–	–	–	–	.50
348		61.5-63.5	.4-.8	.10	–	Rem.	–	–	–	–	–	–	–	.50
350	Medium Leaded Brass 62%	61.0-64.0	.8-1.4	.10	–	Rem.	–	–	–	–	–	–	–	.50
353	High Leaded Brass 62%	59.0-64.5	1.3-2.3	.10	–	Rem.	–	–	–	–	–	–	–	.50
356	Extra High Leaded Brass	60.0-64.5	2.0-3.0	.10	–	Rem.	–	–	–	–	–	–	–	.50
360	Free Cutting Brass	60.0-63.0	2.5-3.7	.35	–	Rem.	–	–	–	–	–	–	–	.50
362		60.0-63.0	3.5-4.5	.15	–	Rem.	–	–	–	–	–	–	–	.50
365	Leaded Muntz Metal, Uninhibited	58.0-61.0	.4-.9	.15	.25	Rem.	–	–	–	–	–	–	–	.10
366	Leaded Muntz Metal, Arsenical	58.0-61.0	.4-.9	.15	.25	Rem.	–	–	–	.02-.10	–	–	–	.10
367	Leaded Muntz Metal, Antimonial	58.0-61.0	.4-.9	.15	.25	Rem.	–	–	–	–	.02-.10	–	–	.10
368	Leaded Muntz Metal, Phosphorized	58.0-61.0	.4-.9	.15	.25	Rem.	–	–	.02-.10	–	–	–	–	.10
370	Free Cutting Muntz Metal	59.0-62.0	.9-1.4	.15	–	Rem.	–	–	–	–	–	–	–	.50
371		58.0-62.0	.6-1.2	.15	–	Rem.	–	–	–	–	–	–	–	.50
377	Forging Brass	58.0-62.0	1.5-2.5	.30	–	Rem.	–	–	–	–	–	–	–	.50
385	Architectural Bronze	55.0-60.0	2.0-3.8	.35	–	Rem.	–	–	–	–	–	–	–	.50
405		94.0-96.0	.05	.05	.7-1.3	Rem.	–	–	–	–	–	–	–	.15
408		94.0-96.0	.05	.05	1.8-2.2	Rem.	–	–	–	–	–	–	–	.15
410		91.0-93.0	.05	.05	2.0-2.8	Rem.	–	–	–	–	–	–	–	.15
411		89.0-92.0	.10	.05	.3-.7	Rem.	–	–	–	–	–	–	–	.15
413		89.0-93.0	.10	.05	.7-1.3	Rem.	–	–	–	–	–	–	–	.15
415		89.0-93.0	.10	.05	1.5-2.2	Rem.	–	–	–	–	–	–	–	.15
419		89.0-92.0	.10	.05	4.8-5.5	Rem.	–	–	–	–	–	–	–	.15
420		88.0-91.0	–	–	1.5-2.0	Rem.	–	–	.25	–	–	–	–	.15
422		86.0-89.0	.05	.05	.8-1.4	Rem.	–	–	–	–	–	–	–	.15
425		87.0-90.0	.05	.05	1.5-2.2	Rem.	–	–	–	–	–	–	–	.15
430		85.0-89.0	.10	.05	1.7-2.7	Rem.	–	–	–	–	–	–	–	.15
432		85.0-87.0	.05	.05	.4-.6	Rem.	–	–	–	–	–	–	–	.15
434		84.0-86.0	.05	.05	.5-1.0	Rem.	–	–	–	–	–	–	–	.15
435		79.0-83.0	.10	.05	.6-1.2	Rem.	–	–	–	–	–	–	–	.15
438		79.0-82.0	.05	.05	1.0-1.5	Rem.	–	–	–	–	–	–	–	.15
442	Admiralty Uninhibited	70.0-73.0	.07	.06	.8-1.2	Rem.	–	–	–	–	–	–	–	.10
443	Admiralty Arsenical	70.0-73.0	.07	.06	.8-1.2	Rem.	–	–	–	.02-.10	–	–	–	.10
444	Admiralty Antimonial	70.0-73.0	.07	.06	.8-1.2	Rem.	–	–	–	–	.02-.10	–	–	.10
445	Admiralty Phosphorized	70.0-73.0	.07	.06	.8-1.2	Rem.	–	–	.02-.10	–	–	–	–	.10
462	Naval Brass 63½%	62.0-65.0	.20	.10	.5-1.0	Rem.	–	–	–	–	–	–	–	.10
464	Naval Brass	59.0-62.0	.20	.10	.5-1.0	Rem.	–	–	–	–	–	–	–	.10

Tables

STANDARD CLASSIFICATION FOR COPPER AND COPPER ALLOYS—
Continued

COPPER ALLOY NUMBER	PREVIOUS COMMONLY ACCEPTED TRADE NAME	Copper	Lead	Iron	Tin	Zinc	Nickel	Aluminum	Phosphorus	Arsenic	Antimony	Manganese	Silicon	Total other elements Ⓐ
									COMPOSITION, PERCENT MAXIMUM (Unless shown as a range or minimum)					
465	Naval Brass Arsenical	59.0-62.0	.20	.10	.5-1.0	Rem.	—	—	—	.02-.10	—	—	—	.10
466	Naval Brass Antimonial	59.0-62.0	.20	.10	.5-1.0	Rem.	—	—	—	—	.02-.10	—	—	.10
467	Naval Brass Phosphorized	59.0-62.0	.20	.10	.5-1.0	Rem.	—	—	.02-.10	—	—	—	—	.10
470	Naval Brass Welding & Brazing Rod	57.0-61.0	.05	—	.25-1.0	Rem.	—	.01	—	—	—	—	—	.50 Ⓒ
472	Brazing Alloy	49.0-52.0	.50	.10	3.0-4.0	Rem.	—	—	—	—	—	—	—	—
482	Naval Brass Medium Leaded	59.0-62.0	.4-1.0	.10	.5-1.0	Rem.	—	—	—	—	—	—	—	.10
485	Naval Brass High Leaded	59.0-62.0	1.3-2.2	.10	.5-1.0	Rem.	—	—	—	—	—	—	—	.10

COPPER ALLOY NUMBER	PREVIOUS COMMONLY ACCEPTED TRADE NAME	Copper+Tin+ Phosphorus (% min.)	Lead	Iron	Tin	Zinc	Nickel	Aluminum	Phosphorus	Arsenic	Antimony	Manganese	Silicon
					COMPOSITION, PERCENT MAXIMUM (Unless shown as a range or minimum)								
502	Phosphor Bronze E	99.5	.05	.10	1.0-1.5	—	—	—	.04	—	—	—	—
505		99.5	.05	.10	1.0-1.7	.30	—	—	.03-.35	—	—	—	—
507		99.5	.05	.10	1.5-2.0	—	—	—	.04	—	—	—	—
508		99.5	.05	.10	2.6-3.4	—	—	—	.01-.07	—	—	—	—
509		99.5	.05	.10	2.5-3.8	—	—	—	.15-.30	—	—	—	—
510	Phosphor Bronze A	99.5	.05	.10	3.5-5.8	.30	—	—	.03-.35	—	—	—	—
518	Phosphor Bronze	99.5	.02	—	4.0-6.0	—	—	.01	.10-.35	—	—	—	—
521	Phosphor Bronze C	99.5	.05	.10	7.0-9.0	.20	—	—	.03-.35	—	—	—	—
524	Phosphor Bronze D	99.5	.05	.10	9.0-11.0	.20	—	—	.03-.35	—	—	—	—

COPPER ALLOY NUMBER	PREVIOUS COMMONLY ACCEPTED TRADE NAME	Copper+Tin+ Phosphorus+ Lead (% min.)	Lead	Iron	Tin	Zinc	Nickel	Aluminum	Phosphorus	Arsenic	Antimony	Manganese	Silicon
					COMPOSITION, PERCENT MAXIMUM (Unless shown as a range or minimum)								
532	Phosphor Bronze B	99.5	2.5-4.0	.10	4.0-5.5	.20	—	—	.03-.35	—	—	—	—
534	Phosphor Bronze B-1	99.5	.8-1.2	.10	3.5-5.8	.30	—	—	.03-.35	—	—	—	—
544	Phosphor Bronze B-2	99.5 Ⓑ	3.5-4.5	.10	3.5-4.5	1.5-4.5	—	—	.01-.50	—	—	—	—
546	Phosphor Bronze B-2 (P 0.50 max.)	99.5 Ⓑ	3.5-4.5	.10	3.5-4.5	1.5-4.5	—	—	.50	—	—	—	—

COPPER ALLOY NUMBER	PREVIOUS COMMONLY ACCEPTED TRADE NAME	Copper+ Elements with specific limits (% min.)	Lead	Iron	Tin	Zinc	Nickel	Aluminum	Phosphorus	Arsenic	Antimony	Manganese	Silicon
					COMPOSITION, PERCENT MAXIMUM (Unless shown as a range or minimum)								
606		99.5	—	.50	—	—	—	4.0-7.0	—	—	—	—	—
608		99.5	.10	.10	—	—	—	5.0-6.5	—	.35	—	—	—
610		99.5	.02	—	—	.20	—	6.0-9.0	—	—	—	—	.10
612		99.5	—	.50	—	—	—	7.0-9.0	—	—	—	—	—
614	Aluminum Bronze D	99.5	—	1.5-3.5	—	—	—	6.0-8.0	—	—	—	1.0	—
616		99.5	—	4.0	.6	1.0	1.0	6.5-11.0	—	—	—	1.5	.25
618		99.5	.02	1.5	—	.02	—	9.0-11.0	—	—	—	—	.10
620		99.5	—	3.2-3.7	—	—	—	9.8-10.5	—	—	—	—	—
622		99.5	.02	3.0-4.25	—	.02	—	11.0-12.0	—	—	—	—	.10
624		99.5	—	2.0-4.0	.20	—	—	9.0-11.0	—	—	—	.30	—
626		99.7	—	2.0-4.5	—	—	3.0-4.5	9.7-10.7	—	—	—	1.5	—
628		99.5	—	1.5-3.5	—	—	4.0-7.0	8.0-11.0	—	—	—	.5-2.0	—
630		99.5	—	2.0-4.0	.20	—	4.0-5.5	9.0-11.0	—	—	—	1.5	.25
637		99.5	.05	.3	.6	1.0	.25	6.5-8.5	—	—	—	—	1.2-2.2
639		99.5	.05	.10	—	—	—	6.5-8.0	—	—	—	—	1.5-3.0
642		99.5	—	4.0	.6	1.0	.25	6.5-11.0	—	—	—	1.5	2.2
647		99.5	.1	.1	—	.5	1.6-2.2	—	—	—	—	—	.4-.8
651	Low Silicon Bronze B	99.5	.05	.8	—	1.5	—	—	—	—	—	.7	.8-2.0
653		99.7	.05	.8	—	—	—	—	—	—	—	—	2.0-2.6
655	High Silicon Bronze A	99.5	.05	1.6	—	1.5	.6	—	—	—	—	1.5	2.8-3.5
656		99.5	.02	.5	1.5	1.5	—	.01	—	—	—	1.5	2.8-4.0
658		99.5	.05	.5	—	—	—	.01	—	—	—	1.3	2.8-3.8
661		99.5	.2-.8	.25	—	1.5	—	—	—	—	—	1.5	2.8-3.5

Tables

STANDARD CLASSIFICATION FOR COPPER AND COPPER ALLOYS—*Continued*

COPPER ALLOY NUMBER	PREVIOUS COMMONLY ACCEPTED TRADE NAME	COMPOSITION, PERCENT MAXIMUM (Unless shown as a range or minimum)												
		Copper	Lead	Iron	Tin	Zinc	Nickel	Aluminum	Phosphorus	Arsenic	Antimony	Manganese	Silicon	Total other elements ⓐ
665	....	80.0-82.0	.05	.10	–	Rem.	–	–	–	–	–	.7-1.5	–	.15
667	Manganese Brass	68.5-71.5	.07	.10	–	Rem.	–	–	–	–	–	.8-1.5	–	.50
670	Manganese Bronze B	63.0-68.0	.20	2.0-4.0	.50	Rem.	–	3.0-6.0	–	–	–	2.5-5.0	–	.10
675	Manganese Bronze A	57.0-60.0	.20	.80-2.0	.5-1.5	Rem.	–	.25	–	–	–	.05-.5	–	.10
680	Bronze, Low Fuming (Nickel)	56.0-60.0	.05	.25-1.25	.75-1.10	Rem.	.2-.8	.01	–	–	–	.01-.50	.04-.15	.50 ⓒ
681	Bronze, Low Fuming	56.0-60.0	.05	.25-1.25	.75-1.10	Rem.	–	.01	–	–	–	.01-.50	.04-.15	.50 ⓒ
685	....	85.0-89.0	.05	1.5-2.5	.10	Rem.	–	3.5-4.5	–	–	–	–	–	.10
687	Aluminum Brass Arsenical	76.0-79.0	.07	.06	–	Rem.	–	1.8-2.5	–	.02-.10	–	–	–	.10
692	Silicon Brass	89.0-91.0	.05	.05	–	Rem.	–	–	–	–	–	–	.8-1.5	.50
694	Silicon Red Brass	80.0-83.0	.20	.10	–	Rem.	–	–	–	–	–	–	3.5-4.5	.50
697	....	75.0-80.0	.5-1.5	.10	–	Rem.	–	–	–	–	–	.40	2.5-3.5	.50

COPPER ALLOY NUMBER	PREVIOUS COMMONLY ACCEPTED TRADE NAME	Copper+ Elements with specific limits (% min.)	COMPOSITION, PERCENT MAXIMUM (Unless shown as a range or minimum)										
			Lead	Iron	Tin	Zinc	Nickel	Aluminum	Phosphorus	Arsenic	Antimony	Manganese	Silicon
702	....	99.7	.05	.10	–	–	2.0-3.0	–	–	–	–	.40	–
703	....	99.5	–	.05	–	–	4.7-5.7	–	–	–	–	.5	–
704	Copper Nickel 5%	99.6	.05	1.3-1.7	–	–	4.8-6.2	–	–	–	–	.30-.80	–
705	Copper Nickel 7%	99.5	.05	.10	–	.20	6.0-8.0	–	–	–	–	.15	–
706	Copper Nickel 10%	99.5	.05	.5-2.0	–	1.0	9.0-11.0	–	–	–	–	1.0	–
707	....	99.5	–	.05	–	–	9.5-10.5	–	–	–	–	.5	–
708	Copper Nickel 11%	99.5	.05	.10	–	.20	10.5-12.5	–	–	–	–	.15	–
710	Copper Nickel 20%	99.5	.05	1.0	–	1.0	19.0-23.0	–	–	–	–	1.0	–
715	Copper Nickel 30%	99.5	.05	.40-.70	–	1.0	29.0-33.0	–	–	–	–	1.0	–
720	Copper Nickel 40%	99.5	.05	1.5-2.5	–	.3	40.0-43.0	–	–	–	–	.8-1.7	–

COPPER ALLOY NUMBER	PREVIOUS COMMONLY ACCEPTED TRADE NAME	COMPOSITION, PERCENT MAXIMUM (Unless shown as a range or minimum)												
		Copper	Lead	Iron	Tin	Zinc	Nickel	Aluminum	Phosphorus	Arsenic	Antimony	Manganese	Silicon	Total other elements ⓐ
732	....	70.0(min)	.05	.6	–	3.0-6.0	19.0-23.0	–	–	–	–	1.0	–	.50
735	....	70.5-73.5	.10	.25	–	Rem.	16.5-19.5	–	–	–	–	.50	–	.50
740	....	69.0-73.5	.10	.25	–	Rem.	9.0-11.0	–	–	–	–	.50	–	.50
745	Nickel Silver 65-10	63.5-68.5	.10	.25	–	Rem.	9.0-11.0	–	–	–	–	.50	–	.50
752	Nickel Silver 65-18	63.0-66.5	.10	.25	–	Rem.	16.5-19.5	–	–	–	–	.50	–	.50
754	Nickel Silver 65-15	63.5-66.5	.10	.25	–	Rem.	14.0-16.0	–	–	–	–	.50	–	.50
757	Nickel Silver 65-12	63.5-66.5	.05	.25	–	Rem.	11.0-13.0	–	–	–	–	.50	–	.50
762	....	57.0-61.0	.10	.25	–	Rem.	11.0-13.5	–	–	–	–	.50	–	.10
764	....	58.5-61.5	.05	.25	–	Rem.	16.5-19.5	–	–	–	–	.50	–	.50
766	....	55.0-58.0	.10	.25	–	Rem.	11.0-13.5	–	–	–	–	.50	–	.50
770	Nickel Silver 55-18	53.5-56.5	.10	.25	–	Rem.	16.5-19.5	–	–	–	–	.50	–	.50
773	....	46.0-50.0	.05	–	–	Rem.	9.0-11.0	–	.25	–	–	–	.04-.25	.50
774	....	43.0-47.0	.20	–	–	Rem.	9.0-11.0	–	–	–	–	–	–	.50
782	....	63.0-67.0	1.50-2.25	.35	–	Rem.	7.0-9.0	–	–	–	–	.50	–	.10
784	....	60.0-63.0	.8-1.4	.25	–	Rem.	9.0-11.0	–	–	–	–	.50	–	.50
786	....	60.0-63.0	1.25-1.75	.35	–	Rem.	8.5-11.0	–	–	–	–	.50	–	.10
788	....	63.0-67.0	1.5-2.0	.25	–	Rem.	9.0-11.0	–	–	–	–	.50	–	.50
790	....	63.0-67.0	1.50-2.25	.35	–	Rem.	11.0-13.0	–	–	–	–	.50	–	.10
792	....	60.0-63.0	.8-1.4	.25	–	Rem.	11.0-13.0	–	–	–	–	.50	–	.50
794	....	59.0-66.5	.8-1.2	.25	–	Rem.	16.5-19.5	–	–	–	–	.50	–	.50

NOTES

ⓐ Analysis is regularly made for the elements for which limits are listed except Zinc. If, however, the presence of other elements is suspected or indicated in the course of routine analysis further analysis shall be made to determine that the total of these "other" elements is not in excess of the limits specified.

ⓑ These are high conductivity coppers which have in the annealed condition, a minimum conductivity of 100% IACS.

ⓒ Small amounts of Cadmium or other elements may be added by agreement to improve resistance to softening at elevated temperature.

● This includes Low Resistance Lake Copper and Electrolytic Copper.

ⓒ This includes Oxygen Free Copper to which Phosphorus has been added in an amount agreed upon.

ⓕ This includes High Resistance Lake Copper.

ⓖ This includes permissible Selenium.

ⓗ This includes Oxygen Free Tellurium Bearing Copper to which Phosphorus has been added in an amount agreed upon.

ⓘ This includes Copper plus Silver plus Tellurium.

ⓙ This includes Copper plus Silver plus Sulfur.

ⓚ Nickel and/or Cobalt .20 minimum.
Nickel plus Cobalt plus Iron .60 maximum.

ⓛ Including Aluminum and Lead.

ⓜ Including Zinc